Along Prehistoric Lines
Neolithic, Iron Age and Romano-British Activity at the Former MOD Headquarters, Durrington, Wiltshire

Steve Thompson and Andrew B. Powell

Along Prehistoric Lines
Neolithic, Iron Age and Romano-British Activity at the Former MOD Headquarters, Durrington, Wiltshire

Steve Thompson and Andrew B. Powell

with contributions by
Alistair J. Barclay, Dana Challinor, Nicholas Cooke, Phil Harding,
L. Higbee, Rob Ixer, Matt Leivers, Jacqueline I. McKinley,
R. H. Seager Smith, Chris J. Stevens and Sarah F. Wyles

Illustrations by
Will Foster and S. E. James

Wessex Archaeology Occasional Paper
2018

Published 2018 by Wessex Archaeology Ltd
Portway House, Old Sarum Park, Salisbury, SP4 6EB
www.wessexarch.co.uk

British Library Cataloguing in Publication Data
A catalogue record for this book is available from the British Library

ISBN 978-1-911137-04-7

Designed and typeset by Kenneth Lymer
Cover design by Will Foster
Copy-edited by Philippa Bradley
Printed by Lightning Source UK

Front cover
Aerial view of Area 1 from the west, showing the line of the Late Iron Age enclosure ditch

Back cover
North–south line of Late Neolithic postholes, viewed from the north

Wessex Archaeology Ltd is a company limited by guarantee registered in England,
company number 1712772. It is also a Charity registered in England and Wales number 287786,
and in Scotland, Scottish Charity number SC042630. Our registered office is at Portway House,
Old Sarum Park, Salisbury, Wiltshire, SP4 6EB.

Contents

List of Figures

List of Plates

List of Tables

Acknowledgements

The work was commissioned by Persimmon Homes (South Coast) Ltd, and Wessex Archaeology would like to thank Stuart Benfield for his help and support throughout the project, along with Steve White (Site Manager). We are also grateful to Clare King of Wiltshire Council Archaeology Service (WCAS) who monitored the work on behalf the local planning authority.

The evaluation was directed by Bob Davis, and the excavation by Steve Thompson and Naomi Brennan. The watching briefs were undertaken by Nick Taylor, Neil Fitzpatrick, Dave Murdie, Elina Brook, Andy Sole and Julia Sulikowska. David Norcott and Nicki Mulhall provided on-site geoarchaeological advice, and Rachael Seager Smith and Matt Leivers advised on the excavation and sampling of artefacts, in particular lithics and pottery. The fieldwork was managed by Andrew Manning and the post-excavation work by Alistair Barclay.

Wessex Archaeology is grateful to Adam Stanford of Aerial-Cam for taking the aerial photographs of the site during the excavation, and also to Jack Gibbs, Royal Navy, for providing photographs taken while flying over the site (jack_gibbs@btinternet.com). Mike Parker Pearson kindly provided information from his own work within and around Durrington Walls. We would also like to thank Josh Pollard for discussing the Neolithic aspects of the site and the worked sarsen. Both Alex Bayliss and Peter Marshall provided useful guidance on the radiocarbon report.

This report was compiled and edited by Andrew Powell and Alistair Barclay, and copy-edited by Philippa Bradley who also oversaw the production of the report. The illustrations are by Will Foster (plans and sections) and Elizabeth James (finds).

The archive (Wessex Archaeology project numbers 47710-4) will be lodged with Salisbury and South Wiltshire Museum, with an accession number agreed upon deposition.

Abstract

Between 2000 and 2012 a programme of archaeological evaluation, excavation and watching brief was undertaken on the site of the former Ministry of Defence Headquarters in Durrington, Wiltshire. The work was undertaken prior to development of the land for residential housing by Persimmon Homes (South Coast) Ltd. The site lies on the west side of the River Avon valley, immediately north-east of the Stonehenge World Heritage Site, and less than 1 km from the major Late Neolithic (c. 2850–2200 BC) henge of Durrington Walls.

During the evaluation a deeply buried Late Glacial soil was observed in the side of a Late Iron Age ditch. This was further exposed during the excavation and shown to date from the relatively brief warmer period of the Windermere (Allerød oscillation) Interstadial (c. 12,000–9500 BC), before a return to the glacial conditions which existed prior to the beginning of the Holocene (c. 9500 BC). There were no associated archaeological remains.

The earliest archaeological evidence dates from the Late Neolithic, when two intersecting straight lines of timber posts were erected across the site. The lines, in which the posts were unevenly spaced, are of uncertain function, although they appear to have separated a group of pits at the south-west, containing Grooved Ware pottery, worked flints and other materials, from activity at a natural solution hollow and a smaller hollow towards the north. At the base of the solution hollow was an adult cremation burial which had been covered by a deposit of flint knapping waste. The solution hollow also had evidence for large-scale flint knapping around its edges.

The only evidence for Bronze Age activity was a cremation burial in an Early Bronze Age Collared Urn, identified during the evaluation and preserved *in situ*. There was little other evidence for activity until the later Iron Age, this being limited to a small number of Middle and Late Iron Age burials, both cremation and inhumation.

A substantial defensive ditch was constructed in the Late Iron Age, following an irregular north-west to south-east line across the site. There were no contemporary settlement features associated with it. Its line beyond the site is not known and it is unclear whether it defined a large enclosure or was some other form of landscape boundary. It may be compared to the ditch bounding the large Late Iron Age 'valley fort' at Figheldean, 2.5 km to the north.

The ditch was deliberately infilled early in the Romano-British period, and a settlement established between it and the river. Although no settlement structures were revealed on the site, the recovery of a small quantity of painted wall plaster and stone roofing tiles suggest there was a substantial building in the immediate vicinity. The settlement was approached from the south by a metalled trackway which crossed the infilled Late Iron Age ditch and led to a series of well-established field or plot boundaries, with a similar orientation to the earlier linear features. These appear to have divided the site into a number of zones, with extensive quarry pits to the west and a number of ovens and pottery kilns to the east. Domestic waste in the form of pottery and animal bone was recovered from storage pits and other features, some of the material being of very late Romano-British or even early post-Romano-British date.

Chapter 1
Introduction

An excavation in 2010–12 on the site of the former Ministry of Defence (MOD) Headquarters in Durrington, Wiltshire, revealed evidence spanning the post-glacial to the post-medieval periods. Twice during prehistory the site was crossed by long linear features – a line of timber posts erected during the Late Neolithic, and a substantial defensive earthwork built towards the end of the Iron Age. Both features had similar orientations (west-north-west to east-south-east), and although both are of uncertain function and extent, each is likely to have had a significant impact on the disposition of contemporary activity in the landscape. In the case of the Late Iron Age defences that impact continued into the Romano-British period.

The site, on the west side the Avon valley in the southern part of Salisbury Plain, covered 2.4 ha centred on NGR 415400 144700 (Figs 1.1 and 1.2). It lies immediately north-east of the Stonehenge part of the Stonehenge, Avebury and Associated Sites

World Heritage Site (WHS). The significant discoveries made during the excavation include a deeply buried Late Glacial (*c.* 12,000–9500 BC) Allerød soil, and a zone of Late Neolithic activity centred on a number of natural solution hollows, posthole alignments and pit groups. Apart from an Early Bronze Age urned cremation burial discovered (and preserved *in situ*) in the south-west part of the site, there appears then to have been little activity until the later Iron Age when a small number of cremation burials were made. The Late Iron Age defences, possibly constructed in the immediate pre-Conquest period and decommissioned soon after, influenced the layout of subsequent Romano-British fields and settlement activity.

The excavation, undertaken prior to the development of the land for residential housing, was the final stage of a programme of work undertaken following consultation with Wiltshire County Archaeology Service (WCAS) and funded by

Plate 1.1 Aerial view of Durrington, showing site under partial excavation, with Durrington Walls at bottom right (photo courtesy of Jack Gibbs and the Royal Navy)

2

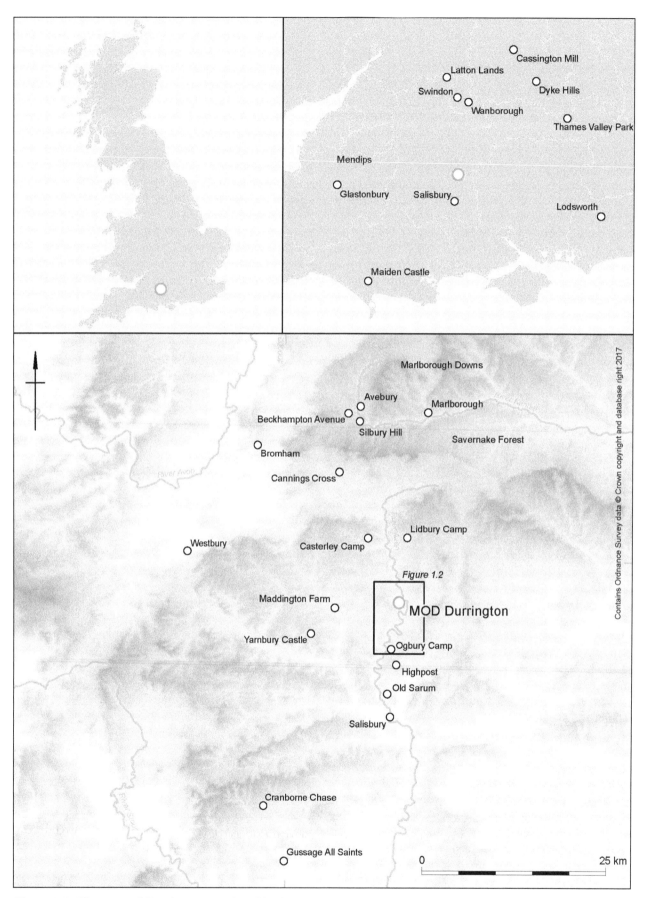

Figure 1.1 Sites around Durrington mentioned in the text

Figure 1.2 Location of the site, showing major sites within the immediate vicinity

4

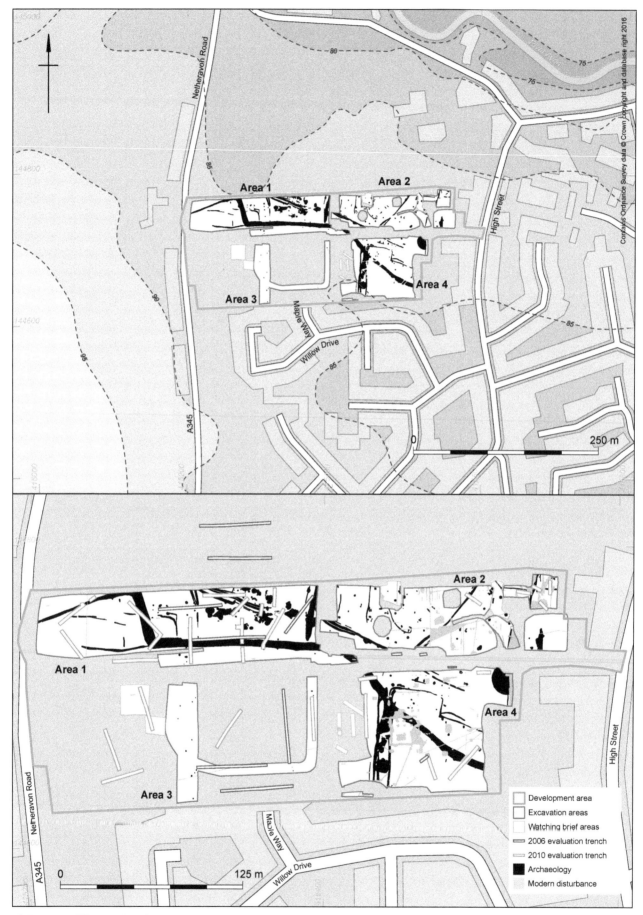

Figure 1.3 The site in relation to the earlier phases of evaluation

Persimmon Homes (South Coast) Ltd. It was preceded by two stages of evaluation – of 12 trenches in 2006, and 23 trenches in 2010 (Wessex Archaeology 2006; 2011) (Fig. 1.3) – which together had revealed a complex, multi-period site. The evaluation results led to the formulation of a mitigation strategy, agreed with WCAS, involving the detailed excavation of all areas to be affected by the proposed development, and an associated watching brief. This work was conducted in four phases (in Areas 1–4) running concurrently with the development ground-works during 2010 to 2012 (Wessex Archaeology 2012). A desk-based assessment of the MOD Buildings including Red House was undertaken in 2004 (Wessex Archaeology 2004; 2012).

Location, Topography, Geology and Soils

The site is located on the north-western edge of the village of Durrington (Fig. 1.2; Pl. 1.1). It lies between properties on the west side of High Street to the east, and Netheravon Road (A345) to the west. To the south are residential properties along Willow Drive and Maple Way, and to the north are a number of fields currently under pasture. Prior to excavation, the site was divided into a number of distinct plots of land: the western half (Areas 1 and 3), formerly cricket and football grounds, was still under pasture; the north-eastern part (Area 2) was occupied by allotments and a car park; and to the south-east (Area 4) there were a number of MOD buildings, including offices, large industrial sheds and storage units.

The surrounding landscape comprises rolling downland typical of Salisbury Plain, which in the vicinity of the site is bisected by the meandering course of the southward-flowing River Avon (Fig. 1.2). The site lies close to the valley floor, to the west of a prominent bend in the river, with higher ground to the east and west. It sits on a low ridge of slightly raised ground running from the west (Fig. 1.3), and levels vary slightly within the site, dropping from 87 m above Ordnance Datum (OD) at the south-west to 84 m along the northern side. To the south-west, at Bulford, is the confluence of Nine Mile River with the River Avon.

The geology is mapped as Seaford Chalk Formation, with superficial Head (coombe deposits) in the bases of the dry valleys and Alluvium (clay, sand and gravel) along the valley floor (British Geological Survey online viewer). On site, the natural deposits varied considerably over short distances, comprising coombe deposits with patches of clay-with-flints and of sand. The coombe deposits, laid down under periglacial conditions before the

beginning of the Holocene (c. 9500 BC), sealed a Late Glacial land surface of the Windermere (Allerød oscillation) Interstadial (c. 12,000–9500 BC). The site also contained a number of natural depressions, known as solution hollows or dolines. These features pre-date the archaeology, although a number appear to have survived as noticeable hollows at least into the Roman-British period.

The soils over the Chalk are mainly brown rendzinas, with typical calcareous brown earths over alluvium and flinty subsoils in the valleys (Jarvis et al. 1984). The topsoil in the western half of site (Areas 1 and 3) consisted of a mid-yellow brown, chalk-rich silty loam, 0.25 m deep. This sealed a mid-brown silty loam subsoil, which was at least 0.3 m thick but increased in depth towards the western and eastern limits of these Areas due to a combination of plough headlands and more recent deliberate levelling of the undulating former ground surface. The south-eastern part of site (Area 4), had similar subsoil deposits sealed by up to 1 m of made ground associated with the former MOD buildings and their subsequent demolition. The north-eastern part (Area 2) had 0.5 m of humic allotment soil, and an area of old MOD car park with 0.3 m of hardcore and tarmac.

The combination of ploughing, both modern and in antiquity, levelling for the cricket and football pitches and the numerous buildings, as well as landscaping associated with the car park and MOD buildings, resulted in the truncation of the archaeological deposits, this being particularly extensive in the eastern half of the site which was the main focus of the MOD estate buildings.

Archaeological and Historical Background

The site lies just outside the Stonehenge WHS in the archaeologically rich landscape of Salisbury Plain, which contains significant remains of prehistoric activity, including funerary and other monuments, settlements and field systems (Fig. 1.2). The Avon valley represents a key north–south communication route through the Plain and was consequently a focus for prehistoric and later activity. Neolithic and Bronze Age material is predominantly represented by ceremonial and burial monuments, as well as stray finds. Neolithic long barrows are present on the slopes of the valleys in Salisbury Plain, and Bronze Age round barrows are found on the floodplain gravels and on the adjacent terraces. One kilometre to the south-west of the site is the causewayed enclosure at Larkhill (Leivers 2017; Anon. 2017, 30–4; Field and McOmish 2017, 56), and large-scale investigations (in advance of a housing development) indicates that the area between contained various isolated barrows, pits and burials of Neolithic and Bronze Age date, as well as features reflecting small-scale Iron Age settlement activity.

Until recently most major settlement sites of these periods have been identified on the higher ground rather than on the floodplain. However, there was a significant settlement in the valley associated with the Neolithic ceremonial complex at Durrington Walls (Wainwright and Longworth 1971; Parker Pearson *et al.* 2008). The large henge enclosure is one of two important Neolithic monuments in the immediate Durrington area, the other being Woodhenge to its south, which sits 1.3 km beyond the eastern end of the Stonehenge Cursus. Other features in this area include Grooved Ware pits, long barrows and flint mines (Lawson 2007).

There are extensive groups of Bronze Age round barrows flanking Nine Mile River to the east and in the landscape around Stonehenge to the west, but relatively few in the immediate vicinity of the site. A small group of ring ditches has been identified approximately 1 km to the north-west, and a larger group approximately 1.5 km to the north-east (Darvill 2005, map 1). A possible barrow group has been identified through aerial photography 450 m south of the site, in a triangle of land between Stonehenge Road and Westfield Close (Fig. 1.2 inset). While field systems and linear boundary ditches of later Bronze Age date are recorded widely across Salisbury Plain, the nearest to the site are those recorded south of Bulford, on Earl's Farm Down (Royal Commission on Historical Monuments England (RCHME) 1979, 29–31; Richards 1990, 277–9; McOmish *et al.* 2002, 51–6).

The site lies between two Late Iron Age settlement sites – the Packway enclosure 600 m to the south and the Figheldean enclosed settlement 2 km to the north (Graham and Newman 1993; McKinley 1999) (Fig. 1.2). Iron Age features were also recorded inside Durrington Walls (Stone *et al.* 1954, 164; Wainwright and Longworth 1971, 312–28), and to its south-west (Wainwright 1971, 82–3). The Iron Age univallate enclosure of Vespasian's Camp (RCHME 1979, 20–2; Hunter-Mann 1999; Jacques *et al.* 2010; Jacques and Phillips 2014, 8) lies further south, just

west of Amesbury. All these sites lie on the western side of the Avon valley. The Figheldean enclosure continued to be occupied into the 2nd century AD, with the addition of a villa and a late Romano-British cemetery.

There is little evidence for Saxon activity in the vicinity, although the Avon valley is likely to have been one of the routes along which Saxon settlement was established. Finds of substantial Saxon cemeteries at Bulford and Tidworth (Anon. 2016) possibly indicate that some contemporary settlements could well be obscured by existing towns and villages. In the medieval period, Durrington village was divided into two parts, related to the presence of two separate manors – East End and West End. This was the origin of the division of the village into two separate groups of buildings, each with a main north–south street, with the village church between the two streets at the northern end of the village. Most farmsteads in the village were on the western street, now called High Street. Until the 12th century, Durrington was part of the King's estate of Amesbury, but by 1120 it had become a separate manor. West End Manor was granted by Henry II in 1155. Eventually the estate was bought by Winchester College and was kept fairly intact until the 20th century.

The 1839 Durrington Parish tithe map shows the site as agricultural plots immediately west of the Red House; to the south-west was the mid-18th-century Parsonage Homestead, later Parsonage Farm (Grade II listed). The 1904 Ordnance Survey (OS) map shows a number of new buildings to the west of Parsonage Farm. These may represent an expansion of the farm complex, although they could be the first MOD structures on the site; some parts of the estate were purchased by the War Department in 1899 and 1902, with the Red House adopted as offices around 1920. By 1945 (as shown on the 1961 OS map), the western half of the site comprised a football ground and cricket ground, while the 1976 OS map shows the Parsonage Farm complex as a Depot, in which the layout of buildings indicates extensive reorganisation.

Chapter 2
Late Glacial

The 2006 evaluation revealed a possible buried ground surface, formed under relatively warm climatic conditions, some 2 m below ground level and sealed by 1.5 m of soliflucted chalk (coombe deposit) indicating a very early date. During the subsequent excavation of Area 1, this palaeosol was further observed during the digging of a slot through a large Late Iron Age ditch (6203, see below), being visible as a layer in the ground into which the ditch was cut. The slot was therefore extended beyond the edge of the ditch in order to reveal the upper surface of the palaeosol (at a height of 83.35 m OD); a narrow sondage was then hand-excavated to reveal its full profile (Figs 2.1–2; Pl. 2.1).

The yellowish-brown palaeosol was formed from three distinct layers: a lower layer of initial soil formation 0.1–0.2 m thick (5995), a middle layer of chalk pieces and soil (5994), also 0.1–0.2 m thick, representing erosion from upslope, and an upper layer of stone-free soil (5993) around 0.2 m thick. These were sealed by a layer of marl-like material (5992) comprising very pale brown silt, 0.1–0.2 m thick (Fig. 2.2). This is likely to represent deteriorating climatic conditions towards the end of the warm

period, with increased rainfall and harder winters leading to rilling and erosion of the chalky substrate, which sealed and choked-off the palaeosol. Above this, were 1.5 m deep deposits of soliflucted chalk and flint (5990–1, 5997, 5989) formed by cryoturbation and indicative of the onset of full periglacial conditions.

The presence of coombe deposits above the palaeosol points to its Late Glacial (Devensian) origins. Massive post-depositional cryoturbation features (ice wedges) were recorded deforming the palaeosol (Pl. 2.1), indicating that it was a land surface formed in the relatively brief warmer period of the Windermere (Allerød oscillation) Interstadial (*c.* 12,000–9500 BC), before a return to the glacial conditions which existed prior to the beginning of the Holocene (*c.* 9500 BC). This date was confirmed by the recovery (during the initial processing of a bulk sample from the palaeosol) of significant numbers of terrestrial snails, including taxa indicative of the Late Glacial period. However, in the absence of any charcoal or artefactual material in the sample from the palaeosol (or noted during the excavation), there is no evidence for human (Late Upper Palaeolithic) activity in the immediate vicinity at this time.

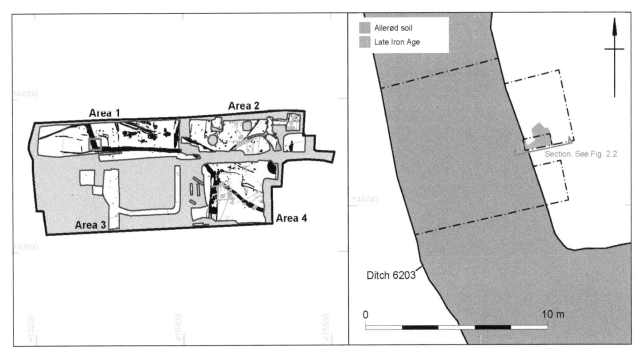

Figure 2.1 Location of the Allerød soil

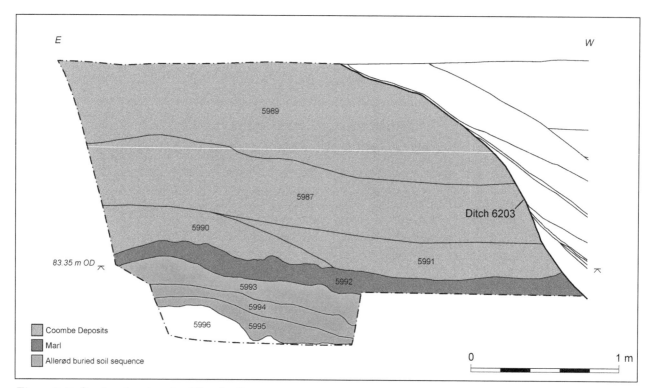

Figure 2.2 Section showing the Allerød soil sequence

Plate 2.1 The Allerød soil visible in the eastern side of ditch 6203 (slot 5199), viewed from the west

Chapter 3
Late Neolithic and Early Bronze Age

Late Neolithic

Activity during the Late Neolithic was represented by two intersecting lines of postholes, a spread of pits some of which contained Grooved Ware pottery and worked flint implements, and by evidence for flint knapping in two natural hollows one of which also contained a cremation burial (Fig. 3.1). Several later features contained residual finds probably dating from this period, including further flint knapping waste. A discoidal fragment of worked 'bluestone' (object number (ON) 36, Fig. 6.2), ground to create a tool of unknown function, was recovered from the northern end a Romano-British ditch (6256, see below).

Posthole Alignments

Two intersecting lines of Late Neolithic postholes were recorded, one (6260) aligned approximately WNW–ESE (referred to here as 'east–west') spanning Areas 1 and 4, the other (6255) aligned north–south in Area 1 (Fig. 3.1). Posthole 5047 appears to belong to both lines; the position of posthole 5106 to the east suggests that the east–west line passes through these two postholes, rather than through posthole 5060 to the south, although the latter is closer to the projected line of the east–west alignment. If posthole 5047 does mark the point of intersection of the two lines, then the east–west alignment appears to make a slight change in orientation at that point.

The component features are identified as postholes (rather than pits) from either the presence of ramps to aid the insertion and erection of posts (Pls 3.1 and 3.2), or clear evidence for packing material, although some had neither. In some, the upper deposits formed a distinct 'weathering cone', similar to those observed in postholes at Durrington Walls (Wainwright and Longworth 1971, 24), indicating that the post had decayed *in situ*.

Nine of the postholes contained Late Neolithic pottery, including Grooved Ware, and others contained worked flint with Late Neolithic characteristics, including a broken oblique flint arrowhead (ON 10, Fig. 6.1, 2) from posthole 5088, another oblique arrowhead (ON 77, Pl. 6.1, Fig. 6.1, 5) from posthole 5060, and a broken leaf-shaped

arrowhead (ON 78, Fig. 6.1, 3) from posthole 5688. Other finds included small quantities of burnt flint and animal bone. The postholes are summarised in Tables 3.1 and 3.2, and a selection are described in detail (east to west for group 6260, and north to south for 6255).

Nine radiocarbon dates were obtained from material in six of the postholes (from three postholes in each line), all of which fall in the Late Neolithic (see Barclay, Chapter 7). Note that in this report the radiocarbon date ranges quoted in *italics* are posterior density estimates derived from mathematical modelling of given archaeological problems; the ranges in plain type have been calculated according to the maximum intercept method (Stuiver and Reimer 1986).

Posthole alignment 6260

This line comprised 16 postholes recorded over a distance of 240 m, and probably continued both east and west beyond the excavation (Fig. 3.1). The postholes were irregularly spaced, between 4.8 m and 27 m apart, although there was a clear group of five more closely-spaced postholes (between 5 m and 7 m apart) at the east. There is a wide apparent gap towards the centre of Area 1 (between postholes 5087 and 5233), although this coincides with a cluster of later features which may have destroyed further Late Neolithic postholes. Among them was a line of four closely spaced features (2305, 2307, 2309 2311), recorded during the evaluation as possible tree-throw

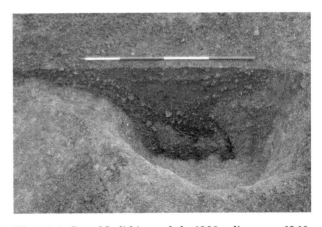

Plate 3.1 Late Neolithic posthole 6882, alignment 6260, viewed from the north-west, note remains of charred post (ON 187) in section

10

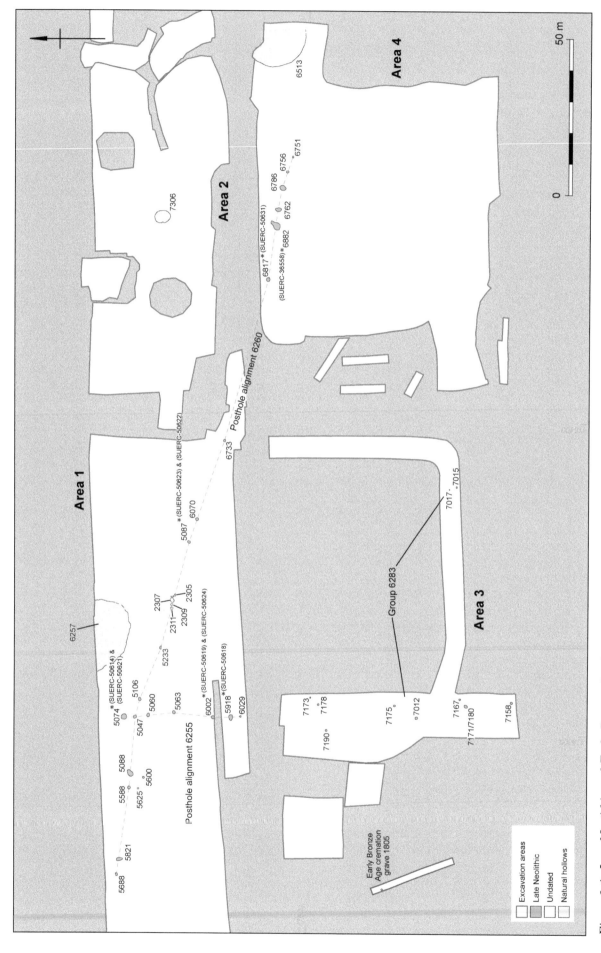

Figure 3.1 Late Neolithic and Early Bronze Age features

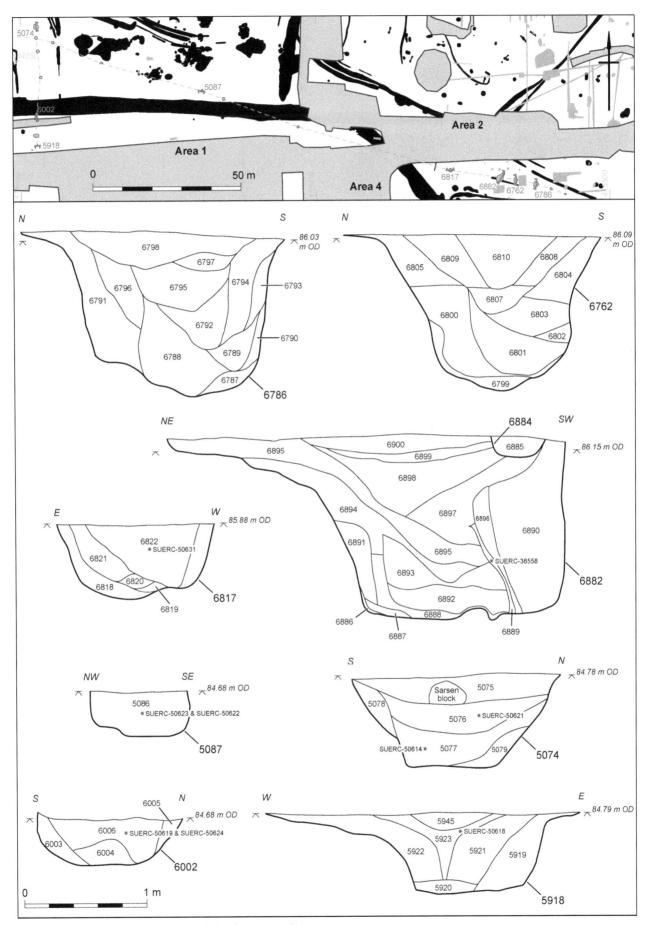

Figure 3.2 Sections of selected postholes from post alignments

Plate 3.2 Late Neolithic posthole 5918, alignment 6255, viewed from the south

holes, which corresponds closely to the alignment, but none had the appearance of a posthole nor contained any finds.

The postholes are summarised in Table 3.1, and selected examples are described below and shown in Figure 3.2. They were predominately subcircular, although those with insertion ramps (eg, 5821, 5088, 6882) had an almost tear-drop shape. They ranged in size from 0.4 m by 0.6 m wide and 0.3 m deep (6751), to 1.9 m by 3.1 m wide and 1.5 m deep (6882). There was no obvious pattern in the distribution of the larger and the smaller postholes, although three large postholes (6882, 6762 and 6786) were adjacent to each other towards the east end of the alignment.

Seven postholes contained packing material (5087, 6070, 6733, 6751, 6762, 6786, 6756). The smaller features contained only one or two fills, with some showing disturbed post-packing with no clear postpipes, suggesting that the posts had been removed rather than decaying *in situ*. Ten of the postholes contained worked flint with Late Neolithic characteristics, while one (6786) contained Grooved

Ware pottery and another (5106) contained less diagnostic pottery albeit of probable Late Neolithic date.

Posthole 5821 contained six Iron Age sherds (27 g) which are likely to be intrusive; their location within the posthole was not recorded, but the layer (5834) from which they were recovered filled all of the posthole apart from a small hollow in the top. A microlith was also recovered from this feature (fill 5833) (Fig. 6.1, 1).

Posthole 6786
Posthole 6786, which had a possible insertion ramp on its northern edge, was oval in shape with near-vertical sides and an irregular base (Fig. 3.2). It had a clear 0.65 m wide central postpipe (6788, 6792, 6795), between packing layers (eg, 6790–1, 6793–4, 6796) lying against the side of the cut. Sherds of Grooved Ware were recovered from the upper part of the postpipe (6795) and, along with worked flint, from the feature's uppermost fill (6798).

Posthole 6762
Posthole 6762 was subcircular in shape with steep to near-vertical sides and a concave base (Fig. 3.2). It had a 0.85 m wide postpipe (6801–3) on its southern side, with clay packing (6800, 6805) to the north, and clear weathering cone deposits at the top (6807–10). It contained small quantities of worked flint and burnt flint.

Posthole 6882
Posthole 6882 was tear-drop shaped with a clear insertion ramp on the north-east side (Fig. 3.2; Pl. 3.1). It had a 1 m wide central postpipe with the charred remnants of an oak post (6889, ON 187) surviving on one edge of it. A radiocarbon date of *2685–2490 cal BC (at 95% probability)* (SUERC-36558, 4060±35 BP) was obtained on the sapwood of this post. The presence of the charred remains and a

Table 3.1 Posthole alignment 6260, features west to east (pottery Late Neolithic unless indicated)

Cut	Width (m)	Length (m)	Depth (m)	No. of fills	Pottery (no/g)	Struck flint (no)	Burnt flint (g)	Animal bone (g)
5688	1.0	1.1	0.8	2	–	23	38	–
5821	1.2	2.1	1.4	2	(6/27 IA)	57	38	42
5588	1.0	1.2	0.8	2	–	2	–	–
5088	1.8	2.5	1.2	2	–	10	230	–
5047†	1.0	1.1	0.7	2	–	1	–	–
5106	0.7	0.9	0.7	2	6/4	–	18	24
5233	1.1	1.2	0.2	1	–	–	–	–
5087*	0.8	0.8	0.4	1	–	1	17	148
6070	0.9	1.1	0.8	1	–	–	–	–
6733	0.8	0.8	0.8	3	–	1	–	212
6817*	1.2	1.5	0.0	7	–	–	–	107
6882*	1.9	3.1	1.5	15	(9/91 RB)	28	1420	118
6762	1.2	2.1	1.2	11	–	5	238	–
6786	1.6	2.1	1.5	12	3/29	8	–	–
6756	0.4	0.9	0.3	2	–	–	–	–
6751	0.4	0.6	0.3	2	–	–	–	–

Key: * radiocarbon date, † posthole on both alignments, IA – Iron Age, RB – Romano-British; postholes in **bold** described in text and illustrated in Fig. 3.2

weathering cone suggest that this post had decayed *in situ*. Intrusive Romano-British sherds were recovered from the uppermost fill (6900), which was cut by a ditch (6884) of probable Romano-British date.

Posthole 6817
Posthole 6817 (west of 6882) had steep, concave sides and an irregular base (Fig. 3.2). It had evidence for post-packing, but it appears that the post had been removed, resulting in the slumping of the packing material. The fill of the resulting void (6822) contained several cattle scapula fragments, one of which was radiocarbon dated to *2570–2460 cal BC (at 95% probability)* (SUERC-50631, 3931±31 BP). It is possible that this bone postdates the removal of the post (see 5087 below).

Posthole 5087
Posthole 5087, towards the centre of the alignment in Area 1, was one of the smallest postholes, and had near-vertical sides and a flat base (Fig. 3.2). Its single fill (5086), which showed no evidence for packing, contained fragments of a probable aurochs femur, radiocarbon dated to *2500–2390 cal BC (at 95% probability)* (SUERC-50622; 3931±31 BP), and a pig vertebra radiocarbon dated to *2580–2465 cal BC (at 95% probability)* (SUERC-50623; 3999±32 BP). Both dates are statistically consistent indicating that the bones could belong to the same depositional event.

Posthole alignment 6255
The north–south line comprised at least seven postholes (including posthole 5047) extending over a distance of 40 m, all of them recorded in Area 1 (Table 3.2; Fig. 3.2). It appears likely that the line continued northwards beyond the excavation; however, at the south, although a number of Neolithic features with a less clearly linear arrangement were recorded in Area 3 (Fig. 3.1), none of these could be shown to definitely form part of the alignment.

The postholes are summarised in Table 3.2, and selected examples are described below and shown in Figure 3.2. They were spaced between 3 m and 13 m apart. Apart from posthole 5918 which was tear-drop shaped, all the rest were subcircular, ranging in size from 0.6 m in diameter and 0.3 m deep (6029) to 1.6 m by 1.8 m wide and 0.9 m deep (5074). It is again likely that some posts were allowed to decay *in situ* while others were apparently removed.

Posthole 5074
The northernmost and largest posthole in this alignment was subcircular, with concave sides and a flat base. It was filled by a series of five dumped and natural erosion deposits (Fig. 3.2). There was no evidence for an insertion ramp or a postpipe, although the uppermost fill (5075) contained a large block of worked sarsen and two smaller flaked pieces (total 17.3 kg) (see Harding and Ixer, Chapter 6, Pls 6.2–6.3) which could represent remnants of packing material disturbed by the extraction of the post. It appears unlikely that the sarsen represents the remains of a standing stone broken on removal, although this possibility cannot be completely excluded. Oak sapwood charcoal recovered from lower fill 5077, probably from the post, was radiocarbon dated to *2680–2500 cal BC (2670–2565 (89%) at 95% probability)* (SUERC-50614; 4091±29 BP), while a cattle radius from the layer above (5076) was dated to *2570–2465 cal BC (at 95% probability)* (SUERC-50621; 4010±32 BP). It can be noted that the cattle radius is younger than the post and probably belongs to a subsequent phase of activity.

Posthole 6002
Posthole 6002 was subcircular, with moderately steep concave sides and a flat base (Fig. 3.2). Its fills included possible post-packing (6003 and 6005) against the sides; towards the centre fills 6004 and 6006 contained fragments of animal bone (including pig and cattle). A sample of oak sapwood charcoal from layer 6006 was radiocarbon dated to *2700–2565 cal BC ((89.1%) at 95% probability)* (SUERC-50619; 4085±29 BP), while a cattle humerus from the same fill was dated to *2495–2355 cal BC ((91.3%) at 95% probability)* (SUERC-50624; 3915±31 BP). As with posthole 5074 the animal bone was later than the post.

Table 3.2 Posthole alignment 6255, features north to south

Cut	Width (m)	Length (m)	Depth (m)	No. of fills	Pottery (no/g)	Struck flint (no)	Burnt flint (g)	Animal bone (g)	Stone (g)
5074*	1.6	1.8	0.9	5	7/6	21	967	93	17,334
5047†	1.0	1.1	0.7	2	–	1	–	–	–
5060	1.0	1.1	0.5	2	43/58	12	15	1	–
5063	0.8	0.8	0.4	3	3/1	4	45	41	–
6002*	1.2	1.4	0.4	4	–	1	309	272	–
5918*	1.3	2.0	0.7	6	41/38	1	21	43	–
6029	0.6	0.6	0.3	4	11	2	–	2	–

Key: * radiocarbon date; † posthole on both alignments; postholes in **bold** described in text and illustrated in Fig. 3.2

Table 3.3 Features in pit group 6283

Cut	Length (m)	Width (m)	Depth (m)	No. of fills	Pottery (no/g)	Struck flint (no.)	Burnt flint (g)	Animal bone (g)	Other (g)
Area 1									
5600	0.7	0.7	0.2	1	–	34	–	–	–
5625	0.6	0.6	0.3	1	–	–	–	–	–
Area 3									
7005	0.8	0.8	0.2	1	–	8	14	–	–
7012	0.9	0.9	0.5	2	138/1863 g	244	3271	5	(st) 410
7015	0.6	0.5	0.2	1	12/68 g	81	582	–	–
7017	0.3	0.3	0.2	1	–	3	–	–	–
7158	0.8	0.7	0.4	1	31/201 g	63	695	2	–
7167	0.6	0.5	0.2	2	9/46 g	139	196	–	(fc) 32
7171	1.2	0.8	0.3	2	8/57 g	110	1112	33	–
7173	0.5	0.4	0.2	1	–	1	131	–	(fc) 3
7175	0.7	0.7	0.2	2	31/53 g	55	1577	–	–
7178	0.7	0.7	0.1	1	–	44	100	–	–
7188	0.6	0.3	0.2	1	–	–	–	–	–
7190	0.7	0.7	0.2	2	–	50	15,768	–	–

Key: st – stone, fc – fired clay

Posthole 5918

Posthole 5918, towards the southern end of the alignment, was tear-drop shaped with steep, straight sides and a flat base, and a long insertion ramp on its western side (Fig. 3.2, Pl. 3.2). It contained redeposited chalk packing (5919) concentrated on its eastern side, while a possible bedding deposit (6920) was observed at the base. The overlying fills were characteristic of weathering cone deposits suggesting that the post had rotted *in situ*. Oak sapwood charcoal from layer 5923 was radiocarbon dated to *2690–2500 cal BC (at 95% probability)* (SUERC-50618; 4110±29 BP).

Pits

Pit group 6283

Several shallow pits were recorded in the western part of Area 3 (Fig. 3.1; Table 3.3). This area of excavation varied in width from 15 to 23 m (east-west), and lay south of posthole alignment 6255. Five of the features recorded in this area contained Grooved Ware with a further three containing probably contemporary worked flint. They were initially considered to be part of, or closely associated with the posthole alignment. However, while this cannot be ruled out for some of these features, their distribution in the narrow excavation area appears largely random, and they are considered more likely to be part of a wider spread of features in the western part of the site. Two further pits (7015 and 7017), for example, were recorded in the south-eastern part of Area 3, and another two (5600 containing 34 flints, and 5625 with no finds but similar in form and fills) were close to the posthole alignments in Area 1, but apparently not part of them. All these pits are considered as a group (6283).

These features, some of which may have been dug as pairs, differed in form from the majority of the

postholes in the alignments, being generally smaller, shallower, and most having single fills (none had more than two). Moreover, as they contained no evidence for having held posts, they are considered to have been small pits, into the majority of which deposits of cultural material were made. They were all subcircular, averaging 0.65 m wide and 0.24 m deep, with bowl-shaped profiles, although pit 7012, the deepest at 0.5 m, had a distinctive conical profile (Fig. 3.4). The pits were filled with homogenous material indicative of rapid deposition. Although some contained charcoal and burnt flint none had evidence for *in situ* burning.

Over 830 pieces of worked flint (nearly 10% of the entire worked flint assemblage) were recovered from the pits. Among them were three arrowheads (ON 191 from pit 7012, Fig. 6.1, 6, Pl. 6.1; ON 201 from pit 7178, Fig. 6.1, 12, Pl. 6.1; and ON 1021 from pit 7175, Fig. 6.1, 11), three scrapers (ON 199 from pit 7167, Fig. 6.1, 7; ON 202 from pit 7173, Fig. 6.1, 8; ON 1023 from pit 7175, Fig. 6.1, 9), a piercer (ON 200 from pit 7175, Fig. 6.1, 10), and, from pit 7012, two hammerstones (ONs 194 and 195).

Other materials recovered included over 240 sherds of Grooved Ware, two rubbing stones (ONs 192 and 193) from pit 7012 and varying quantities of burnt flint (notably almost 15.7 kg from the upper fill of pit 7190, see Chapter 6 and Fig. 6.4), fired clay and animal bone. In addition, eight of the 11 pits that were sampled contained charred hazelnut shells, and a number also contained charred cereal remains.

Two of the pits (5625 and 7188) contained no finds, and a third contained only three pieces of struck flint, but their comparable form, and their proximity to other, dated pits – pit 5625 was just over 3 m from pit 5600 – raises the strong possibility that these were contemporary with the wider group. The cultural material deposited in such pits is likely to have included organic materials that have not survived, so that the absence of finds, although raising

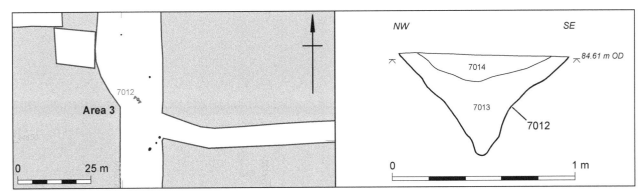

Figure 3.3 Section of Late Neolithic pit 7012

doubts about the phasing of such features, need not be significant.

Pit 7012

Subcircular pit 7012, which had a conical profile (Fig. 3.3; Pl. 3.3), is of particular interest. It contained two deposits (7013 and 7014), which together produced 165 sherds (1832 g) of Grooved Ware representing at least eight different vessels (Fig. 6.4, 1–8). Among the 241 pieces of flint were an oblique arrowhead (ON 191) and two hammerstones (ONs 194 and 195); there was also a fine-grained sandstone sharpening stone (ON 192) and a quartzite or metasediment rubber or grinding stone (ON 193). The pit also contained a cattle tooth, and charred cereal grains and hazelnut shells.

Natural Hollows

Three hollows were recorded on the site – two large solution hollows (6257 in Area 1 and 6513 in Area 4) and a smaller feature (7306 in Area 2) of uncertain origin (Fig. 3.1). Hollows 6257 and 7306 both contained substantial evidence for Late Neolithic flint knapping and were clearly the focus of significant activity. In the larger of them (6257) a layer of flint debitage was associated with a surface of flint gravel which appeared to have been laid down to consolidate the edge of the hollow. In the smaller feature (7306) cremated human remains were sealed by a layer containing some 5000 pieces of struck flint. In contrast, the excavated layers in solution hollow 6513 (excavated to a depth of 1.2 m) produced only a small flint assemblage, with all the material being residual in Romano-British or later contexts.

Solution hollow 6257

The southern half of this large subcircular hollow, a natural sinkhole, lay on the northern edge of Area 1 (Fig. 3.4). It was 23 m wide with gently sloping sides leading to the top of a central, 7 m wide near-vertical solution shaft. The hollow was excavated to a depth

Plate 3.3 Late Neolithic pit 7012, viewed from the south-west

of 3.1 m, revealing the top of the shaft which was filled with natural erosion deposits.

A series of deposits filled the wide bowl at the top of the hollow. Immediately above the natural, around its upper edge, there was a layer of flint gravel up to 4 m wide, with the appearance of a metalled surface (recorded as 6178/6146) (Pl. 3.4). This layer contained 274 pieces of struck flint, while a further 550 pieces were recovered from its surface – recorded as a separate context (6145) but not distinguishable in section.

This flint-rich layer was excavated using a grid of 1 m squares, and 100% sieved for the recovery of finds to allow for their spatial distribution to be assessed (Pl. 3.5). There was a clear concentration of struck flint on the eastern side of the hollow, consisting mostly of unretouched flake debitage, and cores and core fragments, although objects included three scrapers, one serrated flake, 10 pieces with 'miscellaneous' retouch, 16 flakes with edge damage indicative of use, and the end of a narrow bifacially retouched core tool (ON 97). There is very little discernible difference in condition between the material in and on the surface of the layer, the material in it was probably worked into it by traffic, either as the flint was being knapped or during subsequent activity at this location – as indicated by the recovery of later material, and by two later radiocarbon dates on animal bone (SUERC-50628 and SUERC-53037).

16

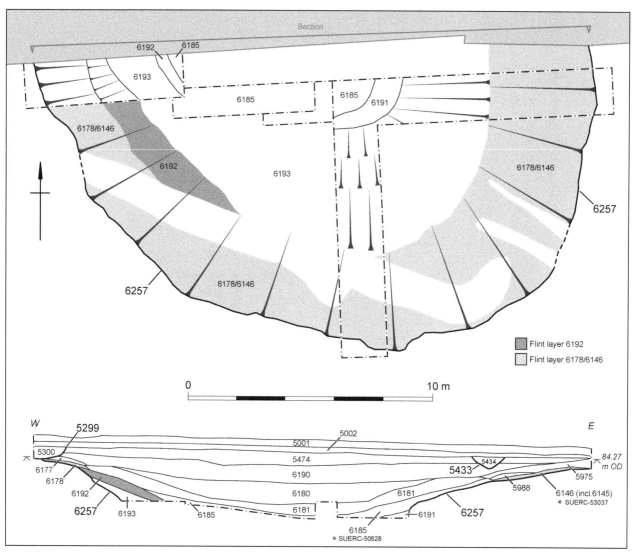

Figure 3.4 Solution hollow 6257

Plate 3.4 Flint gravel surface 6146 on the eastern side of solution hollow 6257; Romano-British field ditches are visible cutting the hollow's upper fills

A number of the grid squares towards the centre of the hollow were excavated into the deposits at lower levels, three of which (6185, 6191 and 6192) contained further struck flint; a fragment of cattle mandible from the uppermost of these deposits (6185) provided a radiocarbon date in the Early–Middle Bronze Age of 1690–1520 cal BC (SUERC-50628, 3327±31 BP, at 95% confidence). Horse bone recovered from layer 6145, on the edge of the hollow, provided a radiocarbon date in the Middle Iron Age of 400–210 cal BC (SUERC-53037, 2260±25 BP, at 95% confidence) (see Chapter 4).

The hollow had been effectively infilled by the Romano-British period, its uppermost fill (5474, below subsoil 5002) being cut by a number of parallel field ditches (Pls 3.4 and 5.1), in one of which (6226) the chronologically diagnostic pottery was of predominantly early Romano-British date; two Romano-British sherds and one medieval sherd from layer 6181 are likely to be intrusive. It may have silted up earlier, given that layer 5474 was also cut by an undated cremation-related feature (5642, see Fig. 4.1), which is suggested to be of Middle Iron Age date (see Chapter 4).

Solution hollow 6513
There is no evidence that hollow 6513, at the north-east corner of Area 4, was a focus for activity in the Late Neolithic – or indeed until the Romano-British period, with only 72 pieces of residual struck flint being recovered from it, along with the large Romano-British finds assemblage (see Chapter 5, Fig. 5.8, Pl. 5.9). It should be noted, however, that unlike hollow 6257 (excavated to over 3 m depth), hollow 6513 was excavated to a depth of only 1.2 m,

and that Romano-British pottery was recovered from throughout the recorded fill sequence, including the lowest exposed fill (6561). There is clearly the possibility, therefore, that the unexposed, pre-Romano-British fills may also have contained evidence for prehistoric activity, comparable to that in hollow 6257. Although much of the Late Neolithic flintwork in hollow 6257 was recovered from relatively high levels around its edge, it is possible that the use of hollow 6513 in the Romano-British period caused its upper edges to erode down to greater depths towards its centre (ie, to below the level of excavation). A potential significance for this feature during the Late Neolithic, therefore, cannot be ruled out.

Hollow 7306 and cremation burial 7531
Evidence for flint knapping was also recorded in a much smaller hollow (7306), measuring 3.7 m by 4.5 m, and 0.4 m deep, in Area 2 (Fig. 3.5, Pl. 3.6). The nature of this hollow (125 m to the east of hollow 6257 and 57 m north-west of hollow 6513) remains unclear. It was interpreted in the field as the upper part of a natural solution hollow, similar to but smaller than hollows 6257 and 6513. However, given its relatively small size and regular shape (and the lack of any recorded evidence for its greater depth), as well as the nature of the basal deposits, an anthropogenic origin cannot be ruled out.

As with hollow 6257, this feature was excavated on a grid of 1 m squares, and 100% sieved so that the spatial distribution of the flints could be assessed. There was a thin layer of possibly trampled soil (7359) on the base, on the surface of which in the centre was a 0.4 m wide concentration of cremated

Plate 3.5 The grid excavation of the fills of solution hollow 6257

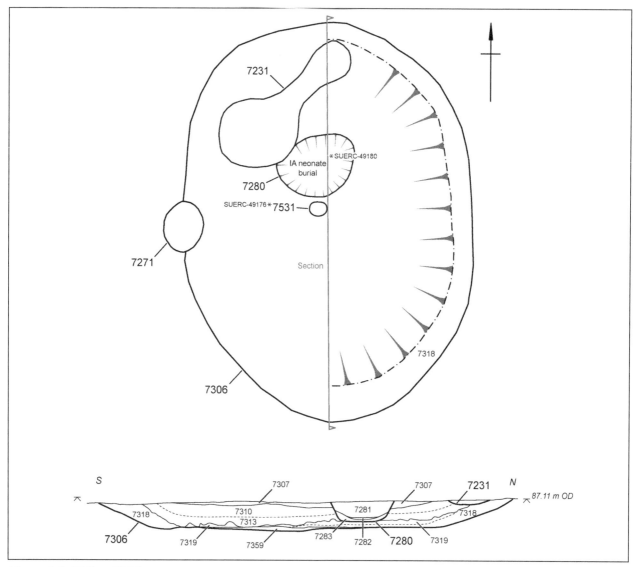

Figure 3.5 Hollow 7306

human bone (7531), of an individual aged 30–50 years. The deposit, which was unurned, was probably in some form of organic container, and the fact that it had not been significantly disturbed suggests that it was covered relatively soon after deposition. A sample of the bone was radiocarbon dated to *2585–2460 cal BC (at 95% probability)* (SUERC-49176, 4000±34 BP).

There was some slumping of the natural gravels at the edge of the hollow (7318), but there was little sign of disturbance to the cremation deposit before it was covered with a deposit of flint knapping waste. This was represented by a thin layer of silty clay (7319) containing 2628 pieces of flint debitage. The flints displayed little evidence for patterning, indicating that it was not the result of *in situ* knapping within the hollow, although the material was concentrated in the south-eastern quadrant, suggesting that it had been deposited from that side. This layer was sealed by a series of natural silting layers containing a further

2729 pieces of worked flint. These flints were more evenly distributed, possibly deriving from surface deposits related to those that had been deliberately deposited, or from further episodes of either flint knapping, or the deposition of knapping waste, over an extended period. The upper fills were cut by an Iron Age feature (7280) containing a neonate burial (see Chapter 4), and by a Romano-British oven (7231) and pit (7271) (see Chapter 5).

Early Bronze Age

The only Bronze Age feature recorded was a small grave (1805) containing a cremation burial in an Early Bronze Age Collared Urn. The grave was identified during the 2010 evaluation and preserved *in situ*; it lies outside the excavation area, west of Area 3 (Fig. 3.1). A small undated feature (5642 in Area 1) containing cremated remains could also be of this

Plate 3.6 Hollow 7306 during excavation, viewed from the north, also showing parts of Middle/Late Iron Age grave 7280 and Romano-British oven 7231

date, but is considered more likely to be contemporary with three Middle Iron Age cremation burials recorded on the site (see Chapter 4, Fig. 4.1).

The only other evidence for activity during the Bronze Age comprised the piece of cattle mandible from solution hollow 6257 (see above) which was radiocarbon dated to 1690–1520 cal BC (SUERC-50628, 3327±31 BP, at 95% confidence), ie, of Early–Middle Bronze Age date, and an abraded sherd of grog and flint-tempered pottery, of probably similar date, recovered residually from the Late Iron Age enclosure ditch 6203 (see Chapter 4).

Chapter 4
Iron Age

There was no evidence from the site for activity during the Early Iron Age, and very limited evidence, predominantly from radiocarbon-dated burials, for Middle Iron Age activity (Fig. 4.1). Only a small quantity of Iron Age pottery (57 sherds weighing 680 g) was recovered. Other finds possibly of this date include a hooked blade (from an otherwise undated pit, 5892, ON 92, Fig. 6.8, 8), three fired clay slingshots (from Romano-British pits 5756 and 7140, and enclosure ditch 6203, Fig. 6.7, 6–7), an antler weaving comb (ON 183 from solution hollow 6513, Fig. 6.10, 1) and two possible worked bone gouges (from the Romano-British trackway and pit 6850) (see Chapter 5, Figs 5.1 and 5.2). It is possible that some of the other undated features, such as pits containing either no finds or variable quantities of worked flint, burnt flint and/or animal bone, also belong to this phase.

There was also a rectilinear arrangement of undated ditches at the north-west of the site (5008, 5012, 6200, 6205, 6206) which could represent part of a late prehistoric field system; the eastern end of ditch 6206 was recorded as being cut by the outer edge of the Late Iron Age ditch (6203, below), although this need not mean that it pre-dates it; a number of similarly orientated ditches in the same area (6207, 6208) are of Romano-British date (see Chapter 5).

Middle Iron Age

Three unurned cremation burials (in graves 7530 and 5206 in Area 1, and 6548 in Area 4) were radiocarbon dated to the Middle Iron Age; one other undated feature (5642 in Area 1) containing cremated human remains is also considered likely to be of this date (Fig. 4.1). A neonate inhumation burial (in grave 7280 in Area 2) provided a radiocarbon date which spanned the Middle and Late Iron Age.

Grave 5206

Grave 5206 (0.3 m by 0.4 m, and 0.1 m deep) (Fig. 4.2), contained the cremated remains of a possible male aged 30–45 years (5221), as well as a few

fragments of possible sheep bone. A sample of human bone produced a radiocarbon date of 360–90 cal BC (SUERC-49173, 2156±34 BP). The grave cut the fill of a small tree-throw hole (5219).

Feature 5642

A small feature (0.4 m by 0.5 m, and 0.07 m deep) (Fig. 4.2), which cut the upper fill (5474) of solution hollow 6257, contained a small quantity (less than 4 g) of cremated human bone from a child aged 4–5 years, as well as a few fragments of charred immature sheep/goat bone, two pieces of burnt flint and a few fragments of charcoal. It is unclear whether this feature was a grave, or whether the material was redeposited, either intentionally or unintentionally. The human remains, found near the surface in the southern part of the feature, clearly represent only part of the individual, but is also likely that the feature had been heavily truncated. There was insufficient bone for radiocarbon dating, and while there is evidence for cremation burial in the Early Bronze Age (see Chapter 3), it is considered more likely that this feature is associated with the Middle Iron Age cremation activity.

Grave 6548

Grave 6548 (0.8 m by 0.9 m, and 0.26 m deep) (Fig. 4.2) contained the remains of a possible female aged 35–45 years (6549), accompanied by fragments of sheep bone. A sample of human bone produced a radiocarbon date of 400–200 cal BC (SUERC-49174, 2240±34 BP).

The grave was recorded cutting the fills of a north–south ditch (6243) which appears to be associated with a Romano-British trackway; the ditch contained 11 sherds (148 g) of predominantly early Romano-British pottery. If the recorded stratigraphic position of the grave is correct, this would suggest either that the radiocarbon determination is wrong (although it is very close to the dates obtained from graves 7530 and 5206), or that the material in the feature was redeposited (see Trackway, Chapter 5).

21

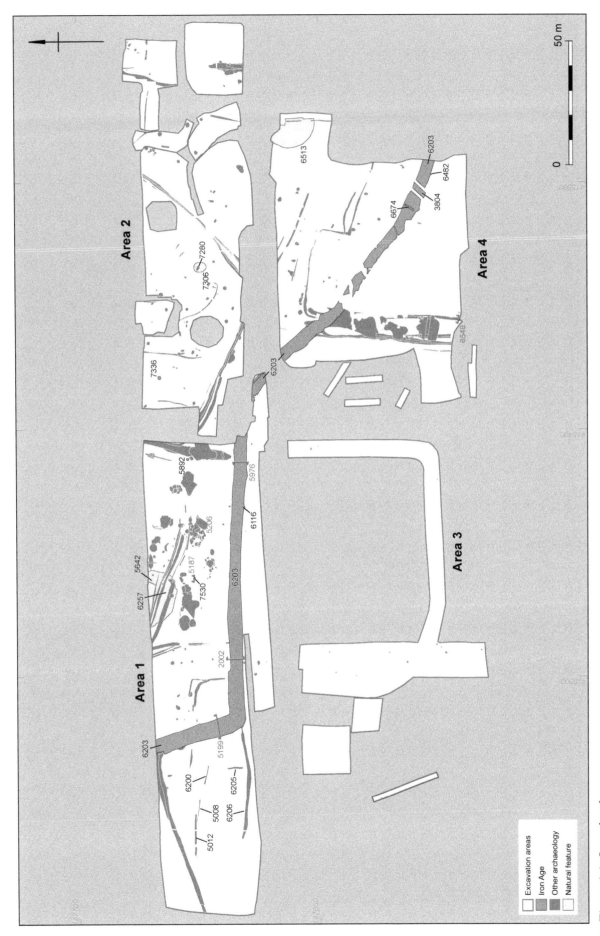

Figure 4.1 Iron Age features

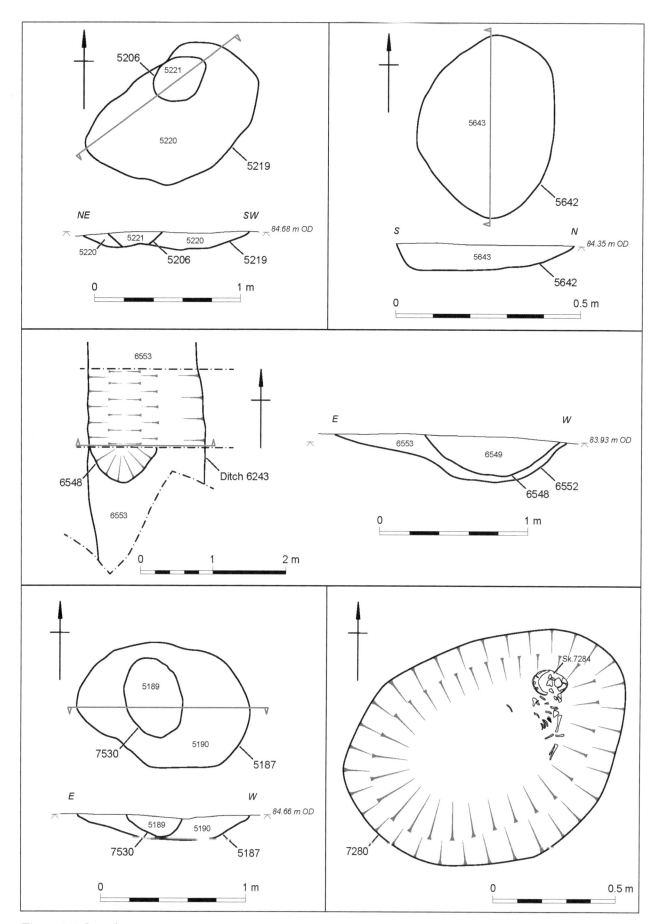

Figure 4.2 Iron Age graves

Grave 7530/Feature 5187

Grave 7530 (0.5 m by 0.7, m and 0.12 m deep) (Fig. 4.2), contained the remains of a child aged 4–5 years, as well as fragments of sub-adult/adult skull, a tooth of a 1–2-year-old and fragments of animal bone. The human bone was recorded both from the grave fill (5189) and from the fill (5190) of a larger feature (5187), possibly a tree-throw hole, into which the grave was cut, perhaps having migrated downwards through natural processes. A sample of human bone (from 5190) produced a radiocarbon date of 410–230 cal BC (SUERC-49175, 2286±34 BP).

Other Middle Iron Age Evidence

A horse metapoidal recovered from layer 6145 in solution hollow 6257 (see Fig. 3.4) was radiocarbon dated to 400–210 cal BC (SUERC-53037, 2260±25 BP, at 95% confidence) which is of a similar date to the cremation burials. While this adds to the evidence for activity on the site at this time, it provides little further information about the nature of that activity beyond cremation and burial.

While some of the Iron Age pottery from the site could be of Middle Iron Age date, sherds from only two diagnostically Middle Iron Age vessels were identified – 22 sherds (216 g) from a handmade, thick-walled, hemispherical cup, and one sherd from a carinated cup – in both cases residual in Late Iron

Age ditch 6203 (below) (contexts 6609 and 6668, respectively). Six Iron Age sherds were intrusive in Neolithic posthole 5821 (see Chapter 3).

Feature 7280

Fourteen Iron Age sherds (215 g) were recovered from a subcircular pit or grave containing a neonate inhumation burial (Fig. 4.2), a sample of bone from which was radiocarbon dated to 210–40 cal BC (SUERC-49180, 2094±34 BP), spanning the Middle and Late Iron Age. The cut was 0.7 by 1.1 m wide and 0.3 m deep, and the flexed inhumation (7284) had been placed on the base against the eastern side, laid on its left side with the head to the north-north-east, facing east (Figs 3.5 and 4.2).

What is notable is that that this feature was cut into uppermost fill of hollow 7306 (see Chapter 3, Figs 3.1, 3.5, Pl. 3.6), which contained a Late Neolithic cremation burial and a large assemblage of Late Neolithic flint knapping waste. While it may be coincidental that the neonate burial was made at same place in the landscape, the possibility that this location retained some special significance cannot be entirely ruled out.

The lowest of three fills in feature 7280 contained small quantities of worked flint, burnt flint and animal bone, but it is likely that some of these finds were residual given the contents of hollow 7306. The other two fills contained a further 41 pieces of worked

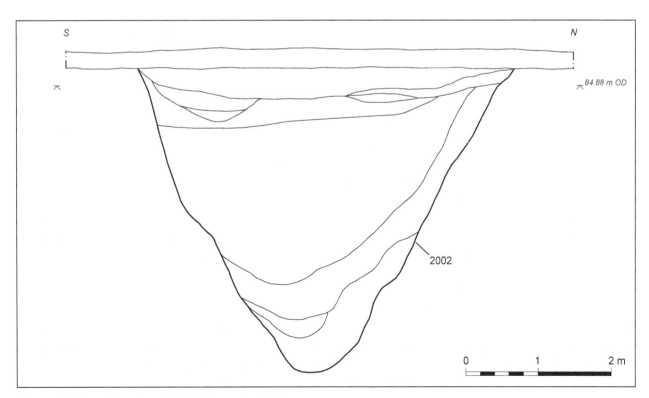

Figure 4.3 Late Iron Age ditch 6203, section 2002

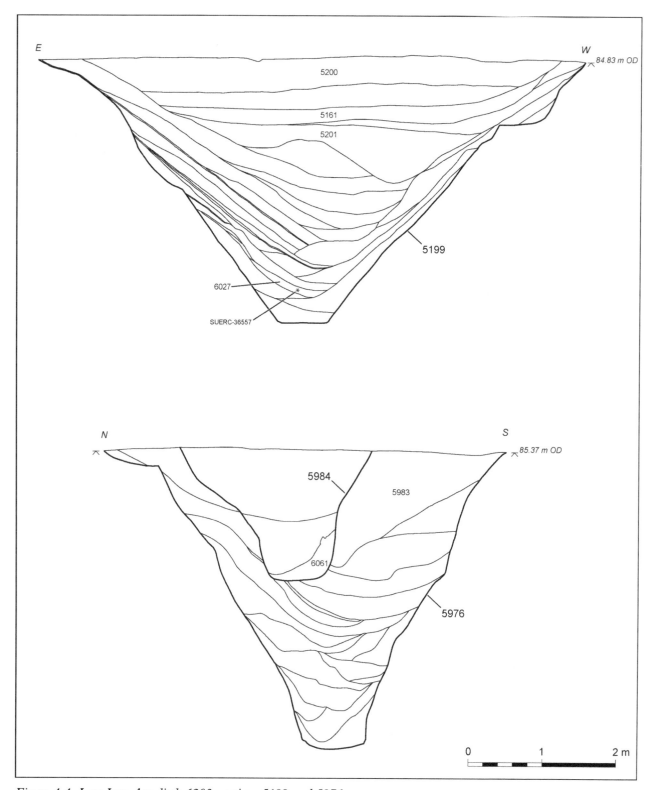

Figure 4.4 Late Iron Age ditch 6203, sections 5199 and 5976

flint, 4535 g of burnt flint and 1050 g of animal bone, including cattle, red deer and sheep/goat, perhaps deliberately deposited. It is uncertain whether to view this feature as a pit in which a neonate had been buried, or a grave in which other materials had been also deposited.

Late Iron Age

Evidence directly dated to the Late Iron Age is also very limited. While it is quite possible that some of the pottery datable only as Late Iron Age/early Romano-British, is of pre-Conquest date, most of this material

Plate 4.1 Enclosure ditch 6203, slot 5199, viewed from the north-west

came from Romano-British features, and those sherds recovered from Late Iron Age ditch 6203 (below) come only from the Romano-British (or later) tertiary fills.

'Enclosure' Ditch and Bank

The dominant feature on the site was a substantial ditch (6203) which followed an irregular north-west to south-east course for 290 m across Areas 1 and 4 (Fig. 4.1). Although it is not yet possible to determine whether it formed part of an enclosure, or some other form of more extensive land boundary, it is referred here to as an *enclosure* ditch. Two lengths, of 9 m and 12 m, lay between the excavated areas but there was no evidence for a clear entrance break in the ditch within the site. The reasons for the sharp change in direction at the west, and a more gradual turn in the centre of the site, are not known.

The full profile of the ditch was revealed in five slots (Fig. 4.1), slots 2002 (Fig. 4.3) and 3804 during the evaluation, and slots 5199, 5976 (Fig. 4.4) and 6674 during the excavation; a number of partial profiles were also excavated. The ditch had a generally V-shaped profile but varied considerably in the steepness of its sides and in its fill sequence, partly a reflection of the highly variable geology across the

site. In slot 2002, for example, where it cut through solid blocky chalk, it was 5 m wide and 4 m deep with very steep sides (Fig. 4.3); in contrast, in slot 5199, where it cut through relatively soft coombe deposit, it was 7.8 m wide and 3.6 m deep with significantly shallower sides (Fig. 4.4; Pl. 4.1). In all the sections, the lower secondary fills derived predominantly from the northern/eastern side (ie, river-side) of the ditch, strongly suggesting that there had been a bank on that side.

There is limited dating evidence for the construction of the ditch, and there were few clear stratigraphic relationships with earlier, dated features. However, animal bone from a small pit (6482) cut by the outer edge of the ditch towards the east of the site, provided a radiocarbon date of *90 cal BC–60 cal AD (SUERC-50629, 2010±30 BP, at 95% probability)*. While it is possible that the pit postdates the construction of the ditch, and was cut only by the subsequent erosion of its edge, a similar but slightly later date, of *20 cal BC–cal AD 80 (SUERC-36557, 1995±35 BP, at 95% probability)*, was obtained from a cattle mandible found low in the ditch (in slot 5199) (Fig. 4.4). The lower secondary fill (6027) containing the dated bone is likely to have been deposited soon after the ditch was dug, when only 0.35 m of eroded material had accumulated on its base, since there is no evidence for any significant maintenance or de-silting the ditch following its construction. A modelled date for the ditch construction based on the three radiocarbon results and the stratigraphy indicates that this could have taken place during *50 cal BC to 70 cal AD (95% probability), possibly during 15 cal BC to 50 cal AD (68% probability).*

The dating above supports an event in the final Late Iron Age, and fits well with archaeological expectation as it is unlikely that such a substantial earthwork would have been constructed after the Roman Conquest. Most of the pottery from the ditch (predominantly Romano-British) was recovered from its upper fills, although in slot 6674 three Romano-British sherds, two of Savernake-type ware and one of greyware, were recovered from secondary fills (6662, 6663 and 6666) in the lower half of the section.

The scale of the ditch and suggested bank indicates that the earthwork almost certainly had a defensive purpose, although without further information about its course beyond the site it is not clear what it was defending. It lies at least 270 m south-west of a large westward meander in the River Avon, and crosses the low spur of ground above 85 m OD that runs east from the western side of the valley (Fig. 1.3). However, it is not yet possible to determine whether it formed part of an enclosure, either flanking or spanning the river, or some other form of more extensive land boundary. What is notable, however, is the almost complete absence of contemporary features, particularly those associated with settlement, in the 'interior' (ie, to its north), although it is possible, if the ditch bounded a very large area, that only part of it was used for settlement activities.

Chapter 5
Romano-British and post-Roman

Early Romano-British

Given the suggested date for the construction of ditch 6203 in the Late Iron Age (possibly late in that period), and the occurrence in one of the excavated slots of Romano-British pottery relatively low in its fill sequence (when filled to approximately one third of its depth), the ditch would certainly have been a significant feature at the start of the Romano-British period (Figs 5.1 and 5.2). However, such a substantial earthwork is unlikely to have had any continuing defensive role, although the area it defined (if it was an enclosure) may have continued to be a focus of activity, including new activities, through the Romano-British period, with different activities apparently organised in different zones.

Precise dating of the Romano-British features is problematical, however, as the Savernake-type wares which constitute most of the pottery remained relatively unchanged from the 1st to the 3rd centuries AD. Although 65% (by weight) of the Romano-British pottery from the site was chronologically undiagnostic, only 8% was diagnostically middle or late Romano-British, suggesting that the main period of settlement activity on the site was likely to be in the 1st and early 2nd centuries AD.

Ditch 6203

In the three slots (5199, 5976 and 6674) through the Late Iron Age ditch excavated to its full depth during the excavation (eg, Fig. 4.4), the bulk of the finds came from the upper (tertiary) fills, for example 95% (by weight) of the pottery, 98% of the burnt flint and 82% of the animal bone. The latter included a number of animal bone groups, such as articulating sheep vertebrae (ABG 1) in slot 2002, and a partial

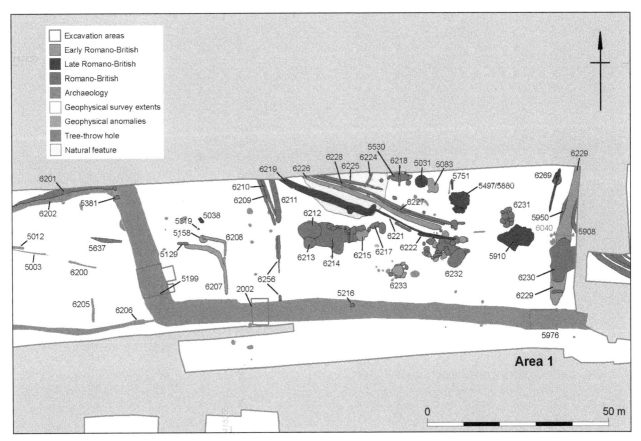

Figure 5.1 Romano-British features in Area 1

28

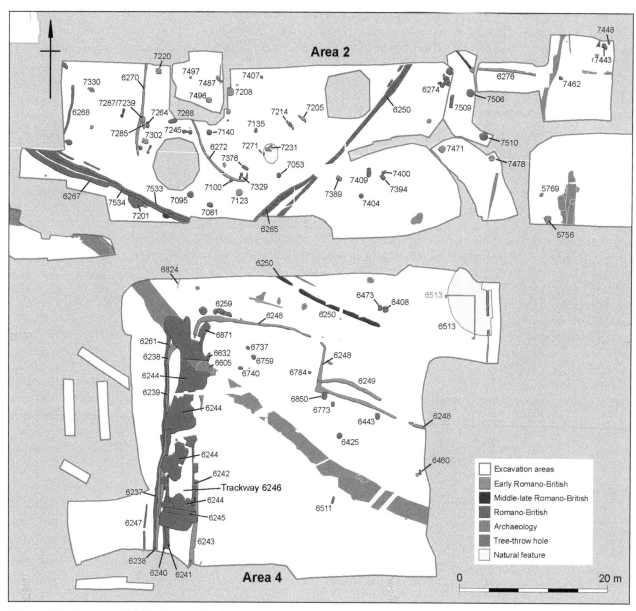

Figure 5.2 Romano-British features in Areas 2 and 4

dog skeleton (ABG 14) in slot 5199. These fills overlay the substantial lower and upper secondary deposits which include those which appear to derive from the bank, and it is possible that there was an episode of deliberate levelling of the bank and infilling of the ditch, effectively decommissioning the feature as a defensive earthwork, early in the early Romano-British period (Pl. 4.1). In the two slots excavated during the evaluation, 2002 (Fig. 4.3) and 3804, the secondary fills were described as the result of deliberate backfilling (Wessex Archaeology 2011, 6).

Of the 775 sherds (15646 g) of pottery from the ditch only two contexts – tertiary fills 5200 and 5201 in slot 5199 (Fig. 4.4) – produced middle or late Romano-British pottery (9.6% by weight); the rest was either early Romano-British or of undiagnostic

Romano-British date. This suggests that the almost complete infilling of the ditch took place during the early Romano-British period.

Possible recuts

There was evidence to suggest that at least parts of the ditch were recut when it was almost completely filled up. No significant recut was observed in either of the slots excavated during the evaluation – 2002 (Fig. 4.3) and 3804 – and there were no obvious discontinuities in the fill sequences in slots 5199 (Fig. 4.4) and 6674. However, a feature (5984) was visible in section cutting the tertiary fill (5893) in slot 5976 (Fig. 4.4), although it was much smaller than the original ditch – just 2.4 m wide and 1.6 m deep – with an asymmetrical profile and a flat base. Some of the

Plate 5.1 Area 1 viewed from the east from a high-elevation camera, showing enclosure ditch 6203 with localised dark upper fills, solution hollow 6257, groups of intercutting pits and some of the field system ditches

early Romano-British sherds from this feature link with material in the tertiary fill of the original ditch. If this was a recut of the ditch it may be associated with a north–south Romano-British ditch (6229), 3–4 m wide and 1.8–2.4 m deep, which terminated to the immediate north of the slot – and which must, therefore, have been dug after the levelling of the bank (Fig. 5.1).

A photograph of ditch 6203 further to the west in Area 1 (Pl. 5.1, taken from a high-elevation camera) shows a narrow band of darker ditch fills which appears to terminate just east of a shallow pit (5216, Fig. 5.1) which cut the uppermost ditch fill, then to continue further – but not as far as slot 2002. This darker soil may simply represent variability in the ditch's uppermost fills, but if it does represent a length of recut ditch, it is possible that there was a break in it at the location of pit 5216. The pit, which was only 0.1 m deep and had a very dark ashy fill, contained Romano-British pottery, burnt flint and animal bone, as well as an iron nail.

A possible north-western terminal for a recut was also recorded in Area 4 (Fig. 5.2), in a partially excavated slot (6605) on the western edge of the Romano-British trackway (see below) which crossed the infilled ditch. The possible terminal was 1.2 m deep and an estimated 2.1 m wide and cut through a chalky, probably secondary ditch fill (6606). Its stratigraphic relationship with a trackside ditch (6632) was not established, however, nor was any opposing terminal recorded to the north-west, although this may have been concealed by the unexcavated length of the trackway surface. Cattle bone from ditch fill 6606 provided a radiocarbon date of *20–140 cal AD (SUERC-50630, 1902±30 BP, at 95% probability)*, although the precise location of the bone in the ditch profile is not known.

In Area 1, at the north-western extent of ditch 6203, a V-shaped cut (5381), 2.7 m wide and 1.1 m deep, was recorded in section in a 1.5 m wide sondage, just cutting the outer edge of the enclosure ditch (Fig. 5.1). If this cut was a ditch, it had clearly diverged from the line of ditch 6203; moreover, it terminated in the sondage (cutting an earlier deep pit, 5386). The stratigraphic relationships at the north-western extent of ditch 6203 were complicated by its intersection at that point with two ditches approaching from the west – Romano-British ditch 6201 and possible medieval ditch 6202. Similarly, during the evaluation, a possible recut was observed (but not excavated) along the outer edge of the enclosure ditch, 10 m further south, but no such recut was evident in slot 5199, a further 15 m to the south.

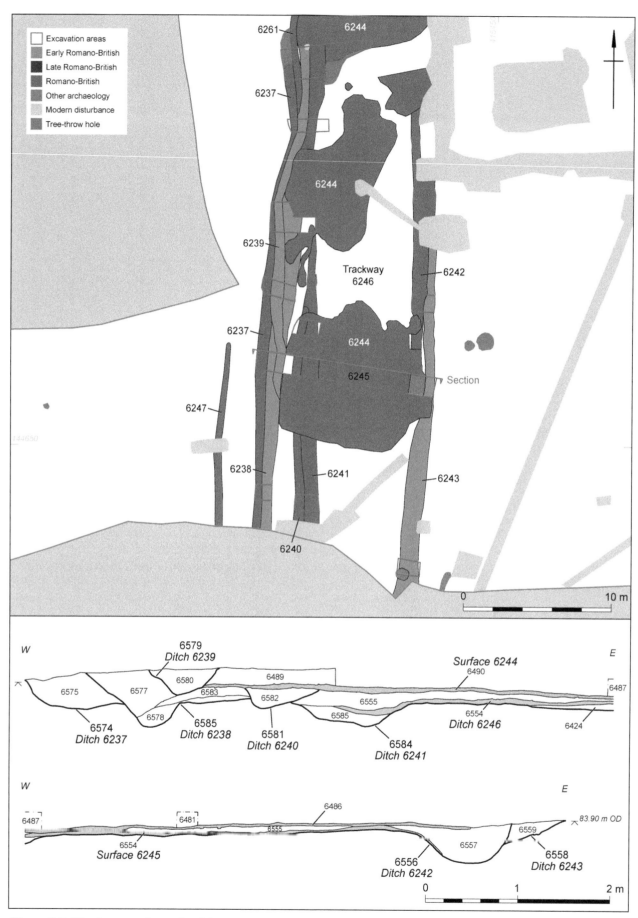

Figure 5.3 Trackway and associated features

Trackway

An important event which followed the infilling of ditch 6203 was the construction of a north–south trackway (6246) that crossed the former boundary at an oblique angle in Area 4, and was traced for at least 50 m (Figs 5.2 and 5.3). It had a metalled surface and was defined by a series of flanking ditches between 6 m and 10 m apart, indicating that its general line had been maintained, but also widened, over time (Fig. 5.3). The trackway was marked on its eastern side by ditch 6243 (recut as 6242), while on its western side there was a sequence of at least six ditch cuts (6237, 6238, 6239, 6240, 6241 and 6261). A short length of undated ditch (6247) which lay parallel to the trackway over 2 m further west may be related to the trackway but not directly associated with it.

As noted above (see Chapter 4), ditch 6243 was recorded as being cut by a cremation grave (6548) from which a radiocarbon date of 400–200 cal BC (SUERC-49174) was obtained on human bone. This would appear to indicate that the ditch was of Middle Iron Age or earlier date, and by implication the trackway also – as well as the enclosure ditch over which it passes. However, as noted above, the recovery from the ditch 6243 of early Romano-British pottery, and the other dating associations, would appear to rule out that possibility, although the reason for this apparent inconsistency remains unresolved.

The trackway itself comprised a sequence of two main surfaces (6245 and 6244), only partially surviving, metalled with angular and rounded pieces of flint, with possible additional localised repairs. Towards the south (Fig. 5.3), the lower surface (6245), the edges of which dipped into the inner trackside ditches (6241 and 6242), was overlain by a layer of trampled soil (6555), which in turn was sealed by an upper metalled surface (6244) that extended across the (by-then infilled) inner ditches (Pl. 5.2, Fig. 5.3). No finds were recovered from the early metalled surface (6245), but the trampled layer and the upper surface, as well as all the trackside ditches, contained Romano-British (and in some cases early Romano-British) pottery. Sealing this second road surface was another trample deposit (6481/6487/6489), from which was recovered the earliest identified coin from the excavation, an *as* of Domitian minted in AD 86 (ON 117).

Towards the north, where the trackway rose slightly onto the spur of higher ground, its line formed a more noticeable hollow in the relatively soft coombe deposit; the fills of this hollow contained pottery of early–late Romano-British date. As it passed across ditch 6203 (Fig. 5.2), the lower metalled surface dipped down approximately 1 m into the infilled ditch, presumably as traffic compacted the underlying fills. Subsequently, this hollow was refilled before the laying down of the upper metalled surface. The trackway also cut into the fills of the terminal of the possible ditch recut (6607, see above).

The upper trackway surface extended less than 2 m north of ditch 6203, although it may originally have continued further, the two outer trackside ditches on the eastern side (6632 and 6871) terminating 2 m and

Plate 5.2 Upper metalled surface 6244 of trackway 6246, overlying infilled ditches 6242 and 6243, viewed from the south; the lower surface 6245 is visible in the section

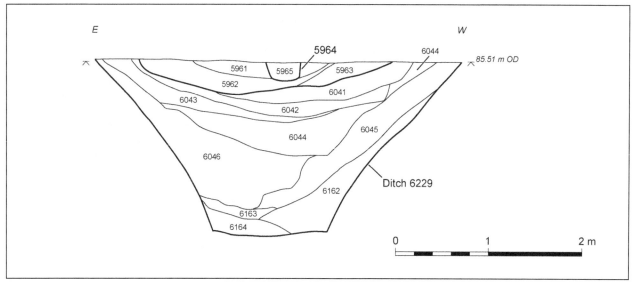

Figure 5.4 Ditch 6229

7 m, respectively, beyond the ditch. The terminal of the outermost ditch (6632) turns slightly to the north-east, possibly matching the line of ditch 6238 on the western side of the trackway, while that of ditch 6871 curved more noticeably to the north-east, matching the line of a possible field ditch (6248) which curves around it towards the east and was part an arrangement of ditches extending to the east.

The northward continuation of the trackway's western ditches may be represented by a short length of truncated undated ditch (6824). However, determining the relationship between the trackway and the more complex array of field ditches to the north is hampered by the 15 m wide unexcavated strip of ground between Areas 4 and 2.

Field Ditches

There was a complex array of Romano-British ditches in Areas 1, 2 and 4, most of them lying to the north and east of ditch 6203 (Figs 5.1 and 5.2). They were of variable size, although most were relatively small (1–1.5 m wide) and they probably represent the boundaries of fields or paddocks, or other small land plots (they are referred to here as *field* ditches). Their layout clearly indicates different phases of organisation of the landscape, although their phasing is hampered by the general lack of stratigraphical relationships between them (other than between recuts). Prominent among them are a series of west-north-west to east-south-east orientated ditches, off which other ditches extend towards the north or north-east, creating a possible 'ladder' arrangement of at least three fields extending to the north.

Other ditches, however, do not fit easily within this pattern, and some may represent an earlier phase

of activity. Among these is north–south ditch 6229, which extended south of the line of those 'ladder' field boundaries (Fig. 5.1). This suggests that at least its southern end may have gone out of use by the time the fields were laid out; one of the field ditches (5908/6267) curved northwards to follow the line of ditch 6229, cutting its fills, although ditch 6229 appears to have cut an earlier possible ditch (5950) on a similar alignment.

The southern terminal of ditch 6229 lay just 1 m from the northern edge of the infilled enclosure ditch (6302), indicating that any bank had been levelled by the time it was dug, and it may have been associated with the possible recut of the enclosure ditch which was observed in the slot to its immediate south (5976, see above, Fig. 4.4). It was more substantial than the other field ditches, being up to 3 m wide and 2.2 m deep, with moderately steep slightly convex sides and a flat base (Fig. 5.4). Approximately half of the pottery from it is of certain or probable early Romano-British date. It was cut by a large shallow hollow (6230), of uncertain nature which extended 12 m along the ditch as well as east beyond the Area 1 excavation area.

In Area 4, to the south-east, a number of ditches were connected to the trackway running up from the south. Ditch 6248, for example, defines what appears to be an arrangement of small subrectangular fields; another length of ditch (6249) may represent their slight modification. Of the pottery from ditch 6248, 89% (by weight) was either Late Iron Age/early Romano-British or early Romano British; and 96% from 6249 was early Romano-British.

Only in Area 1, at the western end of the site, were there field ditches recorded outside the former enclosure (Fig. 5.1). A number of these contained no dating evidence (eg, 5008, 5012, 6200, 6205, 6206), and as mentioned above (see Chapter 4) it is possible that some were of pre-enclosure date, ie, Iron Age or earlier. However, they appear to be closely associated with a number of early Romano-British ditches both outside (5637) and inside the enclosure (eg, 5129, 6207, 6208). Ditches 6208 and 6207, both of which contained early Romano-British pottery, appear to represent the reworking the corner of a small field; the earlier ditch (6208) cut an early Romano-British pit (5158). If some or all these ditches were associated, the early Romano-British field system at the west would appear to have spanned the former enclosure ditch, indicating that it must have been substantially infilled, and therefore no longer an effective boundary, by this time; also, as ditch 6207 terminated just short of ditch 6203, the internal bank must have been levelled by that time.

Although the enclosure ditch was largely infilled in the early Romano-British period, and the bank levelled, its line would still have been known, and it is possible that its general north-west to south-east orientation was reflected in the orientation of the ladder ditches, suggesting some continuity in overall land division (Pl. 5.1). The boundaries of some of these fields appear to have been relatively long-lived as indicated by the repeated recutting of ditches on the same general line (Pl. 5.3). On the basis of the pottery, some appear to be of early Romano-British date, while others continued in use into the late Romano-British period. One of these ditches in Area 1 (6226), for example, contained a significant component (25% by weight) of early Romano-British pottery (and no late Romano-British sherds), while a more substantial, parallel ditch (6219), 2 m to its south, had late Romano-British pottery throughout its fill sequence. That some of these ditches continued in use into the late Romano-British period is also demonstrated by the recovery from (north-west–south-east) ditch 6250 (Area 4) of three coins of the House of Constantine struck between AD 330 and 348.

The southern boundary of the ladder fields was broken by a gap at least 25 m wide at the eastern end of Area 1, although this may have been significantly wider by the late Romano-British period, since late Romano-British ditch 6219 (above) terminated (at a sharp northward turn) some 20 m to the west of the other ditches in this length of boundary. There was a cluster of postholes around the ditch terminals on the western side of the gap. The possibility of entrances into the two fields to the east was obscured by the strip of unexcavated ground between Areas 2 and 4 (Fig. 5.2).

In the central of the three fields (in Area 2) there were a number of other ditches (eg, 6268, 6270, 6272) which may represent either earlier boundaries – two (6270 and 6272) are of early Romano-British

Plate 5.3 Field ditches 6226, 6227 and 6228 (right to left), viewed from the north-west

date – or internal, if irregular, subdivisions. There were comparable short lengths of broadly north–south ditch (eg, 6224, 6218, 5751) in the western field (in Area 1) (Fig. 5.1).

Pits

There are notable differences between the discrete features in Area 1 and those in Areas 2 and 4, suggesting distinct zones of activity developing over time. These zones may have been separated by early Romano-British ditch 6229, with large groups of intercutting pits to its west (Fig. 5.1), and a more dispersed distribution of pits, ovens and other discrete features to its east (Fig. 5.2). Some of the latter were storage pits – circular, steep-sided, or bell-/beehive-shaped, with flat bases – subsequently used for rubbish disposal, while others are of less certain function and more variable in form, including shallow scoops and deeper but irregular features; in addition, 11 subrectangular or sub-square pits were recorded in Area 2 which may have had a particular function.

Intercutting pit groups
In Area 1 there were groups of intercutting shallow scoops and deep pits (eg, 6212–5, 6217, 6231–3), probably bounded by ditch 6229 to the east and by a second boundary (formed by ditches 6209–11 and 6256) to the west (Fig. 5.1). These appeared on the surface as extensive spreads of dark soil, within which individual cuts could often not be discerned (Pl. 5.1). However, the bases of some of these pits were revealed in slots dug through the groups, although the similarities in their upper fills meant that the

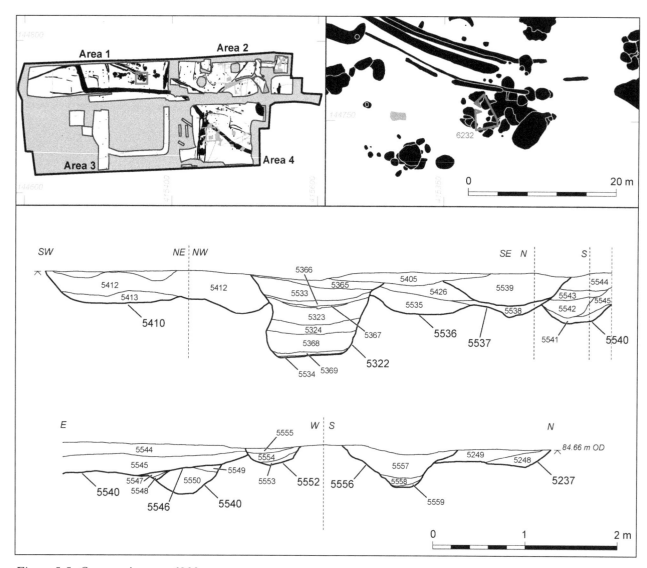

Figure 5.5 Quarry pit group 6232

stratigraphical relationships between them were sometimes unclear. They varied greatly in form and size, having irregular, subcircular and rectangular shapes, and measuring up to 2 m wide and over 1.2 m deep, although most averaged only 0.4 m in depth (Fig. 5.5). The majority had shallow concave sides and concave bases, distinguishing them from the predominantly vertical-sided flat-bottomed pits to the east of ditch 6229. Some similar pits lay just outside the groups.

These features are interpreted as possible quarry pits for the extraction of different raw materials for use in and around the nearby settlement. As they cut through the site's variable geology these materials would have included clay, gravel and soliflucted chalk, for use, potentially, in pottery production, for making daub and cob used in building construction, and for metalling surfaces including along the trackway. However, when viewed in section, it is clear that some of the later pits did not cut into the natural,

but only into the fills of earlier pits suggesting some had other uses. There was evidence for a small fire, with *in situ* burning, at the base of pit 6216 (in group 6215).

Some pits were filled with redeposited natural and contained no finds, suggesting that they had been backfilled soon after excavation, either with their own up-cast, or with that from the excavation of adjacent pits. Others, however, appear to have been used for the dumping of domestic waste. Pit group 6232 (Fig. 5.5), for example, in which at least 30 individual pits were identified in an area measuring 8 m by 13 m, contained (between 20 of its pits) 3562 g of predominantly early Romano-British pottery, 10.6 kg of burnt flint (7.7 kg of it from a single pit: 5566), plus animal bone (3369 g), a mid-1st-century copper alloy brooch (ON 79), and iron hooked blade (ON 50), a group of 39 hobnails (ON 81), and small quantities of fired clay, slag and worked flint, as well as high numbers of charred cereal remains and weed seeds.

Plate 5.4 Quarry pit 5170 (group 6215) containing ABG 35 and pottery discs (ONs 18, 19, 20, 24, 25, 27, 31, and 32), viewed from the north-east

Other finds from these pit groups included four fragments of a Mayen lava quern in pit 5887 (group 6231) and a worked bone awl (ON 60, Fig. 6.10, 4) in pit 5305 (group 6233). A blue glass bead (ON 23; Fig. 6.9) of probable 1st-century BC/AD date was recovered from pit 5170 (group 6215), along with animal bone, including an articulated horse vertebral column (ABG 35), and pieces of pottery clipped into roughly circular shapes (ON 16–20, 22, 24–25, 27, and 31–33), possibly evidence for spindlewhorl production or perhaps discarded gaming pieces, or even 'pessoi' for cleaning after defecation (see Seager Smith, Chapter 6,

Pls 6.5–6.6) (Pl. 5.4); 10 similar objects were recovered from pits 5293 (ON 49) and 5296 (ON 38–44, 48 and 53) in group 6217 to the immediate east.

There was a large possible quarry pit (7201) in Area 2 (Fig. 5.2), which was cut by field ditch 7534, and two small groups of intercutting oval pits in the eastern part of the site, both containing further waste material. Their locations – group 6274 in Area 2 and group 6259 in Area 4 – away from the concentration of possible quarry pits in Area 1, suggest they may have had some other function, possibly simply for waste disposal.

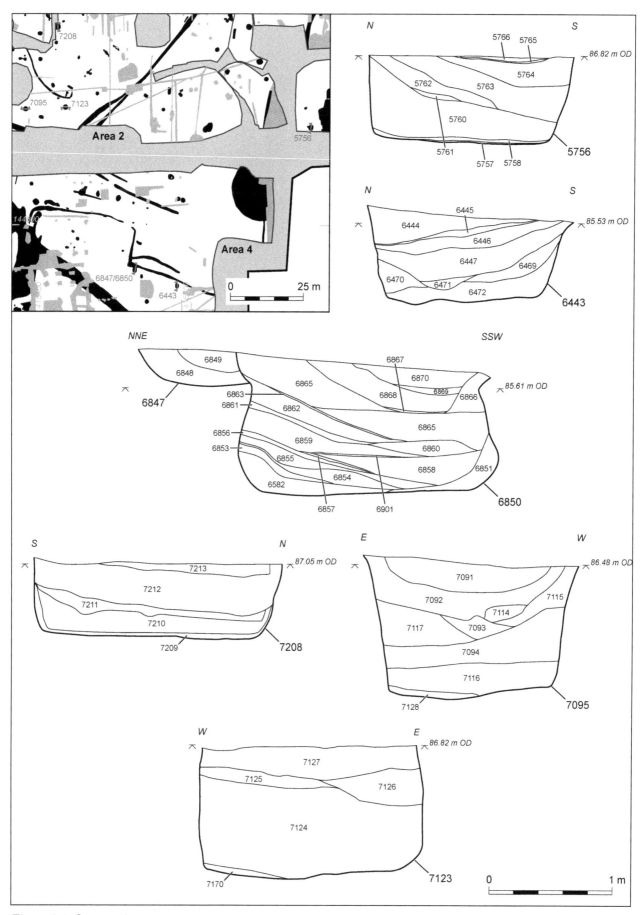

Figure 5.6 Storage pits

Storage pits

Most of the storage pits (87%) were in Areas 2 and 4 – in the zone east of north–south ditch 6229 (Figs 5.2 and 5.6). They are generally spaced well apart, presumably to avoid earlier features in order to minimize the risk of contamination of the stored contents. Those in Area 2, which were close to the ovens/driers (see below), were up to 2 m wide and 1.1 m deep (eg, pit 7123, Fig. 5.6; pit 7081), with variations in recorded depth due in part to the different levels of truncation. Those in Area 1 (Fig. 5.1), which included seven truncated pits close to oven/drier 6174 (Fig. 5.9), were smaller and shallower, measuring 0.8–1.4 m wide and 0.1–0.5 m deep.

After being emptied of their stored contents, the pits were infilled through a combination of erosion and other natural processes, the deliberate backfilling with redeposited natural, and the dumping of settlement waste, so providing much of the evidence for the activities undertaken within and around the associated settlement. The fill sequences varied greatly between the pits, some having evidence for repeated deposits of similar material over time resulting in thick homogenous fills, while other had more variable and heterogeneous deposits. Some deposits were simply thrown in from one side or the other, creating slumping, angled deposits, whereas others had been dumped in and then apparently levelled off into horizontal deposits. A number appeared to contain deliberate deposits of natural, possibly laid down to mask unpleasant smelling waste. A sample of the pits and their deposits are described in detail (see Fig. 5.6) to give an indication of this range of variability.

Pit 5756

Pit 5756 (Area 2) was 1.8 m wide and 0.7 m deep, with near-vertical sides and a flat base. After being emptied of its stored contents the pit was left open for some time, allowing the accumulation of silt on the base (5757 and 5758) which produced a sherd of 1st-century AD pottery. These were sealed by a 0.4 m thick charcoal-rich deposit (5760) sloping down from the north side, which contained nearly 80 kg of burnt flint, along with fragments of fired clay (282 g), cereal processing waste (barley and hulled wheat) and animal bone (pig, sheep/goat and domestic fowl). This layer also had numerous lenses of greenish silty loam, possibly cess. Above this layer was a small deposit of redeposited chalk (5761) followed by three more substantial layers (5762, 5763 and 5764) together containing further early Romano-British pottery and animal bone, burnt flint and fired clay (including a fired clay slingshot of possible Iron Age date and therefore residual), followed by two thin upper fills (5765 and 5766).

Pit 6443

Subcircular pit 6443 (Area 4) was 1.3 m by 1.7 m wide and 0.7 m deep, with near-vertical sides and a flat base. On the base was a layer of dumped soil (6472) containing pottery of probable 1st-century AD date, a disc of Savernake-type ware (ON 132, Pl. 6.7) – possibly a gaming piece or an unfinished spindlewhorl. This was overlain by material collapsed from the pit sides (6470 and 6469), then by further dumped deposits containing numerous cattle, pig and sheep/goat bones. These included a dump of probable hearth waste (6471), a 0.3 m thick layer (6447) containing 1st-century AD pottery and a cattle hind leg (ABG 115), and two charcoal-rich deposits (6446 and 6444) separated by thin layer of redeposited chalk (6445).

Pit 6850

Subcircular pit 6850 (Area 4) was 1.5 m by 2.1 wide and 1.1 m deep, with undercut sides and a flat base, giving it a slight 'bell' or 'beehive' profile. It cut early Romano-British ditch 6248 (cut 6847). Above a small deposit of collapsed natural (6851) on its southern side, there was a series of fills mostly deriving from the northern side (Pl. 5.5), the lowest of which (6582), on the base, contained a worked bone awl (ON 1025, Fig. 6.10, 2) along with pottery, burnt flint and animal bone of cattle, pig and sheep. The overlying 19 fills comprised further dumps of waste material, including a fragment of a dog (or fox) radius (from 6859), interspersed with naturally infilled/eroded layers, suggesting that the pit took some time to be fully infilled.

Pit 7208

Subcircular pit 7208 (Area 2) was 1.8 m by 2.1 m wide and 0.6 m deep, with near-vertical sides and a flat base. It contained five almost horizontal deposits containing 140 sherds of early Romano-British

Plate 5.5 Pit 6850, viewed from the north-east

38

Plate 5.6 Raven skeleton in the base of pit 7123

Plate 5.7 Subrectangular pit 7409

pottery and 170 fragments of animal bone (pig, sheep/goat, red deer and cattle), including a polished, worked bone cylinder, probably a handle fragment (ON 1009, Fig. 6.10, 7). Two pieces of redeposited human bone – the left femur and the left humerus of a neonate (from fills 7210 and 7212, respectively) were also recovered.

Pit 7095
Circular pit 7095 (Area 2) was 1.6–1.7 m wide and 1.1 m deep, with near-vertical, straight sides and a flat base. The lower fills 7128 and 7116 showed evidence for having been levelled off while the remaining eight layers had been dumped in from either side, there being distinct tip lines visible within each fill. Deposit

7116 contained the perforated vertebrae of a fish which may have been used as a bead (ON 1027, Fig. 6.10, 8). The pit contained 27 sherds of Romano-British pottery, 32 pieces of animal bone (cattle and sheep/goat) and 34 kg of burnt flint. There were also charred barley and hulled wheat grain fragments and chaff, indicative of cereal processing.

Pit 7123
Circular pit 7123 (Area 2) was 1.8 m in diameter and 1.1 m deep, with vertical sides and a flat base. On the base against the western edge was the near complete skeleton of a raven (ABG 198; Pl. 5.6), covered by a thin patch of soil (7170) containing fragments of cattle and sheep/goat bones. This was sealed by a thick deposit (7124), possibly resulting from several dumps of largely homogeneous material, which contained over 170 sherds of 1st–2nd AD-century pottery and further animal bone, including dog, pig, sheep/goat, cattle and raven. The fill had no visible tip lines, and its upper surface may have been levelled off. It was overlain by a layer of redeposited natural (7125), then two further layers (7126–7), all three of them containing further animal bone.

Subrectangular pits
Among the pits were a number that were distinctly subrectangular in shape. Most were found in two loose clusters in Area 2 (Fig 5.2), with six (7220, 7264, 7268, 7285, 7287/7239, and 7302) lying between early Romano-British ditches 6270 and 6272, and another four (7389, 7394, 7409, and 7471) in the eastern of the ladder fields; a similar pit (6773) lay to the south in Area 4. These features varied in their orientations, but generally had near-vertical sides and flat bases, and contained similar deposits of organic material and ashy deposits capped or partially sealed by layers of redeposited natural (Fig. 5.7). A north–south aligned rectangular feature (7509) in the Area 2 watching brief area was 0.9 m wide and 3.5 m long and may be related to these pits, although it was only 0.14 m deep. Three of the pits and their deposits are described in detail, and illustrated (Fig. 5.7).

Pit 7409
Pit 7409 measured 1.6 m by 2.5 m and was 1.1 m deep (Pl. 5.7). Its lowest fills (7416 and 7415) had a greenish hue and were gritty in texture, and may derive from cess and/or other decayed organic matter such as compost. They contained high levels of charred cereal remains, including hulled wheat, emmer and spelt, as well as fragments of pig and sheep/goat bone, almost 2 kg of burnt flint, a piece of Romano-British ceramic building material (CBM) and five sherds of pottery; layer 7416 also contained a large piece of apparently unworked stone. The pit was

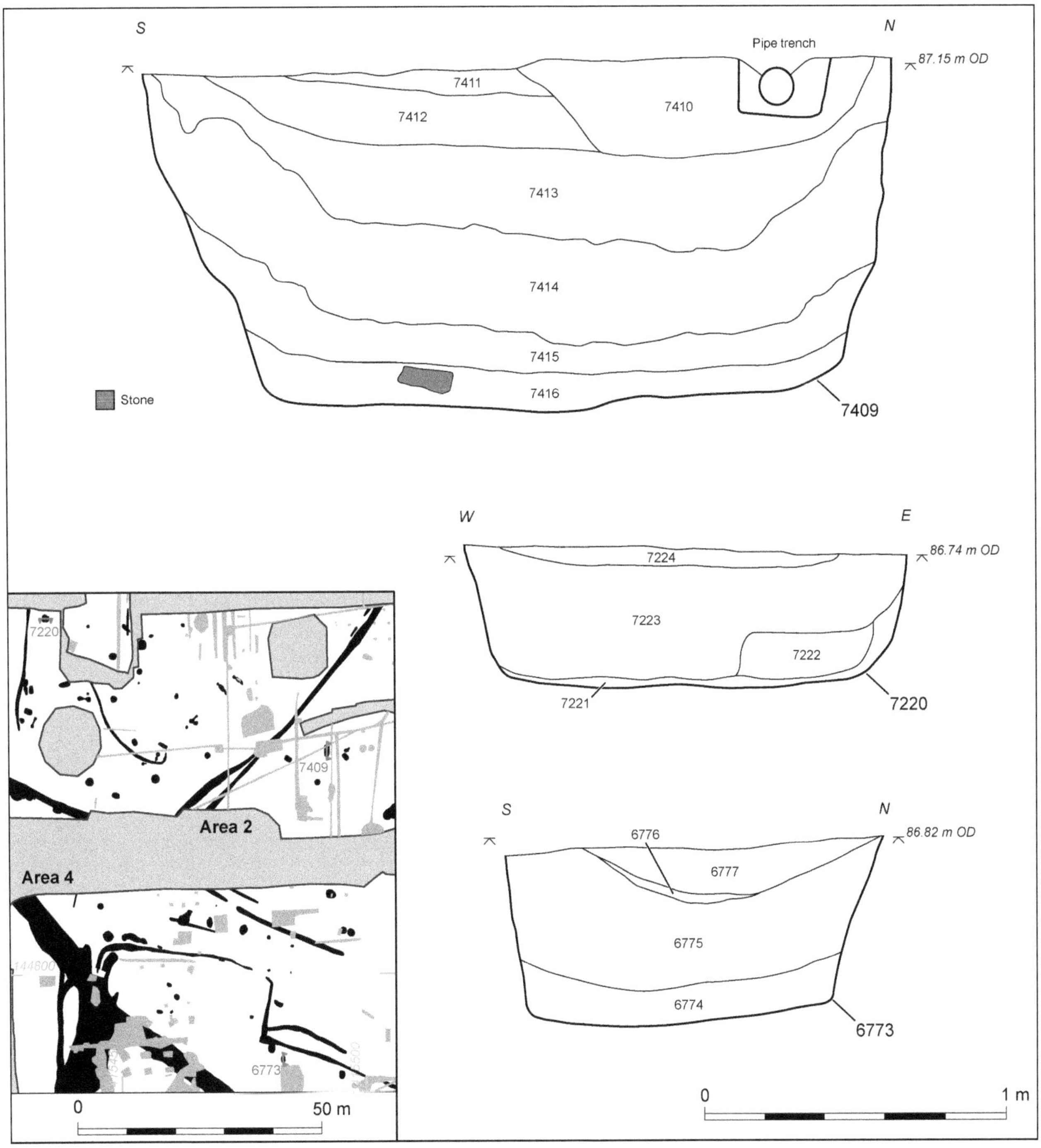

Figure 5.7 Subrectangular pits

subsequently filled with two thick layers of redeposited chalk rubble (7414 and 7413), then further dumps (7412, 7411 and 7410) of waste containing bones of cattle, sheep/goat, pig and roe deer, and 19 sherds of pottery, charcoal and burnt flint.

Pit 7220

Pit 7220 was sub-square, 1.4–1.5 m wide and 0.4 m deep. A very thin cess-like deposit (7221), containing fragments of cattle and sheep/goat bone, covered the base. This appeared to have been deposited from the eastern side as was an overlying dump of possible hearth waste (7222; 0.15 m thick). These were sealed by a thick cess-like organic deposit (7223) containing further animal bone, 1st-century AD pottery, burnt flint and vesicular fuel ash slag, capped by a layer of redeposited soliflucted chalk (7224).

Pit 6773

Pit 6773 measured 0.9 m by 1.3 m long and was 0.6 m deep. Its lowest fill (6774) was an homogenous deposit, a 0.2 m thick, of organic-rich waste material intermixed with ash, suggestive of hearth clearance.

Plate 5.8 The excavation of feature 5530, viewed from the north-west

This had been covered by two layers (6775 and 6777, between which was a thin layer of eroded soliflucted chalk, 6776) comprising repeated deposits of different materials. This resulted in multiple lenses of charcoal-rich and ashy material (interleaved with further layers of redeposited chalk), among which were sherds of pottery, featureless fragments of fired clay and a fragment of render with a rough white surface and a wattle impression preserved in the backing plaster.

Feature 5530

An elongated oval feature (5530), 6.2 m long, 2.1 m wide and 1 m deep, lay north of the quarry pits in Area 1 (Fig. 5.1, Pl. 5.8). It cut the distinctly clay-rich natural, and had steep concave sides apart from a gentle slope from its eastern end. Its function is unclear, although its sloping base suggests it was designed to allow easy access, either by humans or animals. However, its relatively shallow depth and narrow shape suggests it may not have been a waterhole for animals, and it may have had other specific function related to agricultural or craft activity; there was an oven (6174) at its western end – one of a number recorded on the site (see below, Fig. 5.9). Following its period of use it appears to have been partially backfilled then allowed to silt up naturally, its filling containing a small number of early Romano-British sherds, along with fragments of horse, sheep and pig long bones.

Solution Hollow 6513

As noted above (see Chapter 3) this solution hollow, comparable in size to hollow 6257, was excavated to a depth of only 1.2 m (Fig. 5.8, Pl. 5.9). Unless the material in it has continued to subside since the Romano-British period, it must have been a visible hollow at the start of the period since early Romano-British pottery was recovered in its lowest recorded fill (6561), and no pre-Romano-British layers were exposed or excavated.

The hollow, in the north-eastern corner of Area 4 (Fig. 5.2), appeared to be circular and at least 20 m wide, with gently sloping sides leading to a central shaft which, although not exposed, was machine-augered to a depth of 6 m. The exposed fills comprised dumps of Romano-British waste material, interspersed with consolidation layers of coarse flint gravel (6522, 6519 and 6516). The augering indicated that, in the centre of the hollow, the stratigraphically lowest recorded fill (6561), which contained five sherds of Romano-British pottery, overlay a washed-in deposit above further erosion deposits.

The hollow contained dumps of domestic and probably small-scale industrial waste, including kiln

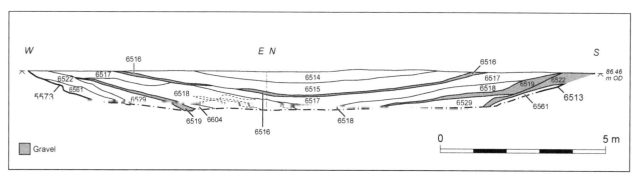

Figure 5.8 Solution hollow 6513

Plate 5.9 Solution hollow 6513, viewed from the north-west

and fire rake-out material, and deposits of decayed organic matter. Together, these contained over 750 sherds of pottery (weighing some 12 kg), and over 18 kg of animal bone – mainly sheep/goat, cattle and pig, but also horse, dog, duck, raven, crane and red deer and roe deer. Also recovered were copper alloy brooches and brooch fragments belonging to the middle of the 1st century AD, including a small complete one-piece or Nauheim-derivative brooch (ON 166, Fig. 6.8, 1) and part of another (ON 148), and parts of two Colchester-type brooches (ON 158 and ON 160). There were also objects of iron, and of worked bone – a decorated knife handle (ON 155, Fig. 6.10, 6) and a weaving comb (ON 183, Fig. 6.10, 1) – as well as quantities of burnt flint, slag, fired clay, and shell. Evidence for a substantial Romanised building in the vicinity can be inferred from the recovery of fragments of discarded painted wall plaster, and a piece of ceramic building material.

Solution Hollow 6257

A number of sherds of Romano-British pottery were recorded from this hollow's tertiary fills (6180 and 5474), and from the layer of Neolithic flints (6146) around its edge (Fig 3.4). However, the hollow appears to have been effectively infilled early in the Romano-British period, its uppermost fill (5474) being cut by a number of the parallel field ditches, one of which (6226), as noted above, contained predominantly early Romano-British pottery. Some

of the ditches, where they crossed the hollow, were covered by a thin layer of possible occupation waste (5489) containing pottery, slag, burnt flint, fired clay and animal bone.

Ovens/Driers

Nine features which had used fire in some agricultural, domestic or industrial function were identified – seven in Area 2 (7100, 7135, 7183, 7231, 7245, 7290 and 7329) and two in Area 1 (5752 and 6174) (Fig. 5.9; Pls 5.10 and 5.11). It is unclear whether these features were used as ovens for cooking or baking or were part of more involved processes, such as grain drying, milling or brewing. Two of the ovens are described in detail below, the rest are summarised in Table 5.1.

Six were roughly keyhole-shaped, consisting of two shallow scooped bowls (stokehole and firing chamber) joined by a central flue; the other three may have been more heavily truncated leaving only the oval chamber. They ranged in size (partly due to truncation) from 0.9 m to 2.7 m long, and were up to 1 m wide and 0.3 m deep. Seven of the ovens cut the natural clay which had been hardened by firing in the chamber, creating a clay bowl, with the hardening extending partly through the flue into the stokehole. Charcoal from feature 7183 indicated the use of birch as fuel.

Their orientations varied, although four were orientated (stokehole to chamber) either NNE–SSW

Table 5.1 Romano-British ovens

Cut	Orientation	Length (m)	Width (m)	Depth (m)	No. of fills	Pottery (no/g)	Animal bone (g)	Burnt flint (g)	Fired clay (g)	Other
5752	(W–E)	0.9	0.8	0.10	1	–	–	–	–	–
6174	NNE–SSW	1.1	0.7	0.15	1	8/74	–	–	674	1 flint
7100	E–W	1.3	0.6	0.16	2	4/32	–	–	–	–
7135	(S–N)	1.2	0.8	0.18	2	11/441	1	54	–	1 flint
7183	NNE–SSW	1.2	0.7	0.20	4	–	–	2	–	–
7231	NE–SW	2.2	1.0	0.07	3	5/37	8	66	87	2 flints
7245	E–W	2.7	0.7	0.29	7	10/38	1	–	28	2 flints, stone (3510 g)
7290	NNE–SSW	2.2	0.8	0.28	7	1/1	408	473	52	ON 213 (Fe nail), ON 214 (Fe hobnails)
7329	SSW–NNE	1.8	0.9	0.23	4	–	53	150	205	2 (Fe), ON 215 (Fe rod) ON 216 (Cu al. scrap)

Key: Orientation: stokehole-chamber (in brackets if uncertain); Fe – iron; Cu al. – copper alloy

or SSW–NNE. It is notable that none were orientated NW–SE, the orientation of the three twin-flued pottery kilns in the same general area of the site (see below), the two types of facility probably operating best under very different wind conditions.

Oven 7245

Oven 7245 was 2.7 m long (east–west) with a 0.7 m wide stokehole at the eastern end linked by a 0.2 m wide flue to the 0.6 m wide western chamber (Fig. 5.10; Pl. 5.10). It cut into degraded Chalk natural and the chamber and flue were fired hard by repeated use, creating a burnt halo (7251) around their edge. Charcoal-rich deposits in the chamber (7246), flue and stokehole (7247) – the residues of the final firing – contained mostly oak charcoal. These layers, which together produced three undiagnostic Romano-British sherds, were sealed by material collapsed from the edges of the oven and its possible superstructure

(7248 and 7249), and a final backfill (7250) which contained seven pieces (3.5 kg) from at least two Portland Limestone polygonal roof tiles; it is unclear whether these had been used as part of the oven structure, but their occurrence provides further evidence for a substantial, Romanised building in the area.

Oven 7290

Oven 7290 was 2.2 m long (NNE–SSW) with a 0.5 m wide stokehole at the north-north-east end linked by a 0.2 m wide flue to a 0.6 m wide chamber (Pl. 5.11). The oven was cut into gravel, and the inner edge of the chamber appeared to have been consolidated with the addition of a chalk block and clay lining (7327) which had been hardened by repeated firing; the gravel had also been heat-affected (7328). Above the lining was a charcoal-rich deposit (7324) containing pig and cattle bone, which was sealed by layers

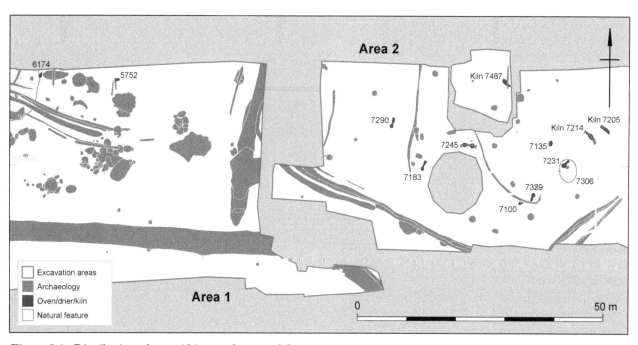

Figure 5.9 Distribution of ovens/driers and pottery kilns

from the collapsed superstructure (7325, 7322 and 7323), and a final backfill (7326) from which the only pottery – a sherd of 2nd-century AD samian – was recovered.

Pottery Kilns

Three pottery kilns were excavated in Area 2, in the same general area as the ovens (Fig. 5.9). Two of the kilns (7205 and 7214) were just 3 m apart, with the third (7487) lying 23 m to their north-west. All were single-chambered, twin-flued kilns, with stokeholes at both ends, aligned NW–SE.

Kiln 7205 (2.7 m long, 0.7 m wide, 0.2 m deep) was heavily truncated, with only the north-western flue and central firing chamber substantially surviving, although remnants of the south-eastern flue were observed. The kiln was cut into the gravel natural which had been consolidated with a partially surviving clay lining (7432). It had a charcoal-rich fill (7206) which contained 33 sherds of early Romano-British 'waster' pottery, fragments from at least 10 fired clay plates probably used to provide temporary 'floors' in the firing chamber, and 2.3 kg of burnt flint.

Kiln 7214 (3 m long, 0.9 m wide, 0.2 m deep) (Fig. 5.11, Pl. 5.12), which was similar in form to kiln 7205, had three fired clay kiln bars (7216; Fig. 6.7, 1–3) positioned centrally on a thin layer of heat-affected clay (7217) on the base of the chamber. Its main, charcoal-rich fill (7215) contained over 100 sherds of early Romano-British 'waster' pottery, and numerous pieces of burnt flint (1 kg) and fired clay (4.6 kg), some of the latter with wattle impressions deriving from the kiln superstructure.

Kiln 7487 (2.8 m long, 0.9 m wide, 0.35 m deep) was also cut into gravel but had no *in situ* traces of a clay lining, although there were fragments of chalk-tempered fired clay in its three charcoal-rich fills (7488, 7489 and 7490). It also contained early Romano-British pottery, burnt flint, fired clay plates (Fig. 6.7, 4–5) and quantities of animal bone (mostly sheep/goat).

The proximity of the kilns, and their position in the same general part of the site as the ovens, suggest the zoning of specific types of activity in relation to the associated, although as yet unlocated, settlement. Their comparable north-west–south-east orientations may have been considered that best suited for maintaining the type of heat required for pottery firing, which appears to have been very different from the type of fire needed for grain drying or similar activities.

The form of the kilns is comparable with the Alice Holt/Farnham type of kiln (Swan 1984, 78, fig. XVIII), as well as Kiln 6 from Whitehill Farm, Lydiard Tregoze, near Swindon (*ibid.*, 118, pl. 42).

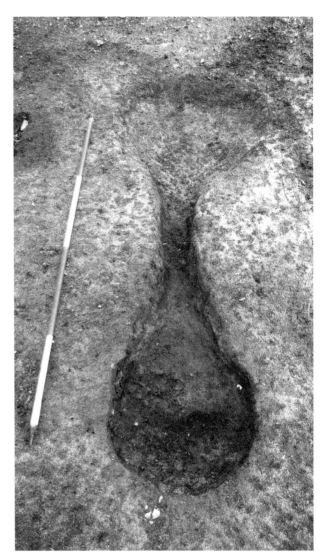

Plate 5.10 Oven 7245, viewed from the west

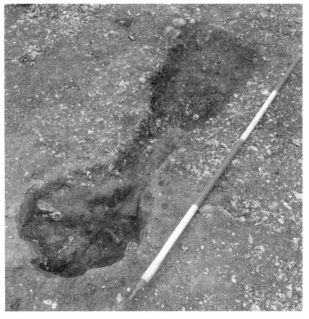

Plate 5.11 Oven 7290, viewed from the south-south-east

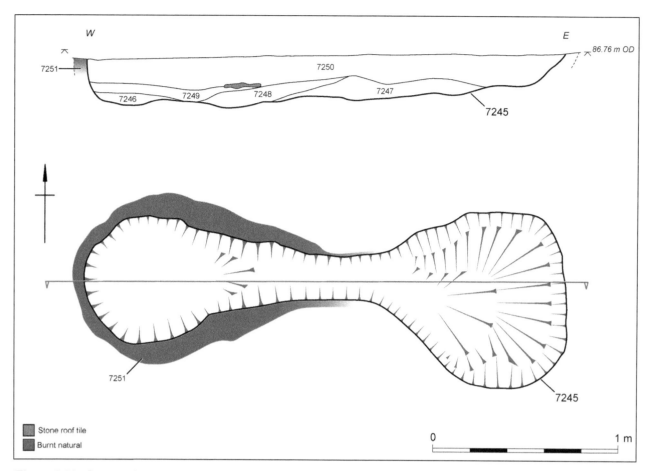

Figure 5.10 Oven 7245

Middle/Late Romano-British

Few features can be confidently dated to the middle–
late Romano-British period, although the recovery of
relatively small quantities of pottery of these dates
indicate some level of continuing activity on the site,
albeit at a reduced level, particularly in the form of the
field system established in the early Romano-British
period, and the activity represented by the
intercutting pit groups.

Plate 5.12 Pottery kiln 7214, viewed from the west

A shallow feature (5031), 3.5 m in diameter and
0.4 m deep in Area 1, contained 166 sherds of pottery
of which 132 were middle Romano-British and all but
one of the rest of general Romano-British date. This
feature accounts for 53% (by weight) of all the middle
Romano-British pottery from the site, with generally
only small quantities coming from a range of other
features. No storage pits date from either the middle
or late Romano-British period, and the single sherd of
middle Romano-British (2nd century) samian from
oven 7290 (Area 2) provides unreliable dating.

The most substantial of the ladder field ditches
(6219) is probably of this period, containing pottery
of predominantly late Romano-British date (492
sherds, 5847 g). It also contained a horse skull and
pelvis (ABG 26), but from different animals, and a
partial dog skeleton (ABG 1001) and a further 4290 g
of animal bone as well as objects of copper alloy, iron
and stone, and quantities of worked flint, burnt flint,
CBM, fired clay and oyster shells. This ditch, which
was over 2 m wide and 1 m deep, with steep straight
sides and a narrow base, was the most southerly of the
sequence in Area 1 (Fig. 5.1). As noted above, it
turned sharply northwards before terminating at its
eastern end (on the edge of the by then infilled
solution hollow 6257), some 18–25 m west of
the terminal of the earlier ditches it appears to

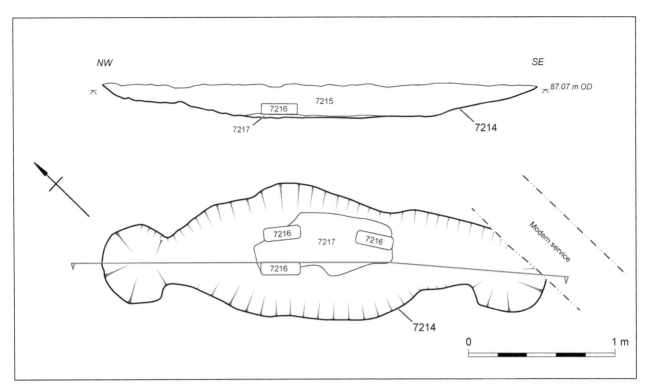

Figure 5.11 Pottery kiln 7214

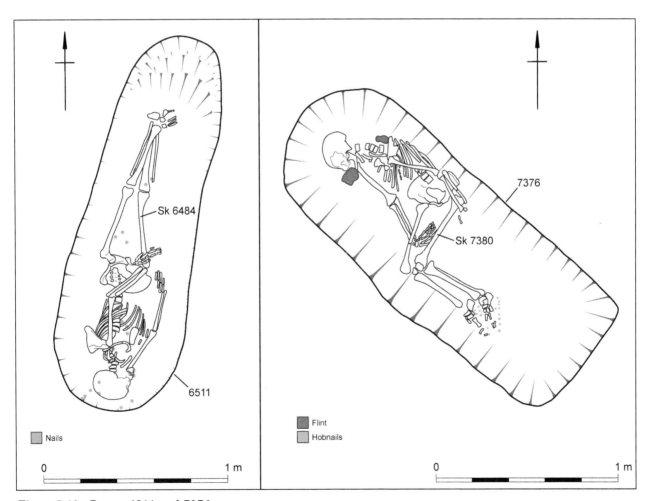

Figure 5.12 Graves 6511 and 7376

46

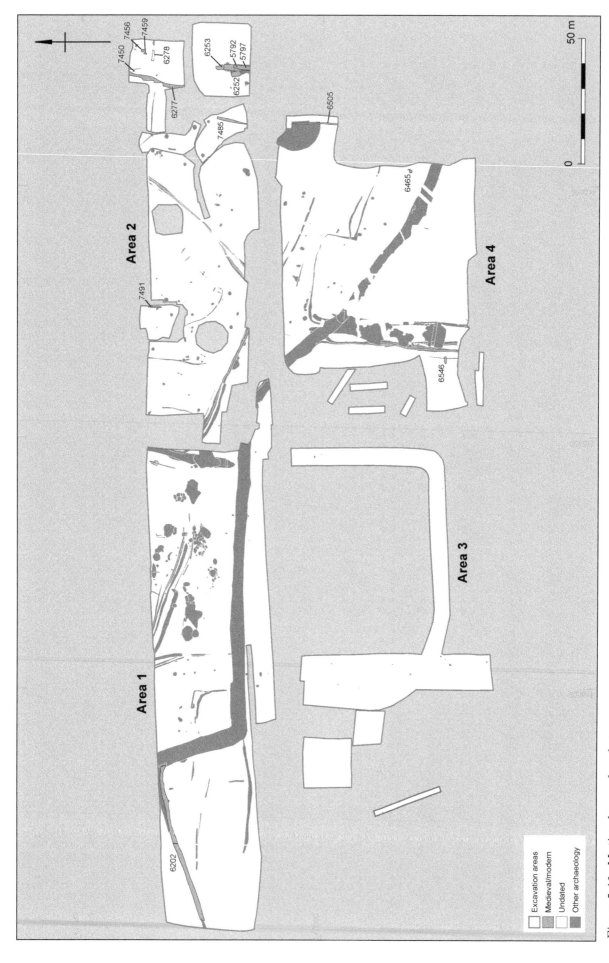

Figure 5.13 Medieval to modern features

have replaced, although its line may have been continued by much smaller ditches of the same period (6221 and 6222).

Two large groups of intercutting possible quarry pits (5497/5880 and 5910), both containing 3rd–4th-century AD pottery, were recorded at the eastern end of Area 1, in the same general area as the earlier, similar groups. They were both located in the gap between ditch 6221 and another small late Romano-British ditch (6269) running to the north, again following the line of earlier ditches.

Burials

Two inhumation burials may belong to this period (Fig. 5.12). Grave 6511, which lay south of the former enclosure ditch in Area 4 (Fig. 5.2), was 2 m long, 0.6 m wide and 0.4 m deep, aligned south-south-west to north-north-east. It contained the extended supine burial (6484) of a woman aged 45–55 years, laid with her head to the south-south-west. The hands were crossed over the right side of the pelvis and the left foot crossed over the right. Twenty-one iron nails were recovered, which were concentrated around the top of the head, across the abdomen and the legs, indicating some kind of wooden covering, but not necessarily a full coffin as none were recovered from the foot of the grave.

Grave 7376, close to the terminal of early Romano-British ditch 6272 in Area 2 (Fig. 5.2), was 2 m long, 0.8 m wide and almost 0.8 m deep, aligned north-west to south-east. It contained the flexed burial (7380) of a probable female, aged over 45 years, laid on the right side with the head to the north-west and the spine flush with the north-east side of the grave. Hobnails were found at the feet, suggesting that the individual had been buried wearing nailed shoes/boots, a practice common from the late 2nd–3rd century AD onwards but with most dated examples dating to the 4th century (Philpot 1991, 167). Pottery recovered from the grave fills included nine sherds of mid-/late 2nd–4th-century date.

Other Features

Two adjacent late Romano-British features in Area 1 (Fig. 5.1) may also have had a ritual function, and possibly be associated. One was a small circular pit (5319), 0.4 m in diameter and 0.13 m deep, containing the partial remains of at least three 10-month-old lambs, 14 sherds of pottery (from two vessels), a hobnail and a late 3rd-century AD coin (ON 116), possibly representing some form of votive offering. Less than 2 m to its north was a subrectangular feature (5038), which was 1.5 m long, 0.9 m wide and 0.4 m deep, with vertical sides and a flat base. Its shape, and the presence of four nails, suggested that it might be a grave, but no human bone was recovered. Other finds from its two fills included a 4th-century coin (ON 82), part of a sandstone whetstone, over 1 kg of pottery and pieces of animal bone.

Medieval, Post-medieval and Modern

There was a concentration of medieval to post-medieval/modern features at the eastern limit of Area 2 (Fig. 5.13), which appear to relate to properties that fronted onto High Street. Two north–south aligned ditches, 6277 and 6253 (recut by ditch 5797), may mark the rear boundaries to the properties, with undated ditch 6278 possibly marking a boundary between two properties. A second north–south boundary, represented by ditches 6505 and 7485, lay some 20 m to the west.

A number of pits (eg, 6252 and 7450) were observed, with others containing animal burials – pits 7019, 7456 and 7459 contained pig burials, and pit 6546 the partial skeleton of a horse (ABG 169).

In Area 1, ditch 6202 cut and replaced ditch 6201 (Fig. 5.1), and potentially formed part of a medieval field system. Finds included a few sherds of early post-medieval Border ware and redwares (along with residual Romano-British sherds).

Worked Flint

by Matt Leivers

Introduction

A total of 8632 pieces of worked flint was retained, as quantified by type in Table 6.1. Of these, 5605 (64.93%) came from hollow 7306, 1118 (12.95%) from solution hollow 6257, and 832 (9.64%) from the Late Neolithic pit group (6283) in Area 1, with a further 135 (1.56%) from posthole alignment 6260 and 42 (0.49%) from posthole alignment 6255; these sub-assemblages are quantified by type and summarised in Table 6.2. The remaining 934 pieces (10.82%) were recovered from various locations across the site, most were redeposited.

Raw material

The whole assemblage consists of nodular flint. The predominant colour of the visible surfaces is dark grey-brown to dark brown with some sandier brown and dark brown/black pieces. Thermal fractures and coarse cherty inclusions occur frequently, but apart from these the material appears to be of good quality. The flint is likely to have been obtained from secondary sources. While some flint may have come directly from the undisturbed natural Chalk (there is a small proportion of pieces with a thick chalky cortex; evidence for the extraction of flint exists locally, between Larkhill Road and Marina Road (Booth and Stone 1952) approximately 500 m to the south of the site), the prevalence of thermally fractured pieces and thin worn cortex suggests that more came from either cryoturbated chalk or the local drift geology.

Condition

Overall, the assemblage is typified by unpatinated pieces, although there is considerable variation between the sub-assemblages, the group from solution hollow 6257 being in markedly worse condition, with the majority having a cream/white patina and some with various mineral stains; many pieces in this group are rolled and abraded. The condition of the rest of the material is varied: pieces from Late Neolithic features are generally fresh (in hollow 7306, especially, mint); other pieces tend to be in poor condition, with frequent edge abrasion, surface gloss, rolling and other indications of redeposited material. Some of the more heavily patinated pieces have blotchy orange iron stains common on pieces from ploughzone assemblages.

Technology

Blanks appear to have been produced using direct hard hammer percussion (Ohnuma and Bergman 1982). Cores reused as hammers were present among the assemblage, as were other possible flint hammers.

Cores were predominantly multi-platform; there are no convincing examples of Levallois-style reduction, the few keeled cores more probably worked-out multi-platform examples. There is some limited evidence for alternate flaking, associated with platform preparation and core rejuvenation techniques, although these are not common.

Microdebitage was recovered from all sieved samples; retouch chips (Newcomer and Karlin 1987) were not noted, suggesting blank production was the predominant activity rather than tool manufacture or modification (tools formed less than 2% of the entire assemblage).

Table 6.1 Composition of the worked flint assemblage

Flint types	No.	% of assemblage
Debitage		
Cores and fragments	226	2.62
Core preparation and rejuvenation	3	0.03
Flakes (incl. broken)	5642	65.36
Blades (incl. broken)	5	0.06
Bladelets (incl. broken)	1	0.01
Chips	2465	28.56
Irregular debitage	120	1.39
Axe thinning flakes	1	0.01
debitage subtotal	8463	*98.04*
Tools		
Scrapers	23	0.27
Notches	4	0.05
Burins	1	0.01
Projectile points	5	0.06
Piercers	3	0.03
Microliths	1	0.01
Miscellaneous retouched pieces	67	0.78
Serrated flakes	3	0.03
Core tools	1	0.01
Denticulates	2	0.02
Rods	2	0.02
Flakes with edge damage	53	0.62
tools subtotal	165	*1.91*
Others		
Hammers/pounders/grinders	4	0.05
Total	8632	100

Table 6.2 Worked flint sub-assemblages

Group	Cut	No. contexts	Flake cores	Broken cores/fragments	Broken blades	Broken bladelets	Flakes	Broken flakes	Rejuvenation tablets	Chips/micro debitage	Scrapers	Other tools	Axe thinning	Projectile points	Denticulate	Core tools	Edge damaged	Piercers	Microdenticulates	Debitage	Misc. retouched	Total	Total per group
6283	5600	1					9			25												34	832
	7005	1		2			6															8	
	7012	2		27			136	17		59		2		1							2	244	
	7158	1		5			22			36												63	
	7167	2		5			69			64	1											139	
	7171	2		4			106															110	
	7173	1												1								1	
	7175	1		5			23			24	1			1								55	
	7178	1					13			30	1											44	
	7190	1								50												50	
	7015	1		1			30	13		33										4		81	
	7017	1					3															3	
6255	5047	1					9			1		1		1								12	42
	5060	2						1														1	
	5063	1					3	1														4	
	5074	3					20	1														21	
	5918	6					1															1	
	6002	1					1	1														2	
	6029	1								1												1	
6260	5087	1					2															2	135
	5088	2		1			6	2												1		10	
	5588	1					16	1		5											1	23	
	5821	2			1		45			6										5		57	
	6733	1					1															1	
	6762	2					5															5	
	6786	1			1		8															9	
	6882	5				1	23	2		1											1	28	
6257	5754						184		1								8			6		199	1118
	6176	96	42	26			706	94		38	6			1		1	10		2	15	20	919	
7306	7306	34	35	31	2		3221	263		1953	7	5	1		2		25	2	1	73	19	5605	5605
Total			77	107	4	1	4668	396	1	2326	16	8	1	5	2	1	43	3	3	104	43	7732	7732

Results

East–west posthole alignment 6260

Nine features in alignment 6260 (excluding 5047 which is counted with alignment 6255, below) contained lithics (Table 6.2), but only five of them (5088, 5821, 5688, 6786 and 6882) contained more than six pieces. Each was typified by groups of debitage with Late Neolithic characteristics.

Of the features containing six or fewer pieces, two contained redeposited earlier material: 5821 contained an A1a (Clark 1934) microlith (ON 1022) (Fig. 6.1, 1), with a distinctive white patina shared by a broken blade from 5087; these two are the only Mesolithic pieces in the assemblage.

Posthole 5088 contained, a broken oblique arrowhead (ON 10, Fig. 6.1, 2) of Clark's (1935) form G (the tip is missing). Posthole 5688 contained a broken bifacially flaked piece of very cherty flint (ON 78) which approximates to a large leaf-shaped arrowhead (Fig. 6.1, 3); its tip also is missing and the piece may be an arrowhead abandoned during manufacture.

North–south posthole alignment 6255

All seven features contained lithics (Table 6.2), only two of which contained more than six pieces – features 5060 and 5074 containing 12 and 21 pieces, respectively. As with alignment 6260, the larger assemblages were typical of Late Neolithic material.

Notable amongst the groups of debitage and cores were several scrapers and arrowheads. Feature 5047 contained a tool (ON 1024) made on the distal end of a heavy flake where two sides with concave semi-abrupt scraper-like retouch intersected to form a blunt hooked nose (Fig. 6.1, 4). Feature 5060 contained a long oblique arrowhead (ON 77, Fig. 6.1, 5, Pl. 6.1) of Clark's form G.

Pit group 6283

Twelve of the pits in pit group 6283 contained lithics (Table 6.2). Pits 7005 and 7017 contained fewer than nine pieces; pits 5600, 7158, 7175 and 7178 contained between 10 and 63 pieces; pit 7015 contained 81 pieces, including some large pieces that could be bifacial thinning flakes; pits 7012, 7167 and 7171 each contained over 100 pieces.

Notable amongst them was pit 7012 which contained two cobble hammers (ONs 194–5) and an oblique arrowhead (ON 191) of Clark's form H (Fig. 6.1, 6, Pl. 6.1). Feature 7167 contained a thin oval end and side scraper on a tertiary blank (ON 199, Fig. 6.1, 7), while 7173 contained a thick end scraper on a secondary trimming flake (ON 202, Fig. 6.1, 8).

Feature 7175 contained an end scraper on a secondary flake (ON 1023, Fig. 6.1, 9), a neatly made piercer on a tertiary flake (ON 200, Fig. 6.1, 10) and a small oblique arrowhead (ON 1021) of Clark's form I (Fig. 6.1, 11). Feature 7178 contained a broken oblique arrowhead (ON 201) of Clark's form H (Fig.

0   10 mm

Plate 6.1 Flint arrowheads (ONs 191, 77 and 201)

6.1, 12, Pl. 6.1); its tip is missing and the 'tang' parallel-sided rather than tapering to a point.

Solution hollow 6257

The fills in the top of the solution hollow's shaft contained 21 flakes, but the fills around the upper edge of the hollow contained 1118 pieces of struck flint. At the base of these latter fills was a layer of flint gravel (6146/6178), with the appearance of a metalled surface, from which 274 pieces of struck flint were recovered, 227 of which were flakes and broken flakes. Among the remainder were two scrapers and nine pieces with 'miscellaneous' retouch. A considerable quantity of struck flint (558 pieces) was found on the surface of this layer (assigned context number 6145), mostly unretouched flake debitage, and cores and core fragments, among which were three scrapers, one serrated flake, 10 pieces with 'miscellaneous' retouch and 16 flakes with edge damage indicative of use.

Following the Neolithic abandonment of the feature, it was filled by a series of natural silting episodes. Many of these contained further lithics, predominantly flake debitage, which were markedly rolled and patinated, indicating the mechanisms by which the feature had filled gradually over time and through which material from the locality had been incorporated within it. The lowest of these layers (6181) contained 141 pieces of unretouched debitage; later layers (5975, 5988, 6177, 6180) contained decreasing quantities of material (96, 65, 11 and 5 pieces, respectively) among which were the butt end of a narrow bifacially-worked chisel (in 5975, Fig. 6.1, 13), a serrated flake (5975, Fig. 6.1, 14), a scraper (6180, Fig. 6.1, 15) and a piece with 'miscellaneous' retouch (5988).

Hollow 7306

This feature contained a small deposit of Late Neolithic cremated human bone lying on a layer of trampled soil which covered the base. Neither the soil nor a slump of eroded natural gravel above it contained any lithics. However, these deposits were sealed by a thin layer (7319) containing 2628 pieces of struck flint, which appears to represent a dump of fresh knapping waste. The distribution of this material suggested that it had been tipped into the hollow from the south-east since the majority of the smaller pieces (over 1000 chips and 1200 flakes) were located in the south-east quadrant, while larger pieces (primarily cores) were more evenly spread, suggesting that they had rolled across the base.

All stages of the reduction sequence are represented, including tested nodules, primary, secondary and tertiary flakes, cores and core fragments, and irregular debitage and microdebitage. Very little of the material is distinguishable from this mass of unretouched flakes and other knapping debris. Retouched pieces are limited to two notched flakes, one piercer, one scraper, one rod and 14 pieces with 'miscellaneous' retouch. Also present are 16 flakes with edge damage indicative of use and a small group of large flakes from the south-west quadrant, all of which are heavily patinated.

A further 2637 pieces were recovered from the gradual infilling of the feature above this primary deposited layer. In these layers (7313 and 7310) flints were more evenly distributed, suggesting that they may have derived from nearby surface deposits, or from more episodic deposition of smaller quantities of waste. There are no traits present to allow the identification of any sub-assemblages, but the fresh nature of the debitage is emphasised by the presence of microdebitage and refitting flakes from the south-west quadrant of layer 7313. As before, the majority of the material is flake debitage. Tools are limited to five scrapers, one rod, two denticulates, one piercer, one serrated flake, three pieces with 'miscellaneous' retouch and nine flakes with edge damage indicative of use.

Other features

Elsewhere on the site, a variety of later and undated features contained lithics, none of which are especially diagnostic, although the prevalence of broad squat flakes indicates a Late Neolithic date. A possible edge-flaked knife and a core used as a hammer (both from Late Iron Age enclosure ditch 6203), a retouched piece with signs of having been used as a scraper (from late Romano-British field ditch 6219), and a large edge-damaged core trimming flake (from Romano-British posthole 3910) all fit within this broad date range.

Discussion

The Late Neolithic assemblage is almost exclusively a flake industry, with few blanks, by-products or techniques of blade production. For the most part, the technology lies well within that which would be expected of a Late Neolithic assemblage.

The assemblage conforms to the composition of similar Late Neolithic groups both locally and nationwide. Wainwright and Longworth (1971, 254–5) calculated the relative frequencies with which various tool types occurred in such assemblages. In their list, scrapers, transverse arrowheads, serrated flakes, knives and piercers were the most commonly occurring, followed by fabricators and denticulated flakes. With the exception of knives and fabricators, these are the most common types of tool present at this site.

Relatively small groups of lithics in pits (or pit groups) containing Durrington Walls-type Grooved Ware are frequently encountered (at, for instance, Amesbury Down (Harding and Leivers forthcoming),

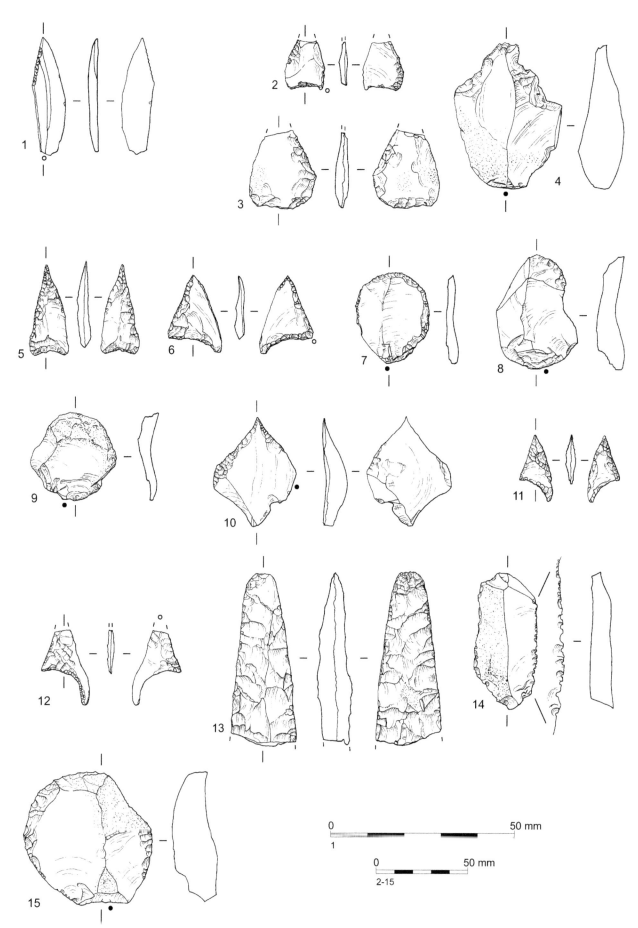

Figure 6.1 Worked flint (1–15)

on Salisbury Plain (Leivers forthcoming) and the Marlborough Downs (Harding 1992)), and in this respect the material is entirely typical.

Less typical, however, are the two large assemblages from the hollows. Large assemblages of lithics are known in Late Neolithic contexts locally – for instance, on the platform in the Southern Circle at Durrington Walls (approximately 3000 pieces, Wainwright and Longworth 1971) and in two adjacent pits on Amesbury Down (approximately 4000 pieces, Harding and Leivers forthcoming), but both of these are rather different in nature, containing significantly higher proportions of tools (3% at Durrington Walls, 3.5% at Amesbury).

List of illustrated flints

Fig. 6.1

1. Obliquely-blunted point, type A1a; posthole 5821, fill 5833, ON 1022
2. Broken oblique arrowhead, form G (Clark 1935); posthole 5088, fill 5089, ON 10
3. Broken and probably unfinished leaf-shaped arrowhead; posthole 5688, fill 5722, ON 78
4. Heavy flake, two sides with concave semi-abrupt scraper-like retouch form a blunt hooked nose; posthole 5047, fill 5049, ON 1024
5. Oblique arrowhead, form G; posthole 5060, fill 5062, ON 77
6. Oblique arrowhead, form H; pit 7012, fill 7013, ON 191
7. Scraper; pit 7167, fill 7168, ON 199
8. Scraper; pit 7173, fill 7174, ON 202
9. Scraper; pit 7175, fill 7177, ON 1023
10. Piercer; pit 7175, fill 7177, ON 200
11. Oblique arrowhead, form I; pit 7175, fill 7177, ON 1021
12. Oblique arrowhead, form H; pit 7178, fill 7179, ON 201
13. Butt end of a narrow bifacially-worked chisel; hollow 6257, layer 5975
14. Serrated flake; hollow 6257, layer 5975
15. Scraper; hollow 6257, layer 6180

Burnt Flint

by R.H. Seager Smith

Approximately 447 kg of unworked burnt flint was found in 223 features and deposits. Most only contained small amounts, with just 40 of the features containing more than one kilogram. Where flint is naturally abundant in the vicinity, its burning was probably an accidental by-product of some other form of agricultural or domestic heating or burning process; it is commonly interpreted as indicative of prehistoric activity, but it is intrinsically undatable

and need not be contemporary with the features from which it was recovered.

However, significant quantities (1215 pieces, 23.4 kg) were found in 10 of the features in Late Neolithic pit group 6283, with particularly large amounts from pits 7012 (3.3 kg), 7171 (1.1 kg), 7175 (1.5 kg) and 7190 (15.7 kg). Burnt flint was also recovered from five of the postholes in alignment 6255 (97 pieces, 1.35 kg) and seven of those in alignment 6260 (146 pieces, 1.9 kg), while an additional 25 pieces (830 g) came from hollow 7306. Overall, the two posthole alignments (6255 and 6260) contained smaller pieces than pit group 6283 (mean weights of 13.9 g, 13.7 g and 19.3 g, respectively) while those from hollow 7306 were larger still (33.2 g), perhaps derived from different processes.

Ten tiny fragments (50 g) found in Middle Iron Age cremation grave 5206 may derive from the pyre site itself, having been accidentally incorporated as the bone was collected prior to burial. Approximately 4.5 kg of burnt flint were found in the upper fills of Middle/Late Iron Age grave 7280, but as this feature was cut into the fills of the earlier hollow 7306, it is possible that all this material is residual. Small quantities (totalling just 280 g) were also recovered from enclosure ditch 6203 (slots 5199, 5619, 5976 and 6605).

The bulk of the burnt flint (373 kg or 83%) was, however, associated with pottery and other artefacts of Romano-British date. Quantities of between 1 kg and 96 kg were noted in features, including storage pits, subrectangular pits and quarry pits, the enclosure ditch and field ditches, as well as solution hollows 6257 and 6513, and kilns 7205 and 7214, although there were no apparent spatial concentrations.

Stone

Neolithic Stone Objects
by Phil Harding and Rob Ixer

Discoidal 'bluestone' object

A discoidal 'bluestone' object (ON 36) with heavily ground and flattened edges (Fig. 6.2) was found in the tertiary fill of the northern terminal of Romano-British ditch 6256 (slot 5145), 7 m from the intersection of the two Late Neolithic posthole alignments (at posthole 5047) (Fig. 3.1). The object, which has a rounded trapezoid shape, is 64 mm wide, 67 mm long and 18 mm thick. It is made from a slab of stone that has developed a light grey surface patina, although a fresh break in one corner suggests a poorly developed conchoidal fracture and is a dark grey colour when freshly worked.

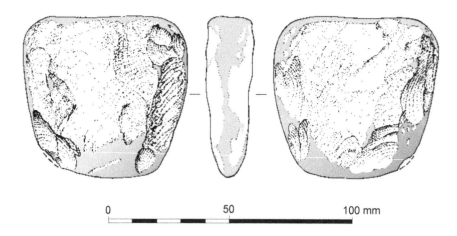

0   50   100 mm

Figure 6.2 Bluestone object (polished areas shown in tone)

Initially the exposed surfaces, cut surface and thin section of the sample were investigated using a x20 hand lens and the Geological Society of America rock-colour. A standard thin section was prepared from the sample by cutting a slice and grinding it to the correct thickness. The section was investigated using transmitted light petrography in plane polarised and crossed polarised light using x6.3 and x12.5 objectives with x12.5 eye pieces giving overall magnifications of x80 and x155.

The lithic is a 'rhyolite with fabric' showing a strong planar, plus a pronounced lensoidal, fabric. These are characteristic of Rhyolite Group C, which has been provenanced to Craig Rhosyfelin on the northern flanks of the Preseli Hills (Ixer and Bevins 2011). This is the most common rhyolitic debitage and is found throughout the Stonehenge landscape (Ixer and Bevins 2013). Hence this is an undoubted piece of 'bluestone' (used in the sense of any non-sarsen lithic used as an orthostat).

Further, thin section petrography shows the artefact to be manufactured from rhyolite with a 'sub-jovian' texture, texturally one of the most extreme (and hence characteristic) of the Craig Rhosyfelin rhyolitic rocks. In hand specimen, this rock-type would be very distinctive.

Relict flake scars confirm that the blank was subjected to rudimentary bifacial flaking around the edges, although it is less certain by how much the sides of the object result from flaking or are products of natural fracture. The edges of the object are all heavily ground, with a distinct flattened facet around the circumference. This flattened facet is a sufficiently recurring feature of similar objects of the type to indicate that it was an original feature and not a subsequent alteration to the edge. Grinding also extended across both sides of the object by as much as 11 mm from the edges.

The function of the object remains unknown; however typologically it seems most appropriate to associate it with other 'bluestone' artefacts that were catalogued from Stonehenge (Montague 1995). This material includes a range of discoidal artefacts that have been manufactured by flaking, both systematic bifacial flaking (bifacially flaked objects) and more irregular flaking (irregularly flaked objects). Artefacts that had been ground around the edges and onto the surfaces, as at MOD Durrington, or showed expedient patches of surface grinding were also listed, as were discs which were also ground around the edges. Precise classification was frequently indistinct, although tabular objects with ground edges were most prevalent at Stonehenge, of which there were 12 pieces.

Two rhyolite slabs with a semi-circular shape (SH08 39.4 (004)) recovered from Aubrey Hole 7 from Stonehenge have been examined and reclassified using the lithic schemes proposed by Ixer and Bevins (2011; 2013). The silicified rhyolites (12.1 g and 3.8 g in weight) have a very strong planar foliation and lensoidal fabric and so too are classed as Rhyolite Group C (Ixer and Bevins forthcoming). It may be significant that these two objects and that from MOD Durrington appear to be very foliated/lensoidal examples of Group C.

'Bluestone' fragments, unequivocally associated with Stonehenge, have been found across the entire Stonehenge landscape; Richards (1990) listed 18 pieces from excavations or surface collection during the Stonehenge Environs Project. Rhyolites were the most prevalent raw material accounting for 13 examples; Rhyolite C samples were dominated by struck flakes or blocks. Four pieces of rhyolite (Richards 1990, fig. 153) were considered to be tools or hammers, which, like the object from MOD Durrington, were characterised by a laminated structure and bifacial flaking around part of the edge. These objects have yet to be examined and reclassified using Ixer and Bevins (2011; 2013) lithic schemes.

Only three pieces of 'bluestone' from the Stonehenge Environs Project, spotted dolerite, were securely stratified. These pieces, from beneath the bank of the North Kite enclosure (W52), were shown to be of Late Neolithic/Early Bronze Age date. Richards (1990) argued that these pieces resulted from 'bluestone' working and were not souvenirs or debris from Stonehenge. Most of the less well-dated specimens of 'bluestone' from the survey area were also associated with Middle/Late Neolithic activity, possibly hinting at direct links to the construction and use of Stonehenge. The discovery at MOD Durrington extends distribution to the River Avon valley and beyond the north-east corner of the Stonehenge WHS, no 'bluestone' having been recorded from the excavations at Woodhenge (Cunnington 1929) or Durrington Walls (Wainwright and Longworth 1971).

On a broader scale, this corpus of 'bluestone' objects finds parallels with a range of other discoidal implements, principally scrapers (Wainwright and Longworth 1971, F23–25) and knives of flint (Clark 1928; Gardiner 2008) which were frequently polished at the edges. In addition, ground-edged flakes (Pitts 1982; Harding n.d.) and scrapers (Harding 1995) were present at Stonehenge, which together with polished-edged flake knives all occur

(Wainwright and Longworth 1971) with Grooved Ware assemblages.

Despite the general analogies of objects made of 'bluestone' with ground-edged objects of flint, there are differences in the treatment of the edge, which might influence any perceived way in which they were used. The edges of the 'bluestone' discoidal object from MOD Durrington, as well as other ground-edged discs from Stonehenge, were ground flat making it difficult to envisage that it may have functioned as a flensing knife (Clark 1928). Bifacially flaked, discoidal stone objects were also manufactured from stone other than 'bluestone', as represented by an unground sandstone disc from Avebury (Smith 1965).

Despite the fact that the 'bluestone' discoidal object from MOD Durrington was found in a residual context, its date of manufacture most probably relates to the use of comparable Late Neolithic artefacts at Stonehenge. It was also indirectly related to the posthole alignments at MOD Durrington, which contained Grooved Ware pottery and associated flintwork and have been radiocarbon dated to the Late Neolithic; Beaker activity was absent at the site. The precise date at which 'bluestone' arrived at Stonehenge remains a subject of discussion but is currently assigned (Parker Pearson et al. 2007) to

Plate 6.2 Sarsen flakes. The smaller broken flake is dulled probably from use as a hammer/pecker (posthole 6882, fill 5074)

Phase 3i of the monument, in the mid-4th millennium BC, during the Late Neolithic.

The typology and raw material of the discoid suggests that it was manufactured during the Late Neolithic, contemporary with the posthole alignments at MOD Durrington and with strong links to Stonehenge where objects of this type are relatively common. However, it is equally possible that it was brought to the site during the Romano-British period given that extensive Romano-British activity has been documented at Stonehenge (Darvill and Wainwright 2009). The 'bluestone' disc could represent a trophy, memento or usable object that was curated from Stonehenge in much the same way that axes were highly prized, collected and reused (Adkins and Adkins 1985; Turner and Wymer 1987) at this time.

Sarsen

In addition to a single fragment (10 g) from Late Neolithic posthole 6882 (posthole alignment 6260), three pieces of red-grey, quartzitic sarsen (Judd 1902; Howard 1982; Montague 1995) were found in the tertiary fills of posthole 5074 in alignment 6255 (Pls 6.2–6.3). The largest of these comprised a sub-angular block weighing 15 kg, with two smaller fragments, both probably broken flakes. The flaking pattern of the large block is unsystematic, demonstrating that it is a by-product of breaking up a much larger boulder. Surfaces demonstrate characteristic points of impact with some crushing of the edge of the striking platform. One small area of the sarsen surface is distinctly more abraded than the fractured flake surfaces with a rounded grain structure. This area seems likely to have been modified and dressed.

This block can best be viewed as an unwanted block that was discarded into a backfilled posthole, when it became impossible to remove additional flakes. The likely original mass of rock makes it unlikely that the sarsen was brought to the site to be broken up; however, the absence of other debris from any parts of the feature suggest that destruction did not take place on the spot, nor that the hole was originally a stone socket. Analysis of sarsen working debris from Stonehenge (Pitts 1982; Harding n.d.) and destruction debris from Avebury (Gillings et al. 2008) has demonstrated that considerable quantities of fractured material are present including within the

Plate 6.3 Large sarsen block with unsystematic flaking and small dressed area (posthole 6882, fill 5074)

6–3 mm sieve fraction. This is typical not only of sarsen working but of any form of stone working. Crushing around the point of percussion and miss-hits all generate quantities of debitage and microdebitage which are absent at MOD Durrington.

The edge of the smallest fragment of sarsen, a broken flake, is dulled and may have been used as a small, expedient hammer/pecker, possibly to dress sarsen. Such usage is entirely in keeping with evidence for stone dressing from the area. Sarsen is indigenous to the Stonehenge area. Large boulders, like the Cuckoo Stone, are present, although blocks of this size are rare. The rock appears much more frequently as small boulders, 0.3–0.4 m in diameter, primarily concentrated in the bottoms of dry valleys (Richards 1990).

Late Neolithic use of sarsen is most closely associated with Stonehenge where stones were extensively shaped and dressed; however, sarsen scatters have been recorded elsewhere across the Stonehenge landscape. An unstratified spread of sarsen fragments was noted on the crest of the King Barrow Ridge (W59) where it was related to Late Neolithic activity. Apparent areas of surface dressing of the type hinted at MOD Durrington have also been noted on stone 424 in the Beckhampton Avenue (Gillings et al. 2008), where pecking removed earlier traces of use as a polisher. Similar limited areas of dressing were also noted on a fractured sarsen incorporated into the structure of Silbury Hill (Pollard 2013).

Sarsen was also recovered in some quantity from areas of Late Bronze Age settlement immediately adjacent to Fargo Wood (W34), where fragments were heavily biased towards broken querns and rubbers. This chronological relationship could be linked to sarsen working in the manufacture of querns on the Marlborough Downs (Gingell 1992).

Evidence for stone breaking is also known from the Stonehenge landscape. Darvill and Wainwright (2009) noted extensive destruction debris and truncated stumps at Stonehenge where Romano-British 'activists' were strongly implicated in the reduction of both sarsens and 'bluestones'. Small-scale stone breaking was also noted at Woodhenge (Cunnington 1929) where a fragment of broken sarsen, approximately 0.30 m across, was found in the upper fill of posthole C6. Cunnington speculated that it had been dumped there to prevent it damaging the plough. However, at Woodhenge, the sarsen block was also associated with burnt chips of sarsen and a hole approximately 2 m across and 0.75 m deep which Cunnington considered to represent a possible stone-hole. Post-medieval stone breaking is also represented at Stonehenge by a line of holes drilled into the surface of the Slaughter Stone but, apart from increased densities around Stonehenge itself, there is little to indicate large-scale stone breaking of the character known from the Marlborough Downs (King 1968; Gillings et al. 2008).

Leary and Field (2013) argued that the use and selection of materials, including sarsen, as deliberate ingredients in prehistoric monument construction was significant at Silbury Hill. It is inadvisable to make too much of one fragment found in the upper part of a Late Neolithic posthole, but it is nevertheless worth reiterating the repeated occurrence of sarsen in local Late Neolithic monuments, most notably at Woodhenge and here at MOD Durrington in an area where sarsen, while indigenous, is not as prevalent as on the Marlborough Downs–Avebury environs.

Other stone objects of Neolithic date
by R.H. Seager Smith
A fine-grained sandstone fragment with a thumb-sized recess apparently worn into its flat, polished surface (ON 192) and a rounded quartzite or metasediment pebble (ON 193) were found in Late Neolithic pit 7012, part of pit group 6283. The sandstone fragment could have been used as a sharpening or polishing stone while three areas of bashed/abraded wear on the edges of the pebble suggest its use as a hammerstone or a rubber/pounder/grinder.

Other Stone Objects
by R.H. Seager Smith

Only items considered to derive from portable stone objects were collected and retained (45 pieces, 16.6 kg). The assemblage includes 16 pieces from at least 12 individual quernstones, two rubstones, two rubbers, a whetstone, a weight and a perforated chalk object of uncertain date and function.

Relatively few rock types were identified, and most are commonly found on other sites in the locality. These include glauconitic sandstones from the Upper Greensand, which outcrops in the Nadder Valley to the south-west and in the Vale of Pewsey to the north, forming part of a broad arc across the north and west of the county, extending eastward into Sussex. Quern production has been suggested in the Vale of Pewsey (Smith 1977, 108), but the only known production site is at Lodsworth, West Sussex (Peacock 1987). A coarse, gritty sandstone used for querns and rubstones may have come from the Bristol/Mendips area or the Forest of Dean, while the sarsen probably derived from a local source although the Vale of Pewsey/Marlborough Downs area (Bowen and Smith 1977, fig. 1) to the north cannot be ruled out. Locally available materials from the Upper Chalk included flint and chalk.

Eight of the quernstone fragments (from at least seven individual stones) were of Greensand, three

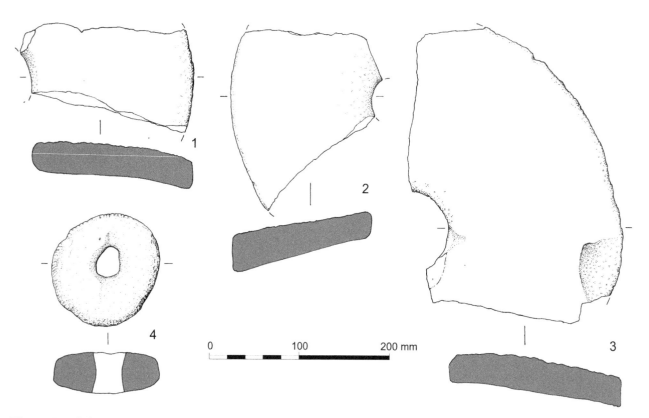

Figure 6.3 Other stone and chalk objects (1–4)

were of sandstone, one of sarsen, and four of Mayen lava, although the latter (ON 76), all from Romano-British pit 5887, are presumed to derive from a single imported quern. One of the sandstone pieces, from field ditch 6219, probably came from a saddle quern or rubstone. Although traditionally considered to be of prehistoric date, the continued use of saddle querns well into the Late Iron Age and early Romano-British period is well attested on sites in central southern England (Brown 1984, 418), although the piece could equally well be redeposited.

Six pieces derived from Curwen's disc-type querns of late or post-Romano-British date (1937, 146, fig. 22 and 23). Two, one of sandstone (Fig. 6.3, 1) and the other Greensand (ON 1007), were found in posthole 3910, while the others came from Romano-British pits 5463 (sarsen; Fig. 6.3, 2) and 5910 (ON 112; Greensand), field ditch 6219 (Greensand) and the subsoil (sandstone; Fig. 6.3, 3). Both stones from pits were associated with late 3rd or 4th-century AD coins from the same layers (Cooke, see below, ONs 7 and 82). Where measurable, these stones were 380–500 mm in diameter and 30–45 mm thick. Parts of the central cavity, up to 80 mm across, survived on the sarsen and the two sandstone pieces but no other evidence for handle holes or rynd-slots were preserved, although the relatively small size of these stones may suggest that they were hand-operated, Shaffrey (2003, 163) noting that the lower limit for millstones is generally in the region of

600 mm in diameter and 10 mm thick. Locally, similar disc-type querns have been found on Amesbury Down (Seager Smith in prep.), in the Avon valley (Mepham 1993, 36) and in the demolition/collapse deposits filling a corn-drying oven at High Post near Salisbury, Wiltshire, where charred wheat representing the final (or near-final) firing of the oven was radiocarbon dated to AD 335–535 (at 95% confidence, 1645±25 BP, SUERC-32322; Powell 2011, 33).

Although too fragmentary to be definitively identified, pieces of Pennant-type sandstone (field ditch 6219) and sarsen (pit 6914) with smoothed, slightly polished surfaces probably derive from rubstones. Two fist-sized, rounded quartzite or metasediment pebbles with slight traces of abraded ware from Romano-British pit 7264 (ON 203) and grave 7376 may have been utilised as rubbers, while a fragment likely to be from a bar-shaped whetstone in fine-grained Pennant-type sandstone came from feature 5038, associated with late Romano-British pottery and a coin dated to AD 330 (Cooke, see below, ON 85). A flat, elliptical chalk weight with a worn, egg-shaped perforation (Fig. 6.3, 4) was also found in field ditch 6219 and although not closely datable, this item is also likely to be of Romano-British date. Four pieces from a smaller perforated chalk object (ON 205) came from Romano-British pit 7285, although the precise nature and date range of this item remain unclear.

List of illustrated stone objects

Fig. 6.3

1. Upper disc-type quernstone; top surface pecked, grinding surface more finely worked and subsequently burnt. Approx. 10% of 380 mm, 30 mm thick, central cavity unmeasurable; sandstone; posthole 3910, layer 3909, ON 1006
2. Upper disc-type quernstone; all surfaces smoothed, grinding surface polished and subsequently burnt. Approx. 15% of 400 mm, 32–42 mm thick, central cavity 70 mm across; sarsen; pit 5463, layer 5462, ON 63
3. Upper disc-type quernstone; top surface pecked, grinding surface smoothed and slightly concave. Approx. 25% of 500 mm, 35 mm thick, central cavity 80 mm across; sandstone; subsoil (302), evaluation trench 3
4. Flat, elliptical chalk weight (631 g; 120 x 110 x 44 mm); slot 5282 of field ditch 6219, layer 5288, ON 37

Early Prehistoric Pottery

by Matt Leivers

The prehistoric pottery assemblage consists of 383 sherds weighing 2477 g. This represents the total of the prehistoric pottery recovered from various phases of work; the material is treated as a single assemblage. It is predominantly Late Neolithic, with only very small quantities of other ceramics. For the most part, ceramics have been dated to at least broad period on the basis of fabric type. A small number of featureless grog-tempered sherds remain imprecisely dated.

The material was analysed in accordance with the nationally recommended guidelines of the Prehistoric Ceramics Research Group (PCRG 2010). Sherds were examined using a x20 binocular microscope to identify clay matrices and tempers, and fabrics were defined on those bases. No petrological analysis has been undertaken. All data have been entered into the project's finds database; illustrated sherds not part of a vessel assigned an object number (ON) are identified below by their pottery record number (PRN).

Of the 25 contexts containing prehistoric ceramics, six contained more than 30 sherds; a further two contexts had 10–19 sherds, and five had 5–9 sherds, and 12 less than five sherds. A total of seven fabrics were defined, belonging to two chronological periods. Fabric descriptions are given in Table 6.3 and a breakdown of their quantification by count and weight in Table 6.4 (fabrics G99 and Q99 are crumbs of grog-tempered and sandy fabrics that cannot be accurately assigned to specific fabrics).

Grooved Ware

Grooved Ware sherds were recovered from five postholes in alignment 6255 (5060, 5063, 5074, 5918 and 6029), and one posthole in alignment 6260 (6786); unidentifiable Late Neolithic scraps were also recovered from posthole 5106. Grooved Ware was also recovered from six pits in pit group 6283 (7012, 7015, 7158, 7167, 7171 and 7175), as well as possible root disturbance (7165) on the edge of pit 7158.

Most of the groups of sherds from individual features are very small, amounting to little more than crumbs; with the exception of the material in pits 7012 and 7158 the assemblage amounts to 175 sherds weighing only 370 g – an average sherd weight of 2 g. Very little of this material is identifiable to type, although sherds forming the complete profile of one unusual vessel, a tiny 'thumb-pot' approximately 40 mm high with a flat base (30 mm in diameter) and a simple, very slightly inturned rim made in a grog-tempered fabric was found in pit 7167 (Fig. 6.4, 13; PRN 38).

Table 6.3 Early prehistoric pottery fabric descriptions

Fabric	Description
G1	coarse quartz sand matrix; sparse fine grog
G2	fine micaceous quartz sand matrix; moderate fine grog
G3	micaceous sand matrix; common medium grog
G4	sand matrix; moderate medium grog
G5	sandy matrix; common medium grog; sparse coarse calcined flint
Q1	quartz sand matrix; sparse coarse calcined flint probably accidental
V1	vesicular

Table 6.4 Early prehistoric pottery fabrics: quantification by count and weight

Fabric	No. sherds	Weight (g)	ASW (g)
Late Neolithic			
G1	164	1162	7.08
G2	113	802	7.10
G3	29	224	7.72
Q1	1	3	3
V1	65	212	3.26
subtotal Late Neolithic	372	2403	6.46
Early Bronze Age			
G4	1	25	25
G5	1	39	39
Unassigned			
G99	8	9	1.12
Q99	1	1	1
Total	383	2477	

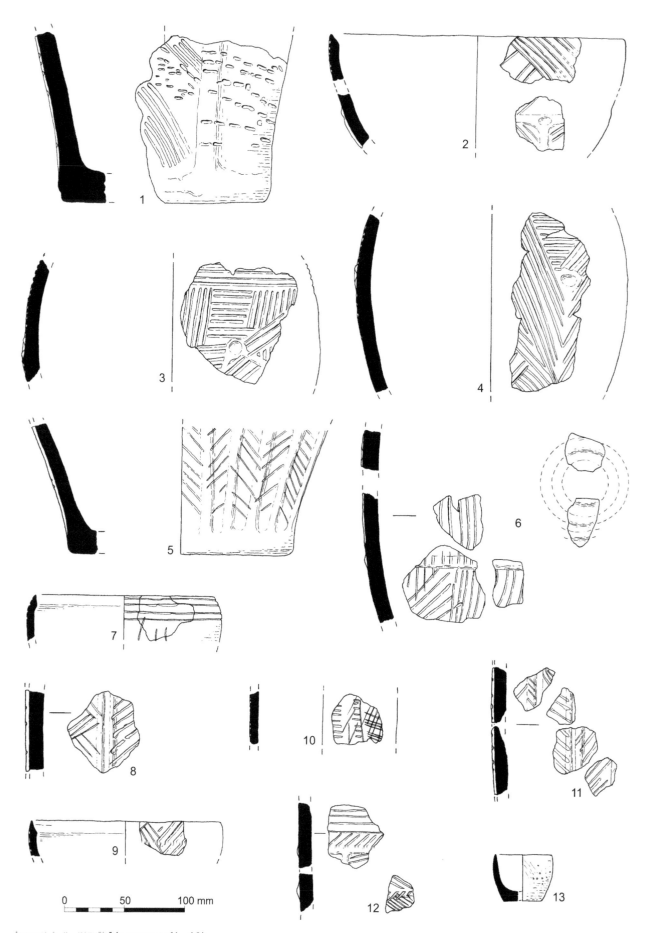

Figure 6.4 Neolithic pottery (1–13)

Rims

Very little variation of rim form is present, with every example being simple and pointed, mostly of upright or inturned attitude. The sample is, however, very small (n=7). Approximately half of the Durrington Walls assemblage was of this type (Longworth 1971, 56).

Bases

All bases are flat, and (whenever identification is possible) simple, without any protrusion or concavity. Again, the sample is very small (n=4).

Decoration

The most frequent decorative techniques employed are grooving/incision (22 examples, not distinguished between) and the application of cordons (12 examples). Other techniques are uncommon, limited to impressed stabs (three examples) and fingertip discs on cordon junctions (three examples). Cord and comb are entirely absent.

Rims

There is only a single instance of a decorated rim, in the form of impressed short linear stabs.

Internal

No internal decoration has been identified. At Durrington Walls, internal decoration occurred primarily immediately beneath the rim or on the rim bevel. The limited frequency of these parts in the present assemblage may account for the lack of internal decoration.

External

Cordons

Sixteen incidences of cordons are recorded, on 13 vessels (seven with vertical cordons, two with horizontal cordons, and four with both). Horizontal cordons occur singly, and divide the vessels into an upper (lesser) and lower (greater) portion. Vertical cordons occur on the lower body at various spacings, creating panels which are variously decorated (some of this decoration spills over onto the cordons). Only one vertical cordon is itself decorated separately to the adjacent panels, with horizontal stabs. On three of the vessels with horizontal and vertical cordons, the junctions are marked by an impressed fingertip disc.

Grooving and incision

These are the most common decorative techniques used on the bodies of vessels. Grooved (blunt) and incised (sharp) lines occur beneath the rim as split filled triangles and groups of horizontal lines; above horizontal cordons as groups of opposed lines, as complex opposed lines, concentric arcs and vertical lines, and zoned diagonal lines; between vertical cordons as filled triangles, opposed groups and opposed lines; and on bodies as vertical lines and filled zoned decoration.

Fingertip

Finger impressions occur only as fingertip discs at cordon junctions on three vessels.

Other impressions

On one vessel, the lower body is divided into panels by applied vertical cordons decorated with transverse stabs. The panels on either side of the cordon are filled with different decorative schemes: to the right with transverse stabs; to the left with alternating diagonal bands of transverse stabs and grooved lines.

Curvilinear

One vessel has what appears to be concentric circular fingertip grooves and incised lines (Cleal's 'distinctive "rosette" motif' (1999, 5)). There are no indications of the place these circular motifs took in any wider design, but parallels from Woodhenge (Cunnington 1929, 120 and pl. 26.2) and Durrington Walls (Longworth 1971, 70) suggest they would have been located either immediately below the rim or immediately below the horizontal cordon.

Significant groups

Pit 7012 Fig. 6.4, 1–8

The largest single group came from this pit, where 165 sherds weighing 1832 g derived from at least eight vessels. These included:

- Fragments of the base (of Longworth's (1971, 58) Type B) and lower wall from a jar with applied vertical cordons decorated with transverse stabs (Fig. 6.4, 1, PRN 14). The panels on either side of the cordon are filled with different decorative schemes: to the right with transverse stabs; to the left with alternating diagonal bands of transverse stabs and grooved lines.
- Very leached fragments of a neutral bowl with a pointed internally bevelled rim (Longworth's Type 18) (Fig. 6.4, 2, PRN 15/16). Below the rim, the external surface is decorated with filled triangles of grooved lines. A horizontal cordon divides the vessel into an upper and lower zone; the lower is further divided by vertical cordons. All of the cordons appear to be plain, but the surface of the vessel is much worn. The junction of the cordons is marked by a fingertip disc. The panels either side of the vertical cordon are infilled with diagonal grooved lines.
- Four joining sherds from a vessel (perhaps a bowl) decorated with filled rectangular zones and triangles of grooved lines (Fig. 6.4, 3, PRN 17). Two applied cordons meet at a fingertip disc.

62

- Four joining sherds from a vessel (perhaps a jar) with a plain horizontal cordon (Fig. 6.4, 4, PRN 18). Above the cordon are grooved filled triangles. Below the cordon, plain vertical cordons with opposed grooved lines infill the panels. The junction of the horizontal and vertical cordons is marked by a fingertip disc.
- Fragments of the base (of Longworth's (1971, 58) Type B) and lower wall from a jar with closely set applied plain vertical cordons (Fig. 6.4, 5, PRN 19/20). The panels on either side of the cordons have opposed incised line filling which spills over onto the cordons in places.
- Fragments of a vessel (possibly a jar) with a plain horizontal cordon with grooved decoration above and opposed filled triangles below (Fig. 6.4, 6, PRN 21/22). From the same vessel are two sherds with concentric circular fingertip grooves and incised lines. There are no indications of the position these circular motifs took in any wider design, but parallels from Durrington Walls (Longworth 1971, 70) suggest they would have been located immediately below the rim. If so, the wall thickness indicates a vessel of some size.
- Fragments from the pointed, internally bevelled rim of a small closed bowl; below the rim are four rather crudely executed incised horizontal lines above groups of incised diagonal lines (Fig. 6.4, 7, PRN 23).
- Fragments from a jar with applied plain vertical cordons with a central thumb groove; to the right of the cordon, a panel of diagonal grooved infill; to the left a panel of grooved filled triangles (Fig. 6.4, 8, PRN 24).

Pit 7158 Fig. 6.4, 9–12
This pit contained 31 sherds weighing 196 g from perhaps six vessels, including:

- A pointed internally bevelled rim (Longworth's Type 18) from a small closed bowl (Fig. 6.4, 9, PRN 29); this had filled triangles of grooved lines on the external surface, very similar to a sherd in pit 7012 (Fig. 6.4, 2).
- A vessel with zoned decoration consisting of parallel rows of transverse stabs and a very fine incised lattice (Fig. 6.4, 10, PRN 30).
- Fragments of a vessel with plain vertical cordons and opposed diagonal grooved infill (Fig. 6.4, 11, PRN 32).
- A vessel with horizontal grooved lines below the (absent) rim, with diagonal grooving above a narrow horizontal cordon; a vertical cordon separated panels of opposed diagonal grooved infill (Fig. 6.4, 12, PRN 33).

Other Early Prehistoric Sherds

The small group of earlier prehistoric sherds include one (25 g) from the decorated collar of a grog-tempered Collared Urn of Early Bronze Age date, used to contain the cremated human remains in grave 1805. The rest of this vessel was left *in situ* because the grave was not directly affected by the current development proposals; the sherd was retained as a guide to its character and date.

A grog and flint-tempered sherd from a secondary fill (6117) within Late Iron Age enclosure ditch 6203 (slot 6116) is also likely to be of Early/Middle Bronze Age date, its rolled and abraded condition confirming that it is residual in this context. A small group of small body sherds and one possible base angle in a grog-tempered fabric are most likely to be of Late Neolithic or Early Bronze Age date, despite being found in modern overburden deposit 6423. Two tiny scraps likely to be of earlier prehistoric date were also found in the secondary fill (7310; sandy) and tertiary deposits (7307; grog-tempered) of the Late Neolithic hollow 7306, but were too small to be more precisely dated.

Discussion

The Grooved Ware from this site takes its place among a large quantity of comparable material in the locality (see Wainwright and Longworth 1971, 55–71, 75–150, 287–97; Longworth and Cleal 1999), with particular concentrations associated with the henges at Durrington Walls (Wainwright and Longworth 1971), which provide the main comparanda, and Woodhenge (Cunnington 1929).

In terms of fabrics, grog temper (with or without additional sand and flint) is common both locally (Cleal 1995) and across southern central England as a whole.

The absence of any open or splay-sided tubs or converging horizontal cordons, coupled with the predominance of vertical cordons and grooved decoration in panels indicates the total lack of any material attributable to either the Woodlands or Clacton substyles. While Clacton-style vessels are not a frequent assemblage trait in the immediate area, Woodlands-style vessels do occur, often in conjunction with large or otherwise special collections of lithic material (see for instance Harding and Leivers forthcoming; Leivers forthcoming; Stone and Young 1948). In this sense, the absence of the type from this site is somewhat surprising; it may be that there is a chronological significance to this.

The material itself is entirely typical of local Durrington Walls assemblages, with the expected range of forms and decorative motifs.

Later Prehistoric, Romano-British and Later Pottery

by R.H. Seager Smith

This assemblage comprises 7327 sherds (122.181 kg). Most (7259 sherds, 121.214 kg) are of latest Iron Age/Romano-British date; while 57 (680 g) are considered to be Iron Age and 11 (287 g) are of medieval and/or post-medieval date (Table 6.5).

Despite some surface abrasion and edge damage, the assemblage survived in moderately good condition, reflected by a mean sherd weight of 16.7 g. Rims account for approximately 10% of the total number of sherds, but most represent less than 5% of the vessel's diameter or are broken at or above the neck/shoulder junction, hampering the identification of form. Most of the sherds also occur in relatively small feature groups; although recovered from 636 contexts in 180 features, only 30 features contained more than 50 sherds. Consequently, detailed fabric/vessel form analysis was only undertaken for the material (256 sherds, 10.194 kg) from kilns 7205, 7214 and 7487 considered to represent on-site pottery production. The remainder of the assemblage was subjected to a detailed scan conforming to minimum archive standards (PCRG, SGRP and MPRG 2016). All the sherds from each context were subdivided into broad ware groups (eg, flint-tempered wares) or known fabric types (eg, Oxfordshire red colour-coated ware) and quantified by the number and weight of pieces (Table 6.5). Vessel forms were recorded using descriptive terms (eg, bead-rimmed jar, flat flanged bowl), where appropriate, cross-referenced to published corpora (such as Fulford 1975; Young 1977), and quantified by the number of examples of each type present; joining sherds were counted as a single example. Other details, such as the presence of unusual sherds, perforations, residues or other evidence for use-wear and graffiti were also noted. Spot dates, used to inform the stratigraphic phasing, were assigned to each fabric group and, in combination with the dating evidence provided by other artefact types, to the context as a whole.

Iron Age

The Iron Age sherds were mostly residual, occurring alongside pottery of Romano-British date. Most are plain body sherds in sand and fine flint-tempered fabrics (Table 6.5). The only recognisable vessel forms comprise a small hemispherical cup with simple beaded rim and a carinated cup (Fig. 6.5, 1 and 2), found residually in enclosure ditch 6203. Both vessels are broadly comparable with the Dorset/Somerset variants of the All Canning's Cross-Meon Hill style group (Cunliffe 1991, 356, A7, 1–3), of the Early/Middle Iron Age (c. 5th–3rd century BC).

However, 13 (157 g) of the sand and fine flint-tempered sherds and a single thick-walled body sherd (58 g) in a sandy fabric are the only sherds recovered from feature 7280. Although no convincing joins exist between them, the sand and flint-tempered sherds probably all derived from the same high-shouldered, bead-rimmed jar, probably of 1st-century BC date, which would be consistent with the radiocarbon date of 210–40 cal BC (SUERC-49180, 2094±34 BP, at 95% confidence) obtained on the neonate inhumation burial made in this feature.

Latest Iron Age/Romano-British (1st–4th centuries AD)

This assemblage is dominated by local coarsewares spanning the entire Roman period (Table 6.5). Overall, 44% of the sherds by count (53% by weight) belonging within this period came from contexts assigned 1st–early 2nd-century AD dates, with smaller quantities from contexts of middle (c. AD 120/130–250/270; 11% by count/9% by weight) and late (c. AD 250/270–410; 13% by count/10% by weight) Romano-British date, attesting to later activity on a reduced scale.

Table 6.5 Later prehistoric, Romano-British and later pottery totals by ware type

Ware	No.	Wt. (g)
Iron Age		
Flint-tempered ware	2	13
Sand and fine flint-tempered ware	50	534
Sandy	5	133
subtotal Iron Age	*57*	*680*
Latest Iron Age/Romano-British		
Samian	25	117
British lead glazed ware	5	15
North Wilts colour-coated ware	6	15
Oxon colour-coated ware	32	139
New Forest colour-coated ware	30	213
New Forest parchment ware	4	81
Oxon colour-coated ware mortaria	3	24
Oxon whiteware mortaria	2	40
Oxidised wares	259	2197
White-slipped red wares	81	541
Savernake-type wares	3546	77841
Sandy grey wares	2652	27279
Black Burnished ware	336	2636
Grog and flint-tempered ware	143	1652
Grog, sand and other inclusions	74	2584
Flint-tempered	55	993
Grog-tempered ware	6	4847
subtotal Romano-British	*7259*	*121214*
Medieval and later wares		
Laverstock-type coarsewares	7	143
Border wares	2	11
Other coarseware	1	76
Redware	1	57
subtotal medieval and later	*11*	*287*
Total	7327	122181

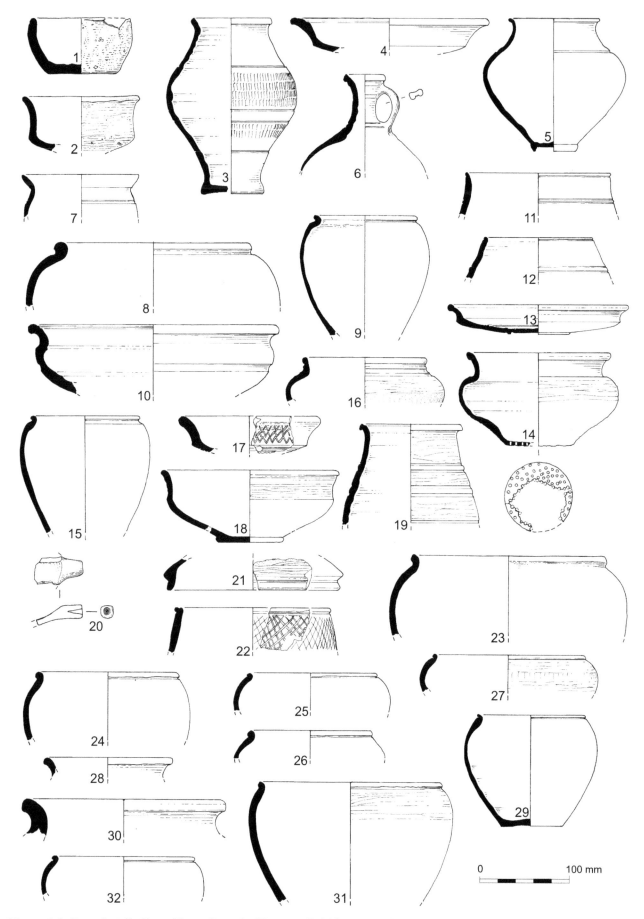

Figure 6.5 Iron Age (1–2) and latest Iron Age/Romano-British pottery (3–32)

Composition

Amphorae and imported mortaria are entirely absent and imported tablewares are limited to samian of later 1st–2nd-century AD date and from Southern and Central Gaulish sources. These wares account for just 0.3% of the Romano-British assemblage by sherd count, a surprisingly low proportion given the early focus of this assemblage, but comparable with that from other sites in the area (Mepham 1993, 28; 1999, 22; Seager Smith 2006, 114; Jones 2011, 58). Sherds from dish forms 18 and 18/31 and cup forms 27 and 33 are present, while a tiny, mould decorated body sherd, probably from a form 37 bowl, was found in pit 6408.

Finewares from British production centres are similarly limited. The five lead glazed ware sherds (pits 5626 and 6408, slot 5199 of enclosure ditch 6203, the upper trackway metalling (6244) and ditch 6276), are all from bowls belonging within the late 1st century AD. The North Wiltshire colour-coated ware beaker sherds (pits 5031 and 5887, ditch 6207 and the upper fills of solution hollow 6257), date from the second quarter of the 2nd century AD (Anderson 1979, 11). Both these fabrics also occur in small amounts on the Salisbury Plain sites (Seager Smith 2006, 116, table 5.5), while the North Wiltshire colour-coated wares have been recognised more widely, for example in the Avon valley (Mepham 1993, 29, fabrics 114 and 118), at High Post, near Salisbury (Jones 2011, 58) and on Amesbury Down (Millard 1996, 32, fabric Q113; Seager Smith in prep).

Together, the products of the large, nucleated British industries represent just 1% of the assemblage by sherd count, emphasising the predominantly earlier Romano-British date of the collection as a whole. During the late Romano-British period, red colour-coated ware bowls were obtained from the Oxfordshire potters, while sherds from the base of a single globular-bodied beaker with rouletted and under-slip barbotine scroll decoration (Young 1977, 154, type C27), were found in field ditch 6250. The New Forest industry also supplied dark colour-coated ware beakers and flagons as well as a smattering of red colour-coated ware bowls. The flagons and bowls are represented by body and base sherds only, while the beakers are mostly of the ubiquitous indented form (Fulford 1975, 52, type 27), although one piece is from a globular-bodied vessel (*ibid.*, 52, type 30) while another has barbotine scale decoration (*ibid.*, 58, type 47). The New Forest Parchment ware sherds include three pieces from a flat, jar-type base with a dark brown slip (quarry pit 5497), while mortaria from the Oxfordshire region, representing the only vessels of this type within the assemblage, include both colour-coated and whiteware forms, although the only diagnostic sherd is a rim (Young 1977, 72,

type M18) of later 3rd-century AD date, found in feature 5824.

The oxidised wares consist of a range of white-, pink-, buff- and orange-firing fabrics, mostly tempered with varying quantities of sand and/or mica, although 12 sherds (78 g) in a very fine, grog-tempered fabric with cream surfaces occurred in solution hollow 6513 and pit 6773. These wares and a smaller number of sherds in similar fabrics with white-slipped surfaces (Table 6.5) remain unsourced but clearly encompass the products of several centres spanning a wide date range. Early (mid-/late 1st century AD) forms include imitation butt-beakers (eg, Fig. 6.5, 3), a shallow, carinated dish with a flat flanged rim (Fig. 6.5, 4), both in fairly thick-walled, coarse sandy fabrics and probably loosely based on Gallo-Belgic prototypes, and finer, Belgic-style, upright-necked cordoned jars/bowls (eg, Fig. 6.5, 5). Later 1st to 3rd-century AD forms include jars with upright and everted rims, bead rim beakers and flagons, including both collared (Fig. 6.5, 6) and ring-necked types. A flared rim beaker sherd (Fig. 6.5. 7), in a hard, wheelmade, red fabric with an external white slip, is directly comparable with a vessel from Durrington Walls, described by Swan (1971, 114, fig. 25, R84) as a possible import from the south Midlands and of late Romano-British date, indicating the continued use of these wares into the late 3rd or 4th centuries AD. Similar fabrics were also noted at Maddington Farm, Shrewton (Seager Smith 1996, fabric Q109), in the Avon valley (Mepham 1999, 22, fabric Q120), and on Amesbury Down (Millard 1996, fig. 16, 4).

The coarse, utilitarian kitchen vessels, which formed the bulk of the assemblage, are dominated by grog-tempered, Savernake-type wares (Table 6.5). Although not unequivocally dated, these first appeared during the second quarter of the 1st century AD and continued, with relatively little typological change, well into the 2nd century AD (Hopkins 1999; Timby 2001, 78–81). Bead-rimmed (eg, Fig. 6.5, 8 and 9) and necked, cordoned jars, both firmly based within the local, indigenous traditions of the area, are the most common forms, with smaller numbers of wide-mouthed bowls (eg, Fig. 6.5, 10), large storage jars, lids, beakers (Fig. 6.5, 11 and 12) and platters (eg, Fig. 6.5, 13). Sherds from the complete profile of a wide-mouthed bowl with small, pre-firing 'strainer' holes in its base (Fig. 6.5, 14) were also found among other early Romano-British sherds in slot 6607 of enclosure ditch 6203. A variety of unprovenanced but probably local, handmade, sandy wares form a significant proportion of the 1st-century AD sherds in this assemblage. Forms are again dominated by bead rim (eg, Fig. 6.5, 15) and 'Belgic' style necked, cordoned jars (eg, Fig. 6.5, 16), along with imitation Gallo-Belgic platters (eg, Fig. 6.5, 17), flared and

Plate 6.4 Fabrics from a) context 7206 (kiln 7205), and b) context 7484 (kiln 7487)

bead rim beakers, carinated bowls (eg, Fig. 6.5, 18), butt beakers (Fig. 6.5, 19) and lids. Other, more unusual early types include a *patera* (Fig. 6.5, 20) with a socketed handle and a 'flanged' lid (Fig. 6.5, 21), both from trackway ditch 6261, as well as a sloping-shouldered jar with a lid-seated bead rim (Fig. 6.5, 22) from solution hollow 6513. Small quantities of flint-tempered ware were also used at this time (Table 6.5), but bead-rimmed jars (eight examples; Fig. 6.5, 23) are the only form recognised in this fabric.

In addition, there is evidence to indicate on-site pottery manufacture during the 1st century AD. The kilns in Area 2 (7205, 7214 and 7487) all contained predominantly grog-tempered 'waster' sherds (33/350 g, 97/1039 g and 74/2584 g, respectively), including numerous laminated flakes and some spalled pieces. Similarly damaged grog-tempered

sherds are known from small-scale, mid-1st-century AD production sites in Northampton (Shaw 1979) and at Thames Valley Park, near Reading (Mepham 1997, 55). Most of the sherds from kilns 7205 and 7214 were moderately hard, predominantly unoxidised (dark grey, brown or black, sometimes with a reddish-brown core and/or margins), and made in fairly fine fabrics tempered with moderate, poorly sorted grog (<5 mm across), rare to sparse calcined flint (<3 mm across) and rare, sub-rounded, translucent quartz sand (<0.5 mm across) in a fine, slightly micaceous matrix (Pl. 6.4a). Some variability in the frequency and size of the grog and flint inclusions is apparent, however, depending on the size and wall thickness of the intended vessel, while the rim sherds tend to include fewer coarse inclusions than those from the lower parts of the vessels. Forms are limited to bead-rimmed (four examples; Fig. 6.5, 24–27) and upright-necked (two examples; Fig. 6.5, 28) jars, while bases are flat and mostly in the region of 60–100 mm in diameter, although one larger example (160 mm) was noted in kiln 7214. Exterior surfaces, including the underside of the bases, are well-burnished to a smooth, glossy finish.

The majority (74 sherds, 2584 g) of sherds from kiln 7487 were made in a very hard, brittle, almost overfired fabric, tempered with moderate, poorly-sorted grog (<5 mm across) and occasional calcined flint, chalk and other inclusions (such as iron particles or organic matter) in a sandy matrix (Pl. 6.4b). Colour varies widely even within a single sherd, and firing clouds abound, but some of the softer sherds found here are also laminated, like those from kilns 7205 and 7214. Most appear to be wheelmade, but vessel forms are again limited to a bead-rimmed jar (Fig. 6.5, 29), with a few fine drying cracks apparent, and medium/large upright-necked jars (seven examples; eg, Fig. 6.5, 30); while surface treatments are restricted to burnishing on the rim and shoulder zones. A very large, everted rim storage jar (6 sherds, 4847 g; Fig. 6.6, 33) made in a coarse, grog-tempered ware may also have been a local product, its size making it difficult to transport any distance, although Savernake-type wares more typical of those made in the north of the county (36 sherds, 954 g, including Figs 6.5, 31, 32 and 6.6, 34), a flint-tempered bead rim jar fragment (20 g) and a sandy plain body sherd (8 g) were also recovered from the fills of this feature.

Overall, the assemblages from the kilns give the impression of competently potted and relatively uniformly fired vessels. Both fabrics were made in the Savernake ware tradition, but although they contain more frequent and conspicuous flint and/or quartz sand inclusions, and tend to be more carefully burnished, the variability inherent within the Savernake Forest wares (eg, Rigby 1982, 153–4, fabric 6; Timby 2001, 75), means that it is very

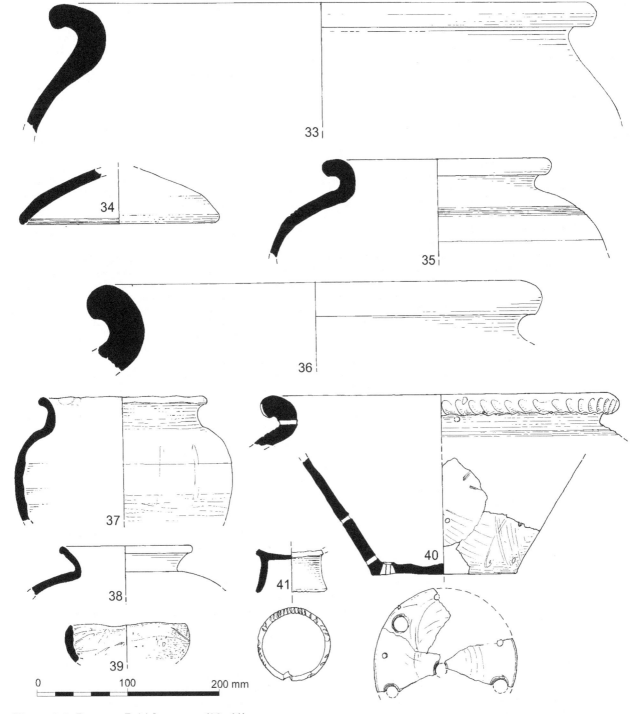

Figure 6.6 Romano-British pottery (33–41)

difficult to distinguish between them (by eye and with the aid of a x20 microscope), even within this assemblage. Small quantities of the kiln products were, however, identified in solution hollow 6513 and in pits 7208, 7496, 7497 and 7510 but the overall paucity of these wares suggest that production here was short-lived.

By the early/mid-2nd century AD, the native-style sandy wares had largely been replaced by a range of more Romanised, wheelmade wares in harder fired,

crisp textured, dark brown or grey, sandy fabrics. These potentially include products of kilns in Westbury (Rogers and Roddham, 1991, 5; Corney *et al.* 2014) and perhaps in Bromham, north-west of Devizes (Wiltshire County Archaeology Service 2004, 6), as well as others as yet undiscovered in the area. Alice Holt/Farnham products (Lyne and Jefferies 1979; Lyne 2012) may also have reached the area, but by the later 3rd and 4th centuries AD, the New Forest industry (Fulford 1975) was probably the major

0   50 mm

Plate 6.5 Pottery discs from pit group 6215 (ONs 16–20, 22, 24–25, 27, 31–33, 1014)

supplier of these wares. South-east Dorset Black Burnished ware was also being used on this site from the later 1st/early 2nd century AD onwards, although the range and frequency of the vessel forms present (Seager Smith and Davies 1993, types 1, 2, 3, 20, 22, 25 and 26) indicate that it became much more common during the late Romano-British period. Overall, the South-east Dorset wares account for approximately 5% of the assemblage by sherd count, a figure comparable with that from other sites in the area (eg, Millard 1996; Mepham 1993; Seager Smith 1996; 2006, 120).

Ceramic production in the Savernake Forest also seems to have suffered a dramatic decline after the middle of the 2nd century AD (Timby 2001, 81), although similar grog-tempered (but often harder fired and paler coloured or fully oxidised) fabrics were subsequently made at sites such as Whitehill Farm, Toothill Farm and Purton, to the west of Swindon, continuing into the 3rd century, perhaps even into the 4th century AD (Anderson 1979, 6 and 13; 1980, 57–8). In this assemblage, large, thick-walled storage jars (eg, Fig. 6.6, 35 and 36) were commonly made in these later wares, along with a range of jars/bowls with upright or slightly everted rim jars (eg, Fig. 6.6, 37 and 38) and straight-sided bowl/dish forms copied from those of the Black Burnished ware industry.

From the 2nd century AD onwards, the range of sandy ware vessel forms also changed to include a wide variety of wide- and narrow-mouthed jars with upright, everted, flared or hooked rims. Large, thick-walled storage jars with everted or rope rims occur in these fabrics, while other forms comprise the full range of straight-sided, flanged, 'casserole'-type bowls/dishes and shallow, circular, plain-rimmed dishes as well as beakers, jugs, flagons and lids. Most of these forms can be paralleled among the repertoire of the New Forest industry (eg, Fulford 1975, 80–103, types 6, 10, 19, 20, 23, 28, 30, 32, 33 and 40) although they were by no means exclusively made there. Other, less common forms included a late Romano-British 'strainer' vessel (*ibid.*, 103, type 37), represented by a flat base with small pre-firing perforations found in pit 5038, and a shallow convex-sided dish (Fig. 6.6, 39) from the upper fill of pit 7506. This form can be paralleled in groups postdating AD 345 at Porchester Castle (Cunliffe 1975, 344, fig.187), and it is possible that it continued into the 5th century

Plate 6.6 Pottery discs from pit group 6217 (ONs 38–44, 48–49 and 53)

AD (M. Lyne pers. comm.). Locally, examples are known from Durrington Walls (Swan 1971, fig. 22, R13 and fig. 23, R25) and Amesbury Down (Seager Smith in prep).

Although present at other sites in the area (eg, Swan 1971, 101; Seager Smith 2006, 118; Seager Smith in prep), no examples of the 4th-century AD 'Wessex' grog-tempered ware (Tomber and Dore 1998, 139, HAM GT) were noted in this assemblage but some of the thick-walled sandy greyware storage jar sherds may provide further evidence for very late Romano-British or early post-Romano-British activity at this site. Most of the sherds from vessels of this type were found in elements of the ladder field system (ditches 6219, 6222 and 6250). Many indicate that the vessels were pierced before being fired (Fulford 1975, 103, fig. 3, type 40.3) and/or had finger-smeared exterior surfaces (*ibid.*, type 40.5). Although these pierced, rope-rimmed vessels are not uncommon in the area (Swan 1971, fig. 22, R10, fig. 24, R45, fig. 25, R70 and fig. 27, R94; Rodgers and Roddham, 1991, 58, fig. 6, 1, 4, 5 and 6; Seager Smith in prep.), sherds probably from a single rope-rimmed vessel found in various contexts in slot 2119 of field ditch 6219 are of particular interest. This vessel, made in the New Forest, is pierced around the neck and through the body, while the base has perforations of two different sizes around its circumference, surrounding a larger, central hole (Fig. 6.6, 40). Similar features are also known on vessels made in a distinctive, coarse, oxidised, South-east Dorset Black Burnished ware fabric of very late 4th or early 5th-century AD date (SEDOWW;

Gerrard 2010; Seager Smith 1997, fig. 108, 13; 2002, 103, fig. 48, 55; Lyne 2012, fig. 149, 13.2, fig. 154, 8 and fig. 155, 1–3). Unfortunately, the function of these vessels remains completely unknown, but it seems reasonable to suppose that they were designed to serve a very particular purpose, perhaps one not previously fulfilled by ceramic vessels. It is therefore likely that the New Forest greyware examples were used in the same way and also belong within a similarly late timeframe; locally, for example, the perforated vessel from High Post (Jones 2011, 61, fig. 27, 30) was found in the same context as a pedestal base sherd of early 5th to 6th-century AD date (Mepham 2011, 62, fig. 27, 34).

Evidence for use, reuse and repair

Evidence for the use, reuse and repair of ceramic vessels is relatively restricted. However, both surfaces of the base and lower walls of the early Romano-British strainer vessel (Fig. 6.5, 14) are pitted and abraded, presumably through use. Surface residues were noted on just eight sherds or groups of associated sherds. Four of these consist of internal limescale deposits, occurring on a large (240–260 mm diameter) bead-rimmed storage jar from ditch 6249, a flat base probably from a similarly sized vessel found in quarry pit 5566 (group 6232) and two body sherds from field ditch 6265, all of Savernake-type ware, as well as New Forest greyware body sherds from a single jar found in quarry pit group 5497. These vessels may have been used to store or boil water. Sooty residues, suggesting cooking or the preparation of foodstuffs and/or other materials, were noted on

0   50 mm

Plate 6.7 Spindlewhorl (ON 175) and disc with post-firing perforation (ON 132)

bead-rimmed jars from ditch 6208 (Savernake-type ware) and slot 6607 of enclosure ditch 6203 (greyware), and on Savernake-type ware body and base sherds from ditch 6249 and solution hollow 6513.

Small, post-firing perforations had been drilled through the shoulder of a bead-rimmed jar (pit 7239) and the neck of a cavetto-rimmed storage jar (trackway 6246), both of Savernake type ware, as well as a greyware jar body sherd (quarry pit 6098, group 6231). These probably indicate the repair of these vessels using metal staples, rivets or organic ties. Various classical authors describe the methods used to repair ceramic vessels in this way (eg, Cato *De agri cultum* 39.1), and although predominantly associated with very large, dolia-type vessels or high quality tablewares, the practice was widespread in Roman Britain on vessels of all types from the mid-1st century to at least the mid-3rd century AD (Peña 2007, 213–49).

One greyware vessel, represented by two worn jar-type base sherds from field ditch 6226, had been modified by the drilling of a large centrally positioned perforation through its base. Such post-firing perforations are generally interpreted as indicative of an intentional change in the use of a vessel and the practice is well known across southern England during all four centuries of Roman rule. It is traditionally associated with the production of cheese (Harding 1974, 88), although such vessels could also have been used to drain solids from liquids in a wide variety of other domestic, agricultural or industrial

contexts, or more exotically, as time-pieces or flower pots, while others may have been rendered useless in more ritualistic ways (Fulford and Timby 2001, 294–6). Two broken vessels may also have been adapted to form new, smaller ones. One of these, a hollow pedestal base in a greyware fabric and probably of 1st-century AD date (Fig. 6.6, 41), may have been deliberately trimmed so that it could be used in an inverted position as a vessel in its own right. Horizontal and diagonal notches, presumably related to this phase of reuse, had also been cut or worn into the top of this new 'rim'. Similarly, a second cup or small bowl may have been created from the base of a New Forest colour-coated ware beaker (field ditch 7356).

An unusually high number (50) of utilised sherds were also recovered. These consist of pieces trimmed to form roughly circular or oval shapes (Pls 6.6–6.7). Most were 30–70 mm in diameter, although two, found in quarry pit 5536 (group 6232; ON 133) and tree-throw hole 7330, were larger (110 mm and 145 mm, respectively) and may have served different purposes, perhaps as pot lids or palettes, for example. All the pieces were 5–15 mm thick, depending on the nature of the original sherd, and most were made from Savernake-type ware, although four were in flint-tempered fabrics, with single examples in a native-style sandy ware, oxidised ware and Romanised greyware. One complete, well-finished spindlewhorl with ground edges (Pl. 6.7; ON 175), was present amongst the utilised sherds, while a second disc (Pl. 6.7; ON 132) had traces of an attempted post-firing perforation in the centre of its interior surface, suggesting it represents a spindlewhorl abandoned during the course of manufacture. It is possible, then, that all these sherds represent unfinished spindlewhorls, although many of them, especially two large groups from pit group 6215 (Pl. 6.5; ONs 16–20, 22, 24–25, 27, 31–33 and 1014) and pit group 6217 (Pl. 6.6; ONs 38–44, 48–49 and 53) seem worn and well handled, suggesting that they were utilised in their current state. Traditionally, such items have been interpreted as gaming pieces, counters or weights, but recent research has suggested that some, known throughout the Greco-Roman world as 'pessoi', may have been used for cleaning the buttocks and anal area after defecation (Papadopoulos 2002; Charlier 2012).

Summary

The range of fabrics and forms recovered is typical of other Romano-British sites in the region (Rathz 1963, Swan 1971; Davies 1990; Jones 2011; Mepham 1993; 1998; 1999; Millard 1996; Seager Smith 1996; 2006; in prep). Overall, the assemblage is dominated by locally-produced, coarse, utilitarian vessels, including the products of the Savernake, New Forest and Black Burnished ware industries. Amphora and imported mortaria are absent, while tablewares are restricted to samian and a small number of types from British production centres, indicating little access to, or perhaps desire for, luxury items. Nothing within the assemblage suggests that it derived from anything other than the activities of an agriculturally based rural community, although two strands of evidence are of particular interest.

The first of these, the evidence for 1st-century AD ceramic production in the Savernake ware style, clearly represents a southerly off-shoot of this industry, perhaps by a migrant or itinerant potter. While only a very restricted range of vessel forms were being made, presumably for immediate local consumption over a short space of time, its presence highlights the hitherto unforeseen potential for further small-scale production centres operating within the Savernake ware tradition at other sites in the south of the county. Although it has proved difficult at this stage to distinguish the kiln products from the Savernake-type wares in general, further detailed petrological, chemical and/or textural analysis may well provide fruitful avenues for future research.

Similarly, the perforated storage jar from ditch 6219 not only provides an indicator of very late Romano-British or early post-Roman activity at this site, but it also highlights the possibility of continued production in the New Forest, at least on a limited scale, into the early decades of the 5th century and something of the connections and influences operating between the New Forest and south-east

Dorset industries at this time. Furthermore, recognition of this form on other sites within the New Forest greyware distribution zone, like that of the SEDOWW vessels in south Dorset, may provide a useful ceramic marker in the identification of features and phases belonging within this difficult to recognise transitional period.

Medieval and Later Sherds

Medieval and later sherds are present in only minimal quantities. Sherds of Laverstock-type coarsewares, including rims from two jars and a shoulder sherd from a similar form, were found in medieval/post-medieval ditches 5797 and 6253, solution hollow 6257 as well as intrusively in Romano-British field ditch 6269. These wares were made on the outskirts of Salisbury between the 12th and 14th centuries. One other coarseware sherd, a burnt or refired handle stump (from a spread of soil, 5373, on the northern edge of Area 3), could be of late Laverstock or early Verwood type of late medieval/early post-medieval date. A thin-walled Border ware sherd with a single spot of glaze could be of similar date, but it occurred with pieces of later, coarser, all-over green glazed Border ware and a Redware strap handle fragment of post-medieval date in the upper fill of ditch 6202.

List of illustrated pottery
Figs 6.5 and 6.6

1. Small hemispherical cup with simple beaded rim; sand and fine flint-tempered ware; slot (6607) of ditch 6203, context 6609
2. Carinated cup; sandy ware; slot 6537 of enclosure ditch 6203, context 6668
3. Globular-bodied, imitation butt beaker; rouletted decoration; oxidised ware; slot 6562 of trackway 6246, context 6565
4. Shallow, carinated dish with flat flanged rim; oxidised ware; slot 6527 of ditch 6239, context 6528
5. Necked, cordoned jar; oxidised ware; solution hollow 6513, context 6518.299
6. Small collared flagon; white-slipped red ware; slot 5299 of field ditch 6226, context 5300
7. Flared rim beaker; white-slipped red ware; slot 5827 of field ditch 6269, context 5828
8. Bead-rimmed jar; Savernake-type ware; pit 5756, context 5764
9. Bead-rimmed jar; Savernake-type ware; solution hollow 6513, context 6518.321
10. Wide-mouth jar/bowl; Savernake-type ware; pit 6914, group 6259, context 6921
11. Necked beaker; Savernake-type ware; slot 6537 of enclosure ditch 6203, context 6538
12. Necked beaker; Savernake-type ware; pit 6425, context, 6427

13. Imitation Gallo-Belgic platter; Savernake-type ware; pit 5756, context 5764

14. Strainer bowl; Savernake-type ware; slot 6607 of enclosure ditch 6203, context 6613

15. Bead-rimmed jar; greyware; slot 6607 of enclosure ditch 6203, context 6613

16. Upright-necked jar; greyware; solution hollow 6513, context 6515

17. Large, imitation Gallo-Belgic platter/carinated bowl; burnished-line decoration; greyware; solution hollow 6513, context 6515

18. Carinated bowl; greyware; slot 6562 of trackway 6246, context 6565

19. Imitation cordoned butt beaker; fine greyware; slot 5052 of ditch 6211, context 5054

20. *Patera*, with socketed handle; greyware; slot 6591 of ditch 6261, context 6592

21. Flanged lid; greyware; slot 6591 of ditch 6261, context 6592

22. Straight-shouldered jar with a lid-seated rim; burnished-line decoration; greyware; solution hollow 6513, context 6517

23. Bead-rimmed jar; flint-tempered ware; evaluation trench 1, ditch 111 (north of Area 1)

24. Bead-rimmed jar; grog, flint and sand-tempered ware; kiln 7205, context 7206

25. Bead-rimmed jar; grog, flint and sand-tempered ware; kiln 7214, context 7215

26. Bead-rimmed jar; grog, flint and sand-tempered ware; kiln 7214, context 7215

27. Bead-rimmed jar; grog, flint and sand-tempered ware; kiln 7214, context 7215

28. Upright-necked jar; grog, flint and sand-tempered ware; kiln 7214, context 7215

29. Bead-rimmed jar; grog, sand and occasional flint/other inclusions; kiln 7487, context 7488

30. Upright-necked storage jar; grog, sand and occasional flint/other inclusions; kiln 7487, context 7488

31. Bead-rimmed jar; Savernake-type ware; kiln 7487, context 7488

32. Bead-rimmed jar; Savernake-type ware; kiln 7487, context 7488

33. Large everted rim storage jar; grog-tempered ware; kiln 7487, context 7488

34. Lid; Savernake-type ware; kiln 7487, context 7488

35. Large cavetto storage jar rim; Savernake-type ware; slot 6607 of enclosure ditch 6203, context 6616

36. Heavy bead-rimmed storage jar; Savernake-type ware; pit 6914, group 6259, context 6921

37. Medium necked jar; Savernake-type ware; possible recut 5984 in slot 5976 of enclosure ditch 6203, context 6061

38. Everted rim jar; Savernake-type ware; pit 6914, group 6259, context 6921

39. Convex-sided dish; greyware; pit 7506, context 7522

40. Storage jar with a pie-crust rim; pre-firing perforations in neck, body and base; greyware; slot 2119 of field ditch 6219, contexts 2104, 2108, 2114 and 2118

41. Hollow pedestal base trimmed for reuse in an inverted position; greyware; solution hollow 6513, context 6518

Fired Clay
R.H. Seager Smith

A total of 2050 fragments (23.629 kg) of fired clay were recorded. All the fabrics contain variable quantities of sand with chalk, grog, organic materials and crushed calcined flint, either separately or in various combinations. Firing varies from fully oxidised to the dark grey/brown colour range and from soft and powdery to almost vitrified.

Approximately 89% of the assemblage by weight (21 kg) derived from Romano-British pottery kilns 7205, 7214 and 7487 and ovens 6174, 7231, 7245, 7290 and 7329. Soft, lightly fired and predominantly oxidised, chalk-tempered fragments were found in the filling of kiln 7487 (2.8 kg) and in smaller amounts in the other kilns (7205, 23 g; 7214, 650 g) and ovens (6174, 674 g; 7231, 87 g; 7245, 28 g, 7290, 87 g; 7329, 205 g). Most are amorphous, but some have a single, flattish, smoothed surface or preserved wattle impressions, suggesting that this material derived from the linings of these structures.

Three more or less complete rectangular kiln bars (220–240 x 70–80 x 60–70 mm), made in hard, dark grey fabrics with chalk, grog, flint and organic inclusions (Fig. 6.7, 1–3) were found on the base of kiln 7214, and may have provided supports for its floor (Pl. 5.12). Numerous thin, surfaceless but often slightly curved fragments (761 pieces, 4.6 kg) in fabrics similar to those used for the bars were also found in kiln 7214. These probably represent the fired remains of clay plastered over the exterior of, and/or between, the turves or sods used to form a temporary dome over the chamber of the structure during firing (*cf* Swan 1984, 37).

Similar pieces also occurred amongst the material from kilns 7205 (1.9 kg) and 7487 (8.4 kg), although the majority of these fragments derive from flat, roughly circular or oval plates. These are made in fabrics tempered with varying amounts of grog, flint, chalk, organic material and sand, variably fired and varying greatly in terms of hardness. Organic impressions are especially frequent on the surfaces of these objects. Although highly fragmentary, the roughly circular plates are in the region of 150–250 mm in diameter and vary from 5 mm to 25 mm thick; the oval examples (eg, Fig. 6.7, 4) tend to be

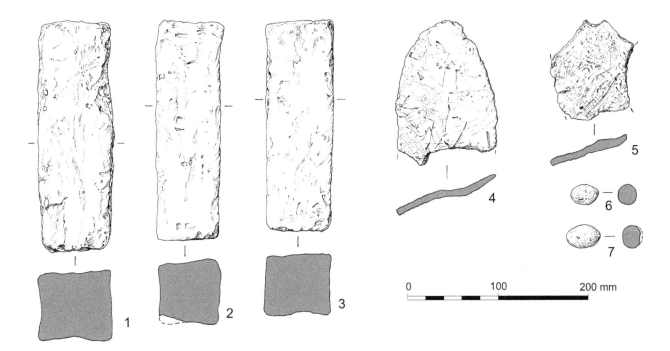

Figure 6.7 Fired clay objects (1–7)

thinner, harder fired and in the region of 200–300 mm long, 100–120 mm wide and 5–10 mm thick. Most appear to be fairly flat, although some warping may have occurred during use, while others are raised towards a central, pre-firing perforation, 200 mm in diameter (Fig. 6.7, 5). Comparable clay plates have been found on numerous Romano-British kiln sites (Swan 1984, 41; 64–5), including those of the north Wiltshire Savernake pottery industry (Hopkins 1999, pl. 3; Timby 2001, 74). They are most likely to have been used as temporary 'floors' or 'setters' to separate vessels horizontally within the firing chamber or to span gaps or to level layers within the load (Swan 1984, 40). Locally, however, similar circular plates have been found in Romano-British settlement contexts at Maddington Farm, Shrewton (Seager Smith 1996, 58), at Figheldean (Mepham 1993, fig. 13, 2 and 3; 1999, 24), at Coombe Down South and Chisenbury Warren on Salisbury Plain (Allen and Seager Smith 2006, 122) and from Amesbury Down (Seager Smith in prep.), for example, although in general these items were not so hard fired. Pieces probably derived from two other clay plates in soft, oxidised sandy fabrics were also recovered from pit 5031 and field ditch 6265 and these may have served alternative functions, perhaps as lids or 'hot plates'.

The only other recognisable objects are three ovoid slingshots, probably of Iron Age date and used for hunting small game. These were found in pits 5756 and 7140 (Fig. 6.7, 6), and in slot 6537 of enclosure ditch 6203 (Fig. 6.7, 7), and can be paralleled in the later phases (cp 6 and 7; c. 400–

100/50 BC) of activity at Danebury and on other Iron Age sites in the area including Yarnbury, Maiden Castle, Glastonbury, All Canning's Cross and Gussage All Saints (Poole 1984, 398, fig. 7.44).

The remainder of the fired clay is amorphous in character, consisting of small, abraded fragments in poorly fired fabrics. The function of these could not be ascertained, although wattle impressions on a number of pieces suggest that many derive from structural materials such as daub.

List of illustrated fired clay objects
Fig. 6.7
1. Kiln bar; kiln 7214, layer 7216
2. Kiln bar; kiln 7214, layer 7216
3. Kiln bar; kiln 7214, layer 7216
4. Flat, oval clay plate; kiln 7487, layer 7488
5. Perforated clay plate; kiln 7487, layer 7488
6. Slingshot; pit 7140, layer 7142, ON 1020
7. Slingshot; slot 6537 of enclosure ditch 6203, layer 6647, ON 180

Coins
by Nicholas Cooke

Thirteen coins, all Roman low-denomination copper alloy issues, were recovered. They are in generally good condition, with little sign of post-depositional corrosion, suggesting a largely stable burial environment. Some show signs of pre-depositional wear, but all could be identified to period (Table 6.6).

Table 6.6 Roman coins

Period	ON	Context	Denomination	Description	Issue Date	Ruler	References
AD 69–96	184	6481	Cu alloy *as*	Domitian/Virtus Augusti type; Rome mint	AD 86	Domitian	RIC II, Domitian, 500
AD 96–118	–	1205	Cu alloy *sestertius*	Trajan/uncertain reverse	AD 98–117	Trajan	–
AD 161–180	30	5186	Cu alloy *sestertius*	Marcus Aurelius/Vota Sol Decennii SC type ; Rome	AD 170–71	Marcus Aurelius	As RIC III, Marcus Aurelis 1014, 1016 and 1017
AD 260–275	13	5373	Cu alloy *antoninianus*	?Radiate copy of Tetricus II/Princ Iuvent type; unknown mint	AD 270–3	?Tetricus II	? Copy as RIC V (Part II) Tetricus II, 260
AD 275–296	82	5462	Cu alloy *antoninianus*	Radiate copy of Tetricus I/Virtus Aug type; unknown mint	AD 270–96	Irregular radiates	–
	117	5321	Cu alloy *antoninianus*	Radiate copy/uncertain reverse; unknown mint.	AD 270–96	Irregular radiates	–
AD 330–348	85	5039	Cu alloy AE 3	Constantine I/Gloria Exercitus type (1 standard); Lyons mint (SLG)	AD 330	Constantine I	LRBC I, 180
	116	6411	Cu alloy AE 3	House of Constantine/Gloria Exercitus (2 standards); Arles mint (Christmas tree/PCONST')	AD 335	Constantine II	LRBC I, 392
	185	6877	Cu alloy AE 4	Copy of Urbs Roma/Wolf and Twins; unknown mint	AD 330–45	House of Constantine	Copy as LRBC I, 51
	186	6877	Cu alloy AE 3	House of Constantine/Victoriaddauggqnn type; unknown mint	AD 341–8	House of Constantine	As LRBC I, 137
	–	6783	Cu alloy AE 3	Constans/Victoriaddauggqnn type; Trier mint (mint mark: D/TRS)	AD 345	Constans	LRBC I, 155
AD 364–378	7	5916	Cu alloy AE 3	House of Valentinian/Securitas Reipublicae type; unknown mint	AD 364–78	House of Valentinian	As LRBC II, 82
	111	5744	Cu alloy AE 3	House of Valentinian/Gloria Romanorum typ; Lyons mint (OF| III / LVG-)	AD 364–78	House of Valentinian	As LRBC II, 279 etc

The assemblage is typical of a small Romano-British rural site, with a small number of coins dating to the 1st to mid-3rd centuries AD and a larger group of late 3rd and 4th-century AD coins. The three early coins all suggest activity in the 1st or 2nd centuries. However, prior to the second half of the 3rd century, the Roman state appears to have had little interest in withdrawing low-denomination coinage from circulation once minted, and these coins could have remained in circulation for some considerable time before their loss. The bulk of the Roman coins, however, date to the late 3rd and 4th centuries – three radiate *antoniniani* of the late 3rd century (including two irregular contemporary 'barbarous' copies) and seven 4th-century coins. The latter comprise five coins of the House of Constantine and two of the House of Valentinian. These indicate that there was coin use on the site into the last quarter of the 4th century.

Metalwork

by R.H. Seager Smith

The metalwork assemblage (375 objects) is dominated by iron (341 items) with just 33 copper alloy objects and a single piece of lead. Many of the objects, particularly the iron, are heavily corroded. Where appropriate, the metalwork has been x-rayed to aid identification and to provide a basic archival record for these inherently unstable material types, but no further conservation cleaning or stabilisation treatments were undertaken.

With the exception of a hooked iron blade from otherwise undated pit 5892 (ON 92), all the metalwork came from features and deposits of Romano-British or later date. These include 20 pits, a posthole, two stakeholes, the trackway, oven/kilns 7290 and 7329, graves 6511 and 7376, a tree-throw hole and 10 ditches and gullies; metal items were especially prolific in the fillings of the field ditches (78 items) and solution hollow 6513 (40 objects).

Personal Items

Items of personal ornament are confined to brooches; the assemblage includes both copper alloy and iron examples, although almost all were residual in the contexts in which they were found. Brooches were especially frequent in solution hollow 6513 where 11 copper alloy fragments were recovered. These include a small, almost complete, one-piece or Nauheim-derivative brooch (ON 166, Fig. 6.8, 1), but the others are all very fragmentary. Part of the bow and catchplate from a second one-piece brooch (ON 148) and pieces of two Colchester-type brooches (ON 158

and 160; head/bow and bow/catchplate, respectively) are the only others that can be assigned to type; both were in use in Britain before the Roman Conquest, but became much more common during the middle decades of the 1st century AD (Bayley and Butcher 2004, 147–9). The other seven pieces (ONs 134–6, 149 and 160–1) comprise small, unidentifiable spring, bow or pin fragments.

Part of a third simple, one-piece brooch (ON 79, Fig. 6.8, 2) was found in quarry pit 5724 (group 6232), while the head, spring and upper part of the bow of another Colchester-type (ON 71, Fig. 6.8, 3) was recovered from field ditch 6228. A mid-1st-century AD Colchester two-piece brooch (ON 182, Fig. 6.8, 4), similar to examples from Wanborough (Butcher 2001, 52–3, fig. 21, 82, 83 and fig. 22, 86), survived complete and in exceptionally good condition in slot 6670 of the enclosure ditch (6203). Part of a composite iron and copper alloy brooch spring (ON 87) was also found in late Romano-British field ditch 6219, while the other copper alloy brooch pieces – a spring fragment (ON 6) and two pins (ON 65 and 109), the latter from a hinged brooch – were from quarry pit group 5910, field ditch 6228 and pit 6408, respectively.

Although iron was the metal least commonly used for items of personal adornment, pieces from at least six iron brooches were also recovered. These include bow fragments from two simple, one-piece brooches from ditch 6208 (ON 11) and pit 5585 (ON 55) and a hinged strip bow brooch (ON 73–74, Fig. 6.8, 5) from field ditch 6219, as well as three pins with flattened, perforated heads, all from hinged forms, found in slot 5199 of enclosure ditch 6203 (ON 21), and in pit 6408 (ONs 101–2). Locally, an iron strip brooch was found at Figheldean (Hutcheson 1999, 20, fig. 5, a) while both types are known from Wanborough (Butcher 2001, 44, fig. 17, 28–34; fig. 18, 38 and 39), dated to the 1st century AD.

Part of a pair of Romano-British copper alloy wire tweezers of very simple form (ON 1002, Fig. 6.8, 6), were also found in field ditch 6219. Tweezers seem to have been used by both sexes for the removal of unwanted facial and body hair (Crummy and Eckhardt 2003), although some may have functioned in a variety of surgical contexts. Although not closely datable, pin or needle shank fragments occurred in both copper alloy (ON 89, unstratified, and two pieces ON 176 from solution hollow 6513) and iron (ON 137; post-medieval ditch 6277).

Household

Part of a tanged iron knife, with a straight back continuing the line of the handle and a straight edge (ON 54, Fig. 6.8, 7), was found in field ditch 6219.

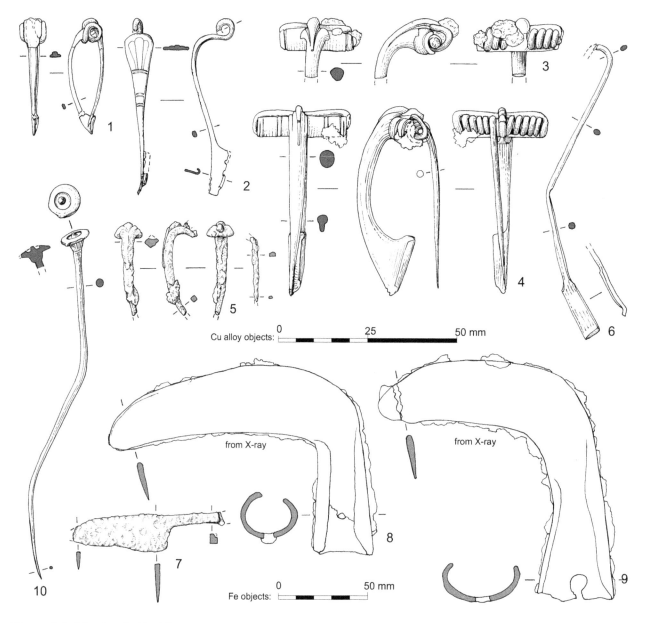

Figure 6.8 Metalwork (1–10)

Manning (1985, 114, type 11) noted that while knives of this type were common in mid-1st-century AD contexts, there is little evidence to suggest that they were an exclusively early type.

Agricultural/Horticultural Items

Two small, socketed, hooked iron blades represent the only identifiable iron tools. One (ON 92, Fig. 6.8, 8) has a blade set at a right angle to the handle (Manning 1985, 53, type 1, pl. 22, F24) and is an early type, probably of Iron Age date; it was the only artefact found in the otherwise undated pit 5892. The other has a more curved blade (ON 50, Fig. 6.8, 9), and is likely to be slightly later (*ibid*, type 2, pl, 22,

F26–29, pl. 23, F30–33). This came from quarry pit 5322 (group 6232), associated with earlier Romano-British pottery and a cattle skull (ABG 51). Both are likely to have been multipurpose tools, for pruning, reaping and cutting leaves and fodder.

Fragments from a rod-like iron object were found in the backfill of oven 7329 (ON 215). This item is 300 mm long with an oval cross-section (12–15 mm across) but is too fragmentary to identify further.

Fastenings and Fittings

The iron assemblage includes 72 nails or nail shank fragments. Where discernible, all are of the flat, round-headed type, with square-sectioned tapering shanks (eg, Manning 1985, 134, type 1b) and of small to medium size (less than 100 mm long). Handmade nails of this type are not closely datable although is likely that that most are Romano-British. The largest concentration (22 nails, many with traces of mineral-replaced wood: ONs 119–131, 142–147) was in grave 6511 (Fig. 5.12), suggesting that the woman (burial 6484) was buried in a coffin. Most are fragmentary, but the more complete examples are 35–60 mm long with heads approximately 15 mm in diameter. Eight had their shanks bent to right angles 20–45 mm below their heads, indicating the thickness of the planks they were driven through.

Concentrations of hobnails with traces of mineral-replaced leather, found around the feet (ON 217, left foot – 34 hobnails; ON 218, right foot – 35 hobnails) of the probable female (burial 7380) in grave 7376 (Fig. 5.12), indicate that she wore heavy nailed boots or shoes and is therefore likely to have been fully dressed at the time of burial. In his survey of Roman burial customs, Philpott (1991, 167) noted that although the practice of including boots/shoes became common from the late 2nd–3rd century AD onwards, the vast majority of datable examples belong within the 4th century AD. Another cluster of 39 hobnails and a single, narrow cleat (ON 81), occurred in quarry pit 5808 (group 6232), while two further groups came from ditch 2919, slots 2119 (ON 1003; 41 hobnails) and 5282 (ON 45; 10 hobnails and ON 46; a cleat), while a single cleat was also found in quarry pit group 5910. These, too, may represent discarded boots/shoes although similar, small, dome-headed nails were also used in upholstery and to decorate woodwork.

The remaining iron objects include part of a double-spiked loop (ON 173, trackway 6246), a fine, square-sectioned rod, 125 mm long, tapering slightly towards the ends (ON 141; surface 6244 of the trackway) as well as a variety of unidentifiable scraps, strips and sheet metal fragments.

Metalworking Waste

Five waste droplets provided evidence for small-scale copper alloy working in the vicinity. These comprise a single piece of high-lead bronze from pit 6408 (ON 108) and four irregularly-shaped fragments from the fills of solution hollow 6513.

Items of Post-Roman Date

A complete copper alloy hair or hat pin (ON 2, Fig. 6.8, 10), probably of late medieval or post-medieval date, was recovered from the subsoil. Other copper alloy items of similar date comprise a square buckle and a riveted ferrule or other fixing from the upper fills ditch 6202. Eight iron nails, all 77–105 mm long, with small, flat round heads (10 mm in diameter), straight, shanks, pointed only at the tip are also of post-medieval/modern date. These were found in pairs intrusive in ditch 6248, modern feature 6465 and two stakeholes associated with it (6452 and 6458). Part of an oval iron link from a chain found in layer 5373 is also likely to be of relatively recent date. A single, undatable lead object (ON 9), an irregularly-shaped waste fragment, now partially folded, was found in the topsoil (context 5001).

Discussion

Overall, the range of metalwork is relatively restricted and the assemblage contains no high quality items, characteristics shared with the material from other Romano-British settlements in the vicinity (eg, Wainwright 1971, 118; Mepham 1993, 34–6; Hutcheson 1999). Although the types are well paralleled locally, the frequency and highly fragmentary nature of the 1st-century AD iron and copper alloy brooches is somewhat curious. Most were found in later features, which may account for their broken state, but the reasons for their presence remain unclear. With the exception of the coffin nails and hobnails found in funerary contexts, none of the metal items appear to have been deliberately deposited, but represent a background spread of utilitarian objects related to small-scale settlement with associated agricultural, craft and industrial activities.

List of illustrated metal objects
Fig. 6.8

1. Copper alloy Nauheim-derivative brooch; complete; 30 mm long; solution hollow 6513, layer 6518, ON 166
2. Copper alloy Nauheim-derivative brooch; bow and beginning of spring; quarry pit 5724 (group 6232), layer 5725, ON 79
3. Copper alloy Colchester two-piece brooch; incomplete, head, spring and upper part of bow only; slot 5416 of field ditch 6228, layer 5418, ON 71
4. Copper alloy Colchester two-piece brooch; narrow arched bow with central rib on upper part, triangular catchplate forming part of bow's curve; crossbar has two grooves at each end and covers spring of at least 11 turns held on central lug; chord passes through crest; slot 6670 enclosure ditch (6203), layer 6672, ON 182
5. Iron hinged strip bow brooch and part of pin; slot 5628 of field ditch 6219, layer 5629, ON 73 and 74
6. Copper alloy wire tweezers; incomplete; circular-

sectioned wire, flattened at end to form rectangular, slightly inturned blade; slot 2119 of field ditch 6219, layer 2114, ON 1002

7. Tanged iron knife; straight back continuing line of handle and straight edge; slot 5490 of field ditch 6219, layer 5493, ON 54

8. Socketed, hooked iron blade; socket perforated and blade set at right angle to handle (Manning 1985, 53, type 1, pl. 22, F24); pit 5892, layer 5894, ON 92

9. Socketed, hooked iron blade; open socketed type with hooked blade with U-shaped edge, back strongly curved (Manning 1985, 53, type 2, pl. 22, F26–29, pl. 23, F30–33); quarry pit 5322 (group 6232), layer 5323, ON 50

10. Copper alloy hair or hat pin with flat, round head decorated with raised central boss; 95 mm long; subsoil 5019, ON 2

Slag
by R.H. Seager Smith

A total of 1522 g of material was initially identified as slag. However, 90% (1368 g) of this material comprises 'Iron Age grey' or 'Midland grey' fuel ash slag. This lightweight, light-coloured (pale to mid-grey) vesicular material, often with a honeycomb-like structure, was formed by the reaction of wood ash with minerals such as sand, and was probably derived from high-temperature, pyrotechnical activities, such as the conflagration of daub-built structures or the materials within a hearth (Bayley *et al.* 2001, 21). Such material has been recorded on numerous late prehistoric and Romano-British sites elsewhere (eg, Andrews 2009; Starley 2014) but does not have any clear association with metalworking. One relatively large piece from solution hollow 6513 (context 6518) has three intact surfaces and the remains of a shallow groove down one side, raising the possibility that it

was part of an oven plate or similar object. All of the other pieces are smaller and generally without diagnostic features or undamaged surfaces. Most of this material (998 g) came from the early Romano-British layers filling the top of solution hollow 6513, but 23 pieces (70 g) from kiln 7487 highlight a possible association with pottery production.

The remaining material (154 g) is all certainly or possibly debris deriving from iron working, probably smithing, although there is no diagnostic slag. It comprises a probable ironstone lump from ditch 6229 (slot 5896) (103 g), and two small smithing slag fragments from ditch 6201 (slot 5379) and solution hollow 6513 (26 g and 25 g, respectively).

Glass
by R.H. Seager Smith

Approximately half a globular, cobalt blue glass bead with small bosses (perhaps vestigial horns) set in two registers and each decorated with an incised spiral (ON 23, Fig. 6.9), was found in quarry pit 5170 (group 6215). In form, this bead is closest to Guido's class 6 (1978, 53–7, fig. 13) of Late Iron Age date, but it is without the white or occasionally yellow trailed and marvered inlay commonly found on beads of this type.

Illustrated object
Fig. 6.9
1. Incomplete cobalt blue glass bead with small bosses (perhaps vestigial horns) in two registers, each with incised spiral (Guido 1978, 53–7, fig. 13); 25 mm in diameter, 15 mm high, perforation 10 mm across; quarry pit 5170 (group 6215), layer 5172, ON 23

Worked Bone
by R.H. Seager Smith

The eight worked bone objects were all found in Romano-British contexts, although some are likely to be of Iron Age date. These include an antler weaving comb (ON 183, Fig. 6.10, 1) decorated with crudely incised chevrons (solution hollow 6513), and two perforated sheep/goat bones, a tibia (ON 1025, Fig. 6.10, 2) and a metatarsal (ON 1026, Fig. 6.10, 3). Although incomplete with their working tips missing, these probably derive from gouges or other points which are common Iron Age tool types at other sites in the area (eg, Sellwood 1984, 382–9; Saunders 1997, 22, fig. 6; Seager Smith 2000, 224–5; Allen and Every 2006, 139).

Two small awls, both made from splinters of bone and associated with 1st–2nd-century AD pottery,

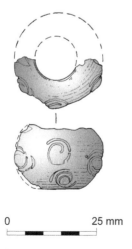

0   25 mm

Figure 6.9 Glass bead

came from pit 5305 in group 6233 (ON 60, Fig. 6.10, 4) and ditch 6249 (slot 6406) (ON 98, Fig. 6.10, 5). Tools of this type were probably used in leather working. Burnt, decorated fragments (ON 155, Fig. 6.10, 6) found in solution hollow 6513 probably came from a Romano-British knife handle and can be compared with examples from Wanborough (Vaughan 2001, 326, fig. 116, 295 and 296). Part of a polished bone cylinder with one original cut end surviving (pit 7208; ON 1009, Fig. 6.10, 7) may also be part of a knife handle; a narrow (2–4 mm wide) longitudinal slot may have taken a folding blade but it is perhaps more likely to represent later, unintentional, damage. The remaining object, a perforated fish vertebra probably used as a bead, was found in pit 7095 (ON 1027, Fig. 6.10, 8) associated with mid-/late 1st-century AD pottery.

List of illustrated worked bone objects
Fig. 6.10
1. Weaving comb (133 x 37 x 12 mm) red deer antler; rectangular teeth (seven originally) with U-shaped notches between and symmetrically tapering points; shaft concavo-convex in cross-section, widest at dentate end, with curving sides and tapering towards expanded, subcircular butt; cortical surface polished and decorated with incised chevrons; trabecular surface unaltered; solution hollow 6513, layer 6522, ON 183
2. Perforated sheep/goat tibia; burnt and incomplete; pit 6850, layer 6852, ON 1025
3. Perforated sheep/goat metatarsal; shaft polished; incomplete; slot 6562 of trackway 6246, layer 6565, ON 1026
4. Awl; complete (32 x 11 x 2 mm); splinter of long bone with a sharp, more or less symmetrical point

and a small, sub-square head; surfaces polished; pit 5305, group 6233, layer 5392, ON 60
5. Awl; complete (48 x 17 x 2 mm); splinter of long bone with a sharp, symmetrical point and a rectangular, paddle-shaped head; upper surface well polished; trabecular bone still apparent on underside; slot 6406 of field ditch 6249, layer 6407, ON 98
6. Pieces from a knife handle decorated with incised obtuse-angled lattice defined by transverse grooves at either end; burnt; solution hollow 6513, layer 6518, ON 155
7. Part of a polished bone cylinder, probably a handle fragment (25 mm in diameter) red deer antler; a narrow (2–4 mm wide) longitudinal slot may have taken a folding blade but more likely represents later, unintentional, damage; pit 7208, layer 7210, ON 1009
8. Perforated fish vertebra probably used as a bead; pit 7095, layer 7116, ON 1027

Building Materials
by R.H. Seager Smith

Identifiable building materials were scarce, emphasising the 'settlement edge' nature of the activity within the excavated area. Although intrinsically undatable, three sand and poorly-slaked lime mortar fragments (100 g) and eight pieces (595 g) of painted wall plaster (white and pale grey) were found in contexts associated with Romano-British pottery and could be of similar date. Eight flat and featureless fragments of Romano-British ceramic building material (155 g) were also recovered, but none is sufficiently complete to allow the

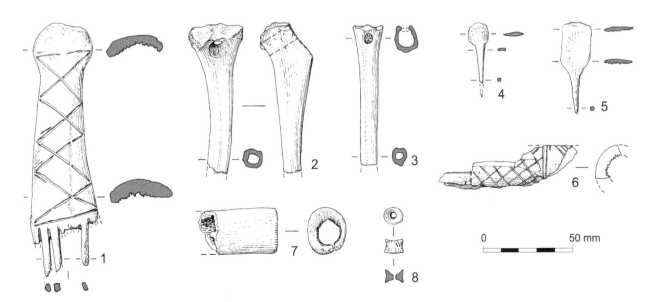

Figure 6.10 Worked bone objects (1–8)

identification of particular brick/tile types. Most of these items came from the fillings of the main field ditches, with isolated pieces in enclosure ditch 6203, pits 6773 and 7409, the uppers layers in solution hollow 6513 and residually in medieval/post-medieval ditch 6277.

In addition, seven polygonal stone roof tile fragments (3.5 kg) were found in the final backfilling layer in oven 7245. These were made from Portland limestone which outcrops in the Chilmark/Tisbury area, 25 km to the south-west of the site; similarly small quantities of this material were recorded at Durrington Walls (Wainwright 1971, 120) and in the Avon valley (Mepham 1993, 36).

Human Bone

by Jacqueline I. McKinley

Introduction

Human bone from 13 contexts was analysed (Table 6.7). Cremated bone was recovered from seven contexts including the remains of four unurned burials, one Late Neolithic and three Middle Iron Age (dated by radiocarbon analysis of bone samples). In the absence of dating evidence or sufficient bone for radiocarbon dating, the cremated bone from feature 5642 has been attributed a Middle Iron Age date by association with nearby cremation-related deposits. Unburnt human bone was found in six contexts, including the remains of three inhumation burials, one of which was radiocarbon dated to the Middle/Late Iron Age, and the other two (one coffined) being late Romano-British. Redeposited unburnt bone was recovered from early Romano-British pit 7208, although the possibility of the individual relating to an earlier phase of activity cannot be discounted.

The mortuary deposits formed small but relatively dispersed clusters and singletons. The Late Neolithic burial remains (7531) were found roughly central to hollow 7306 in Area 2, where they had been laid on the trampled/stabilised lower fill (7359) and sealed by a spread of flint knapping waste (7319) (Figs 3.1, 3.5). Two of the Middle Iron Age cremation graves (7530 and 5206) lay 16 m apart in Area 1, while the third (6548) was situated 140 m to the south-east in Area 4 (Fig. 4.1). Feature 5642, containing redeposited cremated bone, lay 18 m north of the former. The Middle/Late Iron Age inhumation grave 7280 had been cut through the upper fill of hollow 7306 (Figs 3.5, 4.1). One of the Romano-British graves (7376) was situated 6 m south-west of the hollow, the second (6511) was 90 m to the south, south of the Late Iron Age enclosure ditch (Fig. 5.2),

Early Romano-British pit 7208, containing the redeposited unburnt bone, lay 16 m north-west of the hollow (Fig. 5.6).

Recording and analysis of the cremated bone followed McKinley (1994a, 5–21; 2004a). The degree of erosion to the unburnt bone was scored after McKinley (2004b, fig. 6). Age (cremated and unburnt bone) was assessed from the stage of tooth and skeletal development (Bass 1987; Beek 1983; Scheuer and Black 2000) and the patterns and degree of age-related changes to the bones and teeth (Buikstra and Ubelaker 1994). Sex was ascertained from the sexually dimorphic traits of the skeleton (Bass 1987; Buikstra and Ubelaker 1994; Gejvall 1981). Where possible, a standard set of measurements was taken on the unburnt bone (Brothwell and Zakrzewski 2004) to facilitate the calculation of various skeletal indices, including stature and cranial index (Trotter and Gleser 1952; 1958: Brothwell 1972, 88; Bass 1987). Non-metric traits were recorded (Berry and Berry 1967; Finnegan 1978). Details are in the archive.

Taphonomy

The Neolithic remains in hollow 7306 had been sealed by flint deposit 7319 and were undisturbed. The average depth of the Iron Age cremation graves was 0.16 m (range 0.09–0.26 m). No bone was evident at surface level, suggesting the deposits had survived largely or wholly undisturbed and that little, if any bone, will have been lost due to truncation. There was evidence suggestive of plough damage to grave 6548, but this seems to have affected only the upper levels of the 0.26 m deep cut, which appears to have contained a secondary fill of redeposited pyre debris probably made above the burial itself (the horizontal location of the bone is unclear but none was observed at surface level).

The cremated bone is generally in good visual condition, and moderate proportions of trabecular bone (generally subject to preferential destruction in adverse burial environments; McKinley 1997, 245; Nielsen-Marsh *et al.* 2000) were recovered from most deposits. It was observed, however, that the bone from the earliest burial (7531) is in better condition ('sharper', with no evidence for any degree of erosion) than that from the later deposits. This material will not have been in contact with the surrounding soil matrix to the same degree as the later deposits, having been directly covered by a layer of flint knapping debris.

The Iron Age inhumation grave 7280 (0.3 m deep) had been cut by a later feature which had removed the lower limb elements and most of the distal portion of the axial skeleton (Fig. 4.2). The

Table 6.7 Summary of human bone analysis results

Cut (depth)	Context	Date	Deposit type	Quantif. (approx.)	Age (approx.)/ sex	Pathology	Pyre goods	Condition/comment
Cremated bone								
7530 & 5187 (0.14 m)	5189 & 5190	MIA *	unurned burial	180.2 g	infant/juvenile 4–5 yr	–	2.7 g sheep, sheep-sized & immature medium-mammal bone	?intrusive subadult/ adult skull vault & ?2–3 yr infant
5206 (0.09 m)	5221 (incl. 5220)	MIA *	unurned burial	480.3 g	adult 30–45 yr ?male	–	2.3 g sheep-size bone	–
5642 (0.07 m)	5643	?MIA	?R incl. rpd	3.9 g	infant 4–5 yr	–	2.2 g charred immature sheep bone	–
6548 (0.26 m)	6549	MIA *	unurned burial + rpd	223.7 g	adult 35–45 yr ??female	op – 1T bsm, distal femur; enth – proximal femur	1.4 g burnt sheep-sized bone (+ some u/b)	–
7306	7531	L.Neo.*	unurned burial	161.2 g	adult 30–50 yr	op – 1T/L bsm	–	–
Unburnt bone								
6511 (0.42 m)	6484	LRB	coffined burial	99%	adult 45–55yr female	amtl; dental caries; dental abscess; calculus; periodontal disease; osteoarthritis – both 1st & right 12th c-v; Schmorl's node – L1 & 3; ddd – T6; op– C1-2, T2-3, T8 & T10-12 tpj, T4-9 bsm, 3 left & 2 right tarsals, both 1st MrT-P, right distal femur, left shoulder, distal radii, right glenoid fossa, 4 right carpals, acetabulae rims, 5 left & 7 right rib facets; pitting – right 1st MrT-P, left sterno-clavicular, left & right rib facets; calcified rib cartilage; plastic change – right clavicle, tibiae & fibulae shafts; shortened left upper limb bones (?polio); enth – femur & tibiae shafts, patellae, right distal fibula, calcanea; mv – wormian bones, acetabular crease, T10 transverse facet absent, L1 accessory facet left pedicle	n/a	2–3; Fe staining molar, clavicle & proximal tibia, right fibula
7208	7210	?ERB	R ?=7212	left femur	neonate 0–1 weeks	–	n/a	1–2
7208	7212	?ERB	R ?=7210	left humerus	neonate 1–3 weeks	–	n/a	2
7280 (0.30 m)	7284 (incl. 7281)	M/LIA*	*in situ*	25% s.a.u.	neonate 1–4 weeks	–	n/a	1–2
7376 (0.77 m)	7380	LRB	inhumation burial	97%	adult >45yr ?female	amtl; dental caries; dental abscess; calculus; periodontal disease; fracture – min. 2 right ribs; periosteal new bone – right maxilla, left medial nasal process, 5 right ribs, scapulae, femoral & tibiae shafts, fibulae shafts; new bone – right nasal process, humerus & radius shafts, radial heads, left distal humerus articular surface, left prox. ulna; erosive lesions – prox. ulnae, right 3rd MtC; destruction/collapse – right malar, L4-5 (+ new bone; ?TB); plastic changes – right distal humerus & fibula shaft; hypervascularity – endocranial, left distal radius & prox. ulna shafts; osteoporosis – T12; osteoarthritis – T12-L1, distal ulnae, left temporo-mandibular, right acetabulum; Schmorl's node – T12, L1; ddd – L3, 1L; op – 2T apj & 1 bsm, L2 apj, 1L bsm, left 5th prox. IP & 3 distal IP (foot), right distal IP, left prox. ulna & radius, left distal radius & 3rd MtC-P, 4 right carpals, right 1st C-MtC & 5 MtC-P, right 1st prox. & all distal IP (hand), left acetabulum; pitting – 2T & L2 apj, prox. radii & right ulna, 4 right carpals; enth – right prox. humerus, left distal radius, patellae; mv – mandibular M3 5 cusp variation, Vastus notch (left)	n/a	2–3; Fe staining left MtT & right tarsal

Key: * radiocarbon dated; R – redeposited; s.a.u.l. – skull, axial skeleton, upper limb, lower limb (skeletal areas represented where not all are present); sex: ?– probable, ??– possible; amtl – *ante mortem* tooth loss; op – osteophytes; ddd – degenerative disc disease; enth – enthesophytes; mv – morphological variation; bsm – body surface margins; C/T/L/S – cervical/thoracic/lumbar/sacral vertebrae; MtC/MtT – metacarpal/tarsal; MtC/T-P – metacarpal/tarsal – phalangeal joint; IP – interphalangeal joint; apj – articular processes (vertebra); tpj- transverse process (vertebra); prox. – proximal

Romano-British inhumation graves had survived to a relatively substantial depth (0.42–0.77 m) and no bone will have been lost due to horizontal truncation. The bone is in variable condition, showing mild (Grades 1–2; neonatal remains) to moderate (2–3; adult remains) erosion/degradation. As is commonly observed, the trabecular bone (axial skeleton and articular surfaces) had suffered preferential destruction, but skeletal recovery was not substantially affected (Table 6.7). There is heavy fragmentation of the bone from the deepest grave (7376; 0.77 m), much of it of long standing and a consequence of the pressure exerted by the overlying grave fill which had particularly affected the fragile porous trabecular bone; the skull vault had been warped by the same mechanism.

Demographic Data

A minimum of nine individuals are represented within the assemblage (MNI); five cremated (one Late Neolithic, four Middle Iron Age) and four unburnt (one Middle/Late Iron Age, one ?early Romano-British and two late Romano-British; Table 6.7). Although the cremated bone from Middle Iron Age feature 5642 does not appear to derive from the remains of a burial – neither the quantity of bone nor the distribution of the various archaeological components within the feature are commensurate with such an interpretation, fitting rather with that of redeposited pyre debris (McKinley 2013a) – the individual is clearly not represented elsewhere within the assemblage. Grave 7530, 17 m to the south, contained the remains of an individual of similar age, but there is duplication of a skeletal element (maxillary right 2nd permanent incisor) between the two deposits. Consequently, the infant from grave 5642 has been included within the MNI. The two redeposited neonatal bones from early Romano-British pit 7208 could have derived from the same individual. Although the left femur could conceivably have originated from grave 7280 the left humerus could not (duplicate element), and it is more likely that the redeposited elements belong together. Either way, a second neonate to that from grave 7280 is clearly represented within the assemblage and has been included in the MNI.

The Late Neolithic cremation burial 7531 (in hollow 7306) is of note since mortuary deposits of this date are relatively rare in the archaeological record, both regionally and nationally. This may, in part, be due to the paucity of datable artefactual materials within the graves which, until the fairly recent advent of radiocarbon analysis of cremated bone, rendered such burial deposits temporally indistinct. Several small collections of redeposited human bone, mostly

cremated (each <15 g), and the remains of a substantial cremation burial recovered from the ditch fills at Stonehenge (context 3898) in the first half of the 20th century, were attributed a Late Neolithic date (Phase 2) by Cleal *et al.* (1995; McKinley 1995, table 59). The date of one of these deposits, together with two others of unburnt bone from ditch fills, were later confirmed as Late Neolithic by radiocarbon analysis (Parker Pearson *et al.* 2009), but the date of burial 3898 proved to be Middle Neolithic (M. Parker Pearson pers. comm.). A small quantity (41 g; radiocarbon dated) of redeposited cremated bone was recently recovered from pit and posthole deposits at Amesbury Down, 5 km to the south of the Durrington (Powell and Barclay forthcoming).

The nature of the mortuary deposit from hollow 7306 differs from most of these other examples in several respects, noticeably in the form of the deposit. The bone was clearly originally held within some form of organic container (eg, textile/skin bag or basket), the burial was made in a pre-existing feature and, most unusually, it was deliberately sealed by the flint knapping waste. Whether the latter was a response to the perceived personal skills of the deceased, served some other ritual purpose, or simply represented a pragmatic use of available materials cannot currently be deduced with any confidence.

Burial remains of Middle Iron Age date are also relatively infrequent in the archaeological record. The existing evidence suggests that disposal by inhumation of the unburnt corpse formed the dominant rite (possibly with subsequent human manipulation of remains; McKinley 2006a; 2012). At this site, both young immature individuals and adults were present within the cremated bone assemblage suggesting a common communal rite. Although neonates were certainly subject to cremation throughout the temporal use of the rite it is possible that in this instance it was not considered an appropriate mode of disposal for such a young individual. Despite the somewhat dispersed distribution of the Middle Iron Age assemblage, it is not inconceivable that some or all relate to the same small settlement/farmstead.

Late Romano-British cemeteries, small burial groups and singletons are all widespread within the region and, in common with many similar burials, those of the two individuals from this site are likely to have been made on or towards the family's land boundaries, at a distance from but potentially in sight of their home. Both were older adult females. Judging from the extensive ante mortem tooth loss and heavy wear to the remaining teeth, together with widespread degenerative changes to the skeleton, the individual from grave 7376 is likely to have been elderly (ie, >55 years) although other age indicators (sternal rib ends and pelvic traits) suggest she was somewhat younger. The sexual dimorphic traits in this skeleton were also inconclusive, the skull traits were firmly feminine but coupled with ambiguous or mixed pelvic and metric traits.

Skeletal Indices and Non-metric Traits/Morphological Variations

The estimated statures of the two Romano-British adult females are 1.61 m (5 ft 3¼ in; 6484) and 1.63 m (5 ft 4 in; 7380), both of which are slightly above the average of 1.59 m (5 ft 2½ in) given for the period by Roberts and Cox (2003, 163). Both fall within the upper range of heights recorded for 55 late Romano-British females from the Amesbury Down cemeteries (McKinley and Egging Dinwiddy in prep.), where an overall average height of 1.57 m was recorded, a greater mean (1.61 m) being seen in only one of the eight cemeteries (cemetery 4).

Cranial index could be calculated for only one female (6484); at 73.9 falling in the dolichocrany (long-headed) range. A mean value in the dolichocranial range was observed in two of the larger cemeteries at Amesbury Down (32 of 39 female crania), suggesting a general level of homogeneity between 6484 and groups in the wider region.

The platymeric index (demonstrating the degree of anterior-posterior flattening of the proximal femur) was calculated for both females; 6484 (81.8 right/84.7 left) falling in the platymeric range (broad front-back), and 7380 (94.5/96.1) in the eurymeric. The platycnemic index (illustrating the degree of meso-lateral flattening of the tibia) was also calculated for both individuals, both left tibia being in the mesocnemic range and the right tibia from 6484 in the eurycnemic (the right tibia from 7380 could not be measured). The 8.3 point difference between the left and right sides of 6484 suggests uneven stresses acting on each leg; the discrepancy is only evident in the lower leg, however, with close homogeneity between the femora both in terms of the platymeric and the robusticity indices (124.0/126.7).

Variations in skeletal morphology may indicate population diversity. The potential interpretative possibilities for individual traits is complex (Tyrrell 2000); certain traits have been attributed to developmental abnormalities or mechanical modification (ibid., 292; Brothwell 1972, 92, 95–8; Molleson 1993, 156), and some, such as extra ossicles in the lambdoid suture (or wormian bones), are frequently observed. Numerous common and less frequently occurring non-metric traits were observed and recorded in analysis (Table 6.7 and archive), but none were shared between individuals.

Pathology

Pathological lesions were observed in the remains of two cremated individuals (Late Neolithic and Middle Iron Age) and in both Romano-British individuals (Table 6.7). The intrinsic nature of cremation and cremation burial renders the calculation of true prevalence rates (TPR; ie, number/proportion of a specific skeletal element affected by a condition) difficult and potentially misleading (McKinley 2004a). Consequently, the following section deals exclusively with the Romano-British remains.

Dental disease

Two permanent dentitions were available for analysis (19 teeth; 60 tooth positions). Light–moderate deposits of dental calculus (calcified plaque/tartar) were observed in both. Its recorded presence should, however, be viewed as a minimum since there is a tendency for it to become dislodged during excavation and post-excavation processing. Calculus harbours the bacteria which predispose to periodontal disease and the development of dental caries, and lesions indicative of the former were observed in both dentitions; moderate–heavy around the M2 sockets of 6484 and extensive around the mandibular M3 of 7380 (scored according with Ogden 2005). Carious lesions were recorded in between two and three teeth (26.3%). All areas of the dentition were affected, possibly influenced by the extensive *ante mortem* tooth loss (see below). Most lesions had resulted in total destruction of the tooth crown, but where the origin was apparent it was in the contact area. The overall rate is considerably higher than the 7.5% given by Roberts and Cox for the period (2003, table 3.10); however, a great variability in female rates was recorded in the Romano-British cemeteries at Amesbury Down (8.3–38%; McKinley and Egging Dinwiddy in prep.). Both women had also suffered *ante mortem* tooth loss, most probably as a result of carious destruction. The *ante mortem* loss of between eight and 21 teeth was recorded (TPR 48.3%). Both anterior and distal teeth were affected, predominantly the latter. The overall rate is well above that of 14.1% given by Roberts and Cox for their Romano-British sample (29 sites; 2003, table 3.12), probably largely a reflection of the advanced age of the two individuals from this site. It is also above the highest female rate of 36.5% from the Amesbury Down cemeteries (cemetery 3; range 1.6–21.7% for others; McKinley and Egging Dinwiddy in prep.).

The spread of infection from grossly carious teeth to the supportive structures is a common cause of dental abscesses (Hillson 1986, 316–8), and this mechanism appears to have been the source of infection in two of the three cases seen at this site

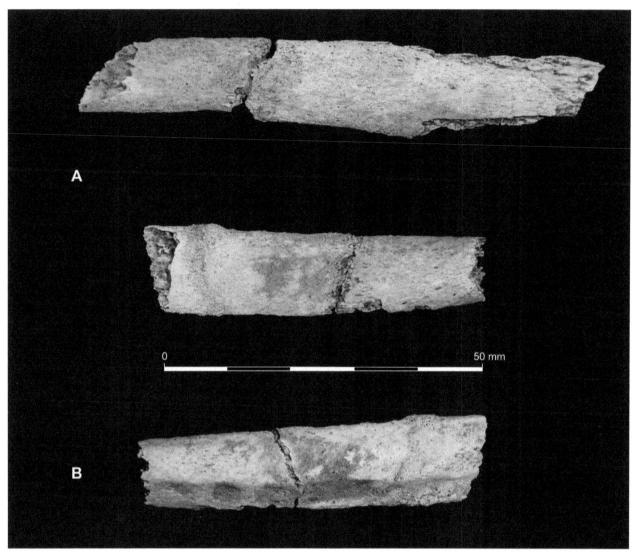

Plate 6.8 Inhumation burial 7380: right rib fragments showing healed fractures and periosteal new bone: a) anterior-lateral surfaces b) visceral surface

(TPR 5%; affecting molar and premolar sockets). The rate is close to that of 3.9% given by Roberts and Cox for the period (2003, table 3.13) and within the range of 2.8–11.5% recorded in the female dentitions from the Amesbury Down cemeteries (McKinley and Egging Dinwiddy in prep.). Infection in the right mandibular M3 socket of 6484 was directly linked to carious infection, active at the time of death, the abscess having exited buccally via the supportive structure. Infection in the maxillary left P1 socket was not associated with dental caries and lamellar new bone indicates the lesion had healed. The origin of infection in the right maxillary M1 socket of 7380 is unclear (*ante mortem* tooth loss), but it had tracked superiorly into the antrum (causing secondary sinusitis) and affected the facial soft tissues. Fine-grained lamellar new bone indicates healing in these areas prior to death, but there had been substantial remodelling of the malar/antrum resulting in a severe

reduction in size and creating a 'collapsed-in' appearance, a 15 mm diameter, 8 mm deep lesion effectively destroying the lower two-thirds of the malar body. Active woven new bone in the right anterior palate and foramen may indicate a spread of infection to these areas from this primary source, as could the small patches of woven new bone seen on the medial (ie, inner) side of the left nasal process and within the trabecular bone of the right (suggestive of a nasal infection).

Dental hypoplasia (developmental defects in the tooth enamel reflective of periods of illness or nutritional stress in the immature individual; Hillson 1979) was observed in one dentition (15.8%). Slight moderate lesions in the form of pitting and faint linear defects were seen in three anterior teeth, suggesting several moderate episodes of arrested growth at around 3–4 years and 4–5 years of age. The rate is above that of 0.1% recorded for the period by Roberts and Cox (2003, table 3.16), but similar to cemeteries 1 and 5 at Amesbury Down (11.2–19.3%) and well below the 27.7–34.5% from three of the other cemeteries (McKinley and Egging Dinwiddy in prep.).

The condition of the teeth can often give indications as to an individual's diet and, potentially, their general wellbeing, but in this case, is likely to be largely reflective of the advanced age of the two women. The level of dental hypoplasia suggests relatively well-nourished children who suffered limited periods of stress during the years of tooth development, but the evidence is likely to have been minimised due to the extensive *ante mortem* tooth loss and heavy tooth wear.

Trauma

Healed fractures were observed in a minimum of two right ribs from 7380. One un-numbered rib (fragments only) had two fractures 22 mm apart and the second (?11/12th?) had a single healed fracture 34 mm from the sternal end. In each case the breaks were at/close to vertical. The x-rays show markedly different bone densities suggesting not all may have occurred at the same time. In each case, the location of the fracture coincided with areas of periosteal new bone which crossed the line of the breaks and affected both sides of the bone (Pl. 6.8, a and b). In all, a potential five right ribs (all fragmentary) have evidence for active and lamellar new bone on the visceral and lateral-anterior surfaces, extending between 10–35 mm along the length of bones and generally across the full depth. In the few cases where the new bone crossed joining fragments, fine-grained new bone was visible infilling the trabecular bone in the broken areas. Healing appears to have occurred with no apparent displacement.

Most rib fractures are caused by direct injury, generally resulting from a fall against a hard object or a blow to the chest (Adams 1987, 107). The former tends to affect the central or lower ribs, as appears to be the case in this instance. Where there is a direct association between the fracture and new bone it appears the latter occurred subsequent to the former, possibly as a consequence of the same traumatic injury. The presence of lesions in at least three ribs where no fractures were recorded could mean that evidence for the latter has been lost in these cases, or that there was extensive soft tissue damage with no direct impact on the bone. The potential for more than one traumatic episode – multiple fractures to one rib with no displacement and indications of differing lengths of healing time for different fractures – is also intriguing (also, see Infection, below).

Enthesophytes are bony growths which may develop at tendon and ligament insertions on the bone. Causative factors include advancing age, traumatic stress, or various diseases (Rogers and Waldron 1995, 24–5). It is not always possible to be conclusive with respect to the aetiology of particular lesions, but they are commonly seen in the anterior surface of the patella and the posterior surface of calcanea, as here, where they reflect activity-related stress. Minor lesions in other areas most probably relate to minor soft tissue trauma (eg, twisted ankle (6484), wrenched shoulder (7380)) or repeated daily stresses (eg, in thigh/leg muscles of 6448).

Over time bone will react to pressures exerted upon it by a number of physical mechanisms including muscle action, increased vascular/neural activity and soft tissue growths. This may simply take the form of the limb on one side being markedly more robust than the other (see above) suggesting preferential use/stress on that side. Marked changes in the right clavicle of 6484 suggest the woman was engaged in an activity requiring strong depression and stabilisation of the shoulder (?weight bearing). Marked lateral bowing in the tibiae and fibulae suggests prolonged flexion and inversion of the foot probably due to the habitual adoption of a particular stance (possibly squatting; medial squatting facets observed). Prolonged inversion of the right foot is suggested by the marked lateral bowing of the fibula from 7380 (left normal), although there is no supportive evidence for the suggested unilateral variation in posture.

Joint disease

Similar lesions – osteophytes and other forms of new bone formation, and micro- and macro-pitting – may develop as a consequence of one of several different disease processes, some also occurring as lone lesions largely reflective of age-related wear and tear (Rogers and Waldron 1995).

Schmorl's nodes (a pressure defect resulting from a rupture in the intervertebral disc; Rogers and Waldron 1995, 27; Roberts and Manchester 1997, 107) commonly affect young adult spines. Shallow lesions of limited extent were observed in two vertebrae in each spine (TPR 10%). There are no lesions above T12, most being in the lumbar region. The rate is lower than the overall average of 17.7% for the period given by Roberts and Cox (2003, table 3.21), probable due to the condition generally being more common in males. However, the rate falls between those of 4.5% and 16% for the females from cemeteries 4 and 5 at Amesbury Down, all substantially lower than the 25% from cemetery 3 (McKinley and Egging Dinwiddy in prep.).

Degenerative disc disease, resulting from the breakdown of the intervertebral disc and reflecting age-related wear-and-tear (Rogers and Waldron 1995, 27), were recorded in one–two vertebrae in both spines (TPR 8%; Table 6.7). The rate is markedly lower than observed at Amesbury Down,

Plate 6.9 Inhumation burial 7380: anterior-superior view of ?4th and 5th lumbar vertebrae showing destructive lesions and new bone

where female rates of 15–28% were recorded in cemeteries 3–5 (McKinley and Egging Dinwiddy in prep.).

Slight lesions, of limited extent, indicative of osteoarthritis (Rogers and Waldron 1995, 43–4) were seen the spine of one female (TPR 5%) and in extra-spinal joints of both (2.2% in right, 1.6% in left; Table 6.7). Spinal lesions affected the lower thoracic and lumbar regions. The extra-spinal joints involved were amongst those commonly affected including the wrist, hip and costo-vertebral joints. The spinal rate is similar to those of 7.6% and 6% for the females from cemeteries 4 and 5 at Amesbury Down, all being substantially lower than the 38% from cemetery 3 (McKinley and Egging Dinwiddy in prep.).

Lone osteophytes often appear to be a 'normal accompaniment of ageing', reflective of wear-and-tear (Rogers and Waldron 1995, 25–6). Mild–moderate lesions were recorded in both spines and 21% of the extra-spinal joints; more sites overall were affected in 6484, but there was a difference in distribution between the two individuals. A higher proportion of spinal joints were involved in the case of 6484 (92% compared with 26%) and conversely a higher percentage of extra-spinal joints in the case of 7380 (26% compared with 16%).

As with osteophytes, macro and micro-pitting in the surfaces of synovial joints may develop in response to a number of conditions and it is not always possible to ascertain the specific cause of individual lesions, although it is probable that they are most commonly reflective of the early stage of osteoarthritis.

Despite evidence for the advanced age of these two women, the comparative rates for the various joint conditions appear relatively low, suggesting they were on a par with their least physically stressed contemporaries buried in the numerous cemeteries at nearby Amesbury Down.

Infection

The long bones (humerus, radius and ulna) of the left upper limb of 6484 are consistently shorter (by 60–70 mm) and markedly less robust than those of the right side. While some variation between sides is not unusual and generally presages a preference in use of one side over the other, in this instance the left limb appears atrophied. A possible cause of such an abnormality could be poliomyelitis, a viral infection which, in the cases where it invades the central nervous system, leads to paralysis in one or more muscle groups (Aufderheide and Rodríguez-Martín 1998, 212; Roberts and Manchester 1997, 134). The attendant atrophy due to muscle weakness/disuse can affect individuals to a variable degree dependent on the age of onset and extent of the condition. Although the disease can strike at any age, the tendency to manifest in early life means it can result in the unequal development of opposite limbs. Were the proposed diagnosis to be correct, the age of onset must have been relatively late, potentially in the woman's mid-teens. Other, equally tentatively suggested contemporaneous cases include individuals from Cirencester, Gloucestershire (Wells 1982) and Baldock, Hertfordshire (McKinley 1993a).

87

Two lumbar vertebrae (?L4–5) from 7380 show extensive destruction in the anterior surfaces with a loss in anterior body height of up to 5 mm (Pl. 6.9). Taphonomic changes render it difficult to be sure of the full nature of the lesions but there is a clear breakdown in the anterior margin of the body, with destructive lesions in the anterior of both and across the superior body surface of the uppermost vertebrae, with irregular new bone formation across the anterior of the bodies (ligament ossification) and some micro-pitting. Overall, the lesions are destructive in nature with incipient kyphosis. The lesions are consistent with spinal changes seen in tuberculous and may represent an early stage of the disease.

Tuberculosis is a chronic bacterial infection caused by *mycobacterium tuberculosis/bovis*, infection resulting from either ingesting infected food or by droplet infection from another individual (Ortner and Putschar 1985, 141–76; Roberts and Manchester 1997, 135–42; Aufderheide and Rodríguez-Martín 1998, 118–41). The condition affects the skeleton in a minority of cases – 3% in modern populations (Ortner and Putschar 1985, 142) – the spine being affected in 25–50% of cases where it tends to include a maximum of two–four adjacent vertebrae, generally in the lower thoracic/lumbar region (Roberts and Manchester 1997, 138–9; Aufderheide and Rodríguez-Martín 1998, 121). Phthisis or pulmonary tuberculosis was recognised by Greco-Roman medical writers as a serious and common problem, particularly amongst the urban poor (Jackson 1988, 180–1). The occurrence of periosteal new bone on the visceral surface of the ribs, generally reflective of a lung infection, is recognised as being indicative of the disease (Roberts and Manchester 1997, 135–42, pl. 7.9), and periostitis elsewhere may also be associated (Roberts and Cox 2003, 235). Although there is an implied connection between the rib fractures seen in the individual from this site and the periosteal new bone see on the ribs, there is no reason why two mechanisms could not be at work and that the lesions on the visceral surface were associated with a lung infection, potential tuberculosis. Similarly, some of the other periosteal new bone noted elsewhere in the skeleton (see below) could also be linked to the disease.

A differential diagnosis of brucellosis may be offered for the vertebral lesions. A recurrent or acute infectious disease caused by any species of *Brucella*, brucellosis is an occupational disease in individuals working with cattle or other animals which may form a host for these intercellular parasitic organisms, infection by which can be debilitating and prolonged (Aufderheide and Rodríguez-Martín 1998, 192–3). Destructive and reparative processes tend to occur simultaneously in brucellosis, however, in contrast to the largely destructive processes in tuberculosis and

vertebral body collapse is not normally associated with the former.

This elderly female (7380) does not fit the profile of the characteristic victim of either disease; both of are more common in males; the onset of tuberculosis tends to be in the young while brucellosis is usually seen in individuals over 30 years of age (Aufderheide and Rodríguez-Martín 1998, 192–3; Roberts and Cox 2003, 229). The diagnosis is, however, considered of sufficient potential to be reported here. There are relatively few recorded cases of tuberculosis from Roman Britain, Roberts and Cox listing examples from 13 sites and giving a crude prevalence rate (CPR) of 0.2% (2003, 119); the writer reported a potential three early Romano-British cases from Essex in 2009 (McKinley 2009).

Periosteal new bone is formed in response to inflammation of the periosteal membrane covering the bone. It is often linked to infection which may be introduced directly to the bone as a result of surface trauma, develop in response to an adjacent soft tissue infection, or the spread of osteomylitis (bone infection). It can also represent a manifestation of a generalised disease, a response to haemorrhage or chronic skin ulcers (Aufderheide and Rodríguez-Martín 1998, 179; Manchester 1983, 36–7; Roberts and Cox 2003, 235; Roberts and Manchester 1997, 126–31). It is not always possible to detect the causative factors involved in individual cases and lesions are frequently classified as indicative of a non-specific infection either active (woven) or healing (lamellar) at the time of death.

Lesions in the facial bones and ribs of 7380 have already been discussed above, with probable and possible links to dental caries and trauma and/or tuberculosis respectively, but further lesions were recorded in upper and lower limb elements of this individual which are less readily ascribed a probable cause. Patches of lamellar new bone were seen along both sides of the spine of the left scapula; a minimum 15 mm anterior-posterior in the supra-spinus area from the superior margin of spine to the edge of the *supraspinatus* attachment, extending from the neck almost to the lateral edge of spine; and across 16 mm depth in the infra-spinus area, straddling between the spine and the blade 43 mm medial-lateral from the acromion neck and ceasing at the edge of attachment for *infraspinatus* attachment. A post mortem fracture at the medial junction between the spine and the blade exposes the presence of very fine-grained new bone infilling within the trabecular bone (as seen in the ribs), which the x-ray indicates as very localised in extent. The right scapula is in poor condition but shows similarly located new bone, although to a much lesser degree and, somewhat oddly, a post mortem fracture between the spine and blade at the same point as in the left. There is no obvious indication of trauma; this area of the scapula is not one normally subject to fracture, the lesions being outside the attachment areas excludes muscle involvement, and the bilateral manifestation would render other direct soft tissue trauma unlikely.

Extensive post mortem damage to parts of the lower limb bones means the extent of some of the lesions is difficult to judge but patches of fine lamellar new bone were observed on the proximal medial shaft of the left femur, and the medial and dorsal side of the distal shaft where some may have extended within the capsule attachment area. Similar but lesser lesions were observed in the right femur. Patches of discontinuous woven new bone were seen on parts of the tibiae proximal shafts. The contours of both fibulae are also roughened, with 'thickening' on the dorsal side of the left proximal shaft and central medial side of the right, which has the appearance of well-healed lamellar new bone. The x-ray shows a potential 2 mm increase in thickness in the right bone, with no associated necrosis.

The new bone observed in the long bone shafts of the upper limb is of a different form (though somewhat similar to that in the tibiae), being coarse/rough and vascular in appearance, and may be reflective of hypervascularity rather than infection. These include changes at the proximal and distal portions of the shafts, sometimes inclusive of the capsule area, of the humeri (both of which have marked radial depressions; right less marked than left), the right distal radius (outside capsule), and the proximal juxta-articular area of the left ulna. Again, there was no necrosis.

These postcranial lesions are difficult to explain. Variations in form and location suggest more than one mechanism at work, possibly at different times. Some are indicative of infection, possibly due to an overlying soft tissue involvement (eg, in the fibulae), others being more suggestive of hypervascularity. All or several could relate to a single systemic problem, potentially the suggested tuberculous infection (see above). Such extensive lesions as are displayed in this individual indicate chronic illness which would have been highly debilitating and painful.

Miscellaneous conditions
As with other forms of new bone, there may be a variety of triggers to the calcification/ossification of cartilaginous material within the body, although in the case of the rib cartilage from 6404 the age of the individual is probable the prime factor.

Endocranial hypervascular activity in the parietal bones of 7380 had created a deep linear depression along the coronal line which had almost penetrated the full depth of the relatively thin vault, on the right

side especially. There is also evidence for generalised endocranial hypervascularity to either side of the sagittal line in the anterior of the bones.

Changes in the left distal humerus, the radial heads and ulnae coronoid processes (ie, both elbow joints) from 7380 all had a similar appearance suggestive of a related condition of uncertain nature. The left humerus has an 8 mm diameter surface defect in the anterior capitulum, with a coarse granular new bone surface of similar appearance to that seen in *osteochondritis dissecans*. The new bone is, however, neither as pale in colour nor fine in form as seen in such cases, and the margins of the feature do not have the sclerotic appearance common to this lesion (although considered an idiopathic metabolic disorder by some workers, *osteochondritis dissecans* is generally believed to be traumatic in origin resulting in localised bone necrosis (Rogers and Waldron 1995, 28–30; Roberts and Manchester 1997, 87–9; Aufderheide and Rodríguez-Martín 1998, 81–3). Both radial heads have similar lesions (16 mm x 6 mm) on the superior anterior margins, where coarse, granular and fairly open new bone may cover some underlying pitting. In the ulnae, the anterior-lateral lips of the coronoid processes are eroded leaving a slightly reduced surface with a roughened and thickened margin of coarse new bone. The form, location and bilateral involvement of these lesions is not consistent with the commonly recorded arthropathies or joint infections.

Pyre Technology and Cremation Ritual

Although most of the cremated bone is white in colour, indicating a high level of oxidation (Holden *et al.* 1995a; 1995b), some variability – hues of grey and blue to black (charred) – symptomatic of differing levels of intra-cremation oxidation, was observed in some bones from all the Iron Age deposits. The variability is fairly extensive, affecting several fragments of between one and four elements from each of the four skeletal areas in the graves (excepting grave 5206 where very little axial skeleton was identified). In some cases affecting the smaller bones (eg, finger phalanges from grave 7530) the whole element is uniformly poorly oxidised, but in most elements the level of oxidation is inconsistent. A variety of factors may have an impact on the efficiency of oxidation (McKinley 1994a, 76–8; 2004c, 293–5; 2008), but this persistent level of intra- and inter-cremation involvement suggests a systemic shortfall, probably linked to the routine use of insufficient fuel in the construction of the pyres to achieve full oxidation of the bone. The latter may not have been considered necessary in order to fulfil the ritual, and some level of variability is frequently observed, but there is an interesting contrast in this case between the Late Neolithic remains (all white) and the Middle Iron Age ones.

As discussed above (see Taphonomy) the weights of bone recovered from the cremation burials are likely to be closely representative of the quantity initially included in the grave, although there may have been some post-depositional loss of trabecular bone in at least one (5221) of the Middle Iron Age deposits. The infant/juvenile is relatively well represented, but the quantity of bone from the Neolithic burial and the maximum weight from the Middle Iron Age adult burials represent approximately only 10% and 30% by weight, respectively, of the average total expected from an adult cremation (McKinley 1993b). In both cases it appears that, as is frequently observed, not all the bone remaining at the end of cremation was collected for inclusion in the burial. Some may have remained unrecovered at the pyre site, some may have been collected for secondary deposition elsewhere or curated for other purposes, and other fragments may have been distributed amongst the relatives of the dead as *memento mori* (see below).

The largest cremated bone fragment (78 mm) was found amongst the Late Neolithic burial remains, a range of 38–56 mm being recorded amongst the largest fragments from the Middle Iron Age burials. In all three adult burials, the majority of the bone was recovered from the 10 mm sieve fraction (77% by weight in the Neolithic; 51–68% in the Iron Age); the majority in the immature burial fell in the 5 mm sieve fraction (54% by weight). There are a number of factors which may affect the size of cremated bone fragments the majority of which are exclusive of any deliberate human action other than that of cremation itself (McKinley 1994b). The protective effect of the flint deposit on the Neolithic remains was discussed above (see Taphonomy) and is further reinforced by this data. Amongst the Iron Age remains, the young age of the immature individual and original small size of the bones was an obvious intrinsic influence. As is commonly observed, there is no indication of deliberate fragmentation of the bone prior to burial.

Between 37% (Middle Iron Age female) and 79% (Neolithic) by weight of the bone from each burial deposit was identifiable to skeletal element (the proportion is generally 30–50%, pers. obs.). As usual, identifiable fragments from all skeletal areas were included in each, the proportions being closest to a 'normal' distribution only in the case of burial 6549; 29% skull (normal 18%), 13% axial skeleton (normal 20%), 18% upper limb (normal 23% normal), and 40% lower limb (normal 38%). Elsewhere, the

frequently recorded bias in favour of skull elements, generally at the expense of elements of axial skeleton, reflects the comparative ease of identification of even small fragments of the former against the taphonomic fragility of the latter (McKinley 1994a, 5–6). There is no evidence to suggest the preferential recovery of certain elements for burial.

The small bones of the hands and feet and tooth crowns/roots no longer *in situ* are routinely recovered from cremation burials, and the writer has discussed elsewhere how their frequency of occurrence may provide some indication of the mode of recovery of bone from the pyre site for burial (McKinley 2004c, 300–1). Between two (Late Neolithic; hand and foot bones) and 37 elements (Middle Iron Age infant/juvenile; 18 lone tooth crowns/roots and 19 hand/foot bones) were found amongst each of the burial remains. The Middle Iron Age adult graves contained far fewer such elements than that of the child, with a total of five (hand/foot bones) from the male burial and 14 (four tooth roots and 10 hand/foot bones) from that of the female. This suggests there may have been both a temporal and inter-phase variation in how the bone was recovered from the pyre sites for burial. The high number of elements from grave 7530 suggests collection was facilitated by the raking off and winnowing of the cremated remains, thereby easing the recovery of the smaller skeletal elements as well as the larger ones, while those from the other burials were subject to hand-recovery of individual fragments.

The deliberate inclusion of pyre debris in the fill of cremation graves is frequently observed, and whether representative of a purely practical 'cleaning up' process or part of the 'closure' of the burial, its presence suggests the relative proximity of the pyre site to the place of burial. Redeposited pyre debris (including fuel ash, burnt clay and burnt flint) was recovered from grave 6548, where it seems to have formed a secondary deposit over the burial made (probably in an organic (?textile) container) in the south-eastern portion of the grave.

Pyre goods, in the form of a small quantities of cremated animal bone, were recovered from all of the Middle Iron Age deposits (Table 6.7). Where species could be identified it comprised sheep, sometimes an immature animal (species identifications by L. Higbee). The presence of cremated animal bone amongst the burial remains is a characteristic of the mortuary rite across the temporal range (McKinley 2006b, table 5.1), with a wide variation in the numbers involved from different cemeteries both between and within different periods. Comparative data for the Middle Iron Age is not forthcoming, but data from Late Iron Age burials suggests small quantities are the norm, with pig and sheep/goat being the more commonly occurring species (McKinley *et al.* 1995).

Quadrant excavation of the Middle Iron Age burials allowed some analysis of the burial formation process. The location of the burial and inclusion of pyre debris within grave 6548 has already been discussed. In the case of grave 5206 the bone appears to have been concentrated in the western half, prominently towards the south. In grave 7530, the bone was concentrated in the northern half with a western bias. Given the small size of the assemblage it cannot be deduced if these placings are simply fortuitous or potentially influenced by the age/sex of the deceased.

A tooth from grave 7530 appears to derive from an individual several years younger than is suggested by the rest of the bone, and a few fragments of skull vault seem to represent those of a much older individual. It is possible that these few elements could be intrusive to the deposit, possibly from a reused and ineffectively cleared pyre site. They could, however, represent deliberately included 'token' elements from other individuals. The use of the word 'token' in respect to the mortuary rite of cremation is problematic, the term 'token burial' having been used to cover a multitude of undoubtedly different types of deposit containing small quantities of bone. The writer has argued for tighter definition in its usage, limiting it to single skeletal elements or very small quantities of bone added at or potentially shortly after burial, and representing symbolic or *memento mori* deposits from earlier cremations, retained by the deceased's friends or relatives and included in later burials (McKinley 2013a). A few such 'tokens' are believed to have been recognised in cremation burials from various periods, predominantly prehistoric but also Romano-British and Anglo-Saxon (eg, McKinley 2004d; 2006c; 2013b; 2015).

Animal Bone
by L. Higbee

Introduction

The animal bone assemblage comprises 9899 fragments (or 89.298 kg); this is a raw fragment count and once conjoins are considered the total falls to 5658. Most (89%) of the assemblage was recovered by hand during the normal course of excavation and the rest was retrieved from the residues of 71 bulk soil samples. Bone was recovered from all phases of occupation and activity at the site. The Romano-British assemblage is the largest stratified group from the site, and accounts for 82.3% of the total assemblage (Table 6.8).

The following information was recorded for each identifiable fragment: species, element, anatomical zone (after Serjeantson 1996, 195–200; Cohen and Serjeantson 1996, 110–12), anatomical position, fusion state (after O'Connor 1989), tooth eruption/wear (after Grant 1982; Halstead 1985; Hambleton 1999; Payne 1973), butchery marks (after Lauwerier 1988; Sykes 2007), metrical data (after von den Driesch 1976; Payne and Bull 1982), gnawing, burning, surface condition, pathology (after Vann and Thomas 2006) and non-metric traits. This information was directly recorded into a relational database (in MS Access) and cross-referenced with relevant contextual information.

Quantification methods applied to the assemblage include the number of identified specimens (NISP), minimum number of elements (MNE), and minimum number of individuals (MNI). As an additional means of assessing the relative importance of livestock species, meat weight estimates (MWE) were also calculated based on the following live weight values: 275 kg for cattle, 37.5 kg for sheep and 85 kg for pig (after Boessneck *et al.* 1971 and following Bourdillon and Coy 1980; Bond and O'Connor 1999; and Dobney *et al.* 2007).

Caprines (sheep and goat) were differentiated on the bases of morphological criteria following Boessneck (1969), Payne (1985) and Halstead *et al.* (2002). As most of the positively differentiated caprine bones belong to sheep, this term will be used throughout the report to refer to all undifferentiated caprine bones.

Preservation and fragmentation

Bone preservation is extremely variable between periods, features and even within individual contexts. The Late Neolithic assemblage is fragmented and poorly preserved, and this has inevitably effaced surface details such as butchery evidence and hindered the positive identification of bones to species and skeletal element. The Romano-British and later assemblages are better preserved, and in general, bones show little or no sign of physical weathering. However, some contexts include bones in different states of preservation and this is generally an indication that residual material has been incorporated into later contexts. In contexts where residual bone is present it is only a minor component of the total recovered from each context. The sieved assemblage is more fragmented than the hand-recovered assemblage, and includes large numbers of small, unidentifiable splinters of bone.

Species represented

Thirty-six percent of the 5658 fragments recovered from the site are identifiable to species and skeletal

Table 6.8 Animal bone: number of identified specimens present (or NISP) by period

Species	Late Neolithic	Middle–Late Iron Age	Early Romano-British	Mid–Late Romano-British	Medieval, post-med., modern	Undated	Total
Cattle*	24	63	394	100	7	7	595
Sheep/goat	6	97	653	150	107	11	1024
Sheep	–	2	3	2	1	1	9
Goat	–	1	–	–	–	–	1
Pig	15	4	99	22	17	1	158
Horse	5	14	87	41	3	2	152
Dog	–	5	28	13	3	2	51
Dog/fox	–	–	1	–	–	–	1
Aurochs**	1	–	–	–	–	–	1
Red deer	–	2	8	–	–	–	10
Roe deer	–	1	3	–	–	–	4
Deer	–	1	1	–	–	–	2
Domestic fowl	–	–	2	2	–	–	4
Goose	–	–	2	–	–	–	2
Duck	–	–	2	1	–	–	3
Crane	–	–	1	1	–	–	2
Raven	–	–	30	–	–	–	30
Crow/rook	–	–	2	9	–	1	12
Salmo sp. (?trout)	–	–	1	–	–	–	1
Total identified	*51*	*190*	*1317*	*341*	*138*	*25*	*2062*
Large mammal	52	101	784	170	31	27	1165
Medium mammal	6	40	643	118	112	27	946
Small mammal	–	–	1	1	–	–	2
Mammal	72	115	974	295	22	5	1483
Bird	–	1	3	1	–	–	5
Amphibian	–	–	5	–	–	–	5
Total unidentifiable	*130*	*257*	*2410*	*585*	*165*	*59*	*3606*
Overall total	*186*	*430*	*3727*	*926*	*303*	*84*	*5656*
% Overall total	*3.2*	*7.6*	*66*	*16.3*	*5.4*	*1.5*	*100*

Key: * Two Early to Middle Bronze Age cattle bones have not been included; ** probable aurochs based on thickness of cortical shaft

element. Fifteen different species have been identified and the large Romano-British assemblage is the most diverse in terms of species range (Table 6.8).

Bones from livestock species dominate the assemblage and account for 87% NISP. Sheep is the most common species overall, followed by cattle and then pig, and this pattern is consistent for most periods, with the exception of the Late Neolithic, which is largely composed of pig and cattle bones.

Horse bones are also relatively common at 8% NISP, followed by dog at 2% NISP, while bones from wild mammals are rare (<1% NIS), but include probable aurochs and two species of deer. The bird bone assemblage, which accounts for 3% NISP, includes domestic poultry, corvids, and crane.

Late Neolithic

Animal bone was recovered from Late Neolithic posthole alignments 6255 and 6260, and hollow 7306.

The material from the posthole alignments was distributed between 15 features and was highly fragmented; indeed only 28 of the 156 fragments recovered from them are identifiable to species. Pig bones dominate at 57% NISP, the assemblage being largely composed of loose teeth and foot bones, but also including two complete mandibles (from posthole 5106, alignment 6255); the mandibles are from animals aged 2–7 months and 21–27 months (MWS B and E).

The majority (39%) of the other identified bones from the posthole alignments belong to cattle. The range of skeletal elements is more varied than for pig, although it also shows a slight bias towards foot and ankle bones. Most of the cattle bones have unfused epiphyses and are from juvenile and neonatal animals, suggesting that dairying played some role in the management strategy for cattle.

Posthole 5087 (alignment 6260) contained a fragment of femur shaft with extremely thick cortical bone. The fragment has been identified as probably aurochs and radiocarbon dated to 2560–2300 cal BC (SUERC-50622, 3931±31 BP, at 95% confidence).

Table 6.9 Associated bone groups (or ABGs)

Period	ABG	Context	Cut	Group	Species	Comments
Early	1	2005	2013	6204	cattle	articulating vertebrae
Romano-British	14	5161	5199	6204	dog	part skeleton
	35	5171	5170	6215	horse	articulating vertebrae
	51	5324	5322	6232	cattle	skull
	61	5405	–	–	horse	mandible
	57	5426	5536	6232	horse	mandible
	115	6447	6443	–	cattle	articulating left hindquarter
	159	6518	6513	–	cattle	skull
	198	7170	7123	–	raven	complete skeleton
Middle/Late	26	5186	6219	6273	horse	skull and pelvic girdle
Romano-British	47	5300	5299	6226	crow/rook	part skeleton
	52	5320	5299	6226	sheep/goat	part skeletons three neonatal lambs
	1001	2114	2119	6219	dog	articulating lumbar vertebrae and pelvic girdle
Modern	–	5007	5006	–	sheep/goat	partial remains six individuals
	169	6547	6546	–	horse	partial skeleton

One of the large-mammal long bone shaft fragments recovered from posthole 5074 (alignment 6255) shows signs of burning and breakage consistent with the technique generally referred to as 'burn and smash' (see for example Serjeantson 1995, 442–7; 2006, 127–30; 2011, 60–2; Albarella and Serjeantson 2002, 41).

Two cattle bones, a loose lower tooth and a right metatarsal, were recovered from hollow 7306, together with a small number of large-mammal long bone shaft fragments.

Early to Middle Bronze Age

Two cattle bones, a left mandible and axis vertebra, were recovered from solution hollow 6257 (NB these bones have not been included in Table 6.8). The mandible was radiocarbon dated to 1690–1520 cal BC (SUERC-50628, 3327±31 BP, at 95% confidence).

Middle to Late Iron Age

A large proportion of the Middle to Late Iron Age (55%) assemblage came from ditches, in particular the lower fills (ie. 5720, 6027, 6144, 6661 and 6664) of large enclosure ditch 6203. The assemblage comprises just 190 identified fragments, most (89%) of which belong to livestock species. Sheep were of prime importance and account for 58% of livestock. Cattle were also of some significance 39%, but pigs were of minor importance and were only kept in small numbers.

Both sheep and goat have been positively identified from the assemblage, and it is assumed that sheep are more common than goats given the general underrepresentation of the latter species in the British archaeological record. The sheep bone assemblage includes a range of different body parts from a minimum of at least six animals. Most of the sheep postcranial bones have fused epiphyses and are therefore from skeletally mature animals. What is a relatively small sample of mandibles comes from animals aged between 1–2 years, 2–3 years, and 4–6 years (MWS D, E and G).

The cattle bone assemblage also includes a range of different elements and these are from at least four separate animals. Based on epiphyseal fusion it would appear that most cattle were slaughtered when they had reached full body size. Only three complete mandibles were recovered and these are from an immature animal aged 8–18 months, a subadult aged 30–36 months, and an adult animal (MWS C, E and G). The latter is from the lower secondary fill of enclosure ditch 6203 (slot 5199) and provided a radiocarbon date of 100 cal BC–cal AD 80 (SUERC-36557, 1995±35 BP, at 95% confidence), likely to be soon after the construction of the enclosure. Butchery marks consistent with skinning, filleting, and disarticulation were noted on a small number of cattle bones. Most of the marks, including those intended to disarticulate joints, were made using a knife.

As indicated above, pigs were of minor importance and only three bones were recovered, a scapula, third phalanx and the canine tooth from a male. Horse bones account for a further 9% NISP, and most were recovered from ditch deposits. Three of the horse bones recovered came from layer 6145 around the edge of solution hollow 6257. The bones include a first phalanx, the distal end of a metacarpal, and three teeth. The metacarpal provided a radiocarbon date in the Middle Iron Age of 400–210 cal BC (SUERC-53037, 2260±23 BP, at 95% confidence).

Deer antler and postcranial bones were also identified; they include a fragment of roe deer pelvis and antler from ditch 6256, a fragment of red deer pelvis from grave 7280 and a piece of antler from gully 6248.

Romano-British

Most of the Romano-British assemblage is from pits (43%) and ditches (32%). Large groups of animal bone were recovered from pits 6443, 7123 and 7409, and the secondary and tertiary upper fills of enclosure ditch 6203. The rest of the assemblage is from a range of features including solution hollows 6513 and 6275 (12%), kilns (6%), and trackway 6244/6246 (4%).

The assemblage comprises 1658 identified fragments. This figure has been adjusted to take account of associated bone groups (ABGs) (Table 6.9). The assemblage is dominated by bones from livestock species which together account for 86% NISP. Sheep were of prime importance to the pastoral economy of the site according to NISP, MNE and MNI (Fig. 6.11). They account for between 55% and 59% of livestock depending on which quantification method is used. Cattle were of secondary importance (31–36%), while pigs were of minor significance (8–10%).

Livestock

All parts of the sheep, cattle and pig carcass are represented in the assemblage, the only underrepresented elements are small bones and loose teeth, and these could easily have been overlooked during hand-recovery. The body part information, therefore, indicates that whole carcasses are present and that livestock were slaughtered and butchered on the site for local consumption. Common sheep bones include the tibia and mandible, and these are from a minimum of 59 animals. Mandibles, metapodials, scapulae and humeri are all common in the cattle bone assemblage, while the pig bone assemblage includes a relatively high number of mandibles and scapulae. These are all robust elements that generally show good survival and recovery rates in most animal bone assemblages.

The cattle bone assemblage includes four ABGs – a section of articulating vertebra (ABG 1) from enclosure ditch 6203 and an articulating left hindleg (ABG 115) – and two skulls (ABG 51 and 159), one from quarry pit 5322 and the other from solution hollow 6513.

Epiphyseal fusion data indicate that 8% of sheep died or were slaughtered before 10 months of age, the majority of the rest were slaughtered at 1–3 years, and only a small fraction (7%) survived beyond 4 years (Fig. 6.12). The mortality profile for mandibles

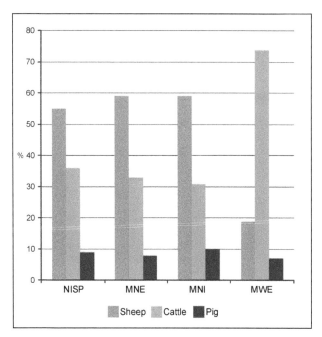

Figure 6.11 Romano-British: relative importance of livestock species by NISP, MNE, MNI and MWE

(Fig. 6.13) shows a main peak (44%) of slaughter at 2–3 years, and a minor peak (24%) at 1–2 years (MWS D and E), with only 26% of sheep surviving beyond 3 years. The mortality pattern suggests that sheep were intensively managed to provide prime meat, although the presence of mandibles from older sheep, aged 3–8 years (MWS G and H), indicates that secondary products such as wool were also important.

The disarticulated remains (ABG 52) of at least three 10-month-old lambs were recovered from pit 5319, together with a 3rd-century coin and other finds. There are similarities between this deposit and those commonly found at some temple/shrine sites (see King 2005) indicating perhaps that the lambs and coin were intended as a votive deposit albeit in a secular context.

The epiphyseal fusion data for cattle indicate that the majority were slaughtered as adult animals over 3.5–4 years of age (Fig. 6.12). A similar pattern is suggested by mandibles, most (54%) of which are from older animals (MWS G–I). A few of the mandibles are from calves aged 1–8 months and 8–18 months (MWS B and C). Overall the age information for cattle suggests that the husbandry strategy was primarily geared towards secondary products and the use of cattle as traction animals. The age information for pigs indicates that they were generally slaughtered between the ages of 14–21 months and 21–27 months (MWS D and E). Pigs provide no secondary products, have large litters and reach full body weight when still immature, this means that they are generally slaughtered at a younger age than other livestock species.

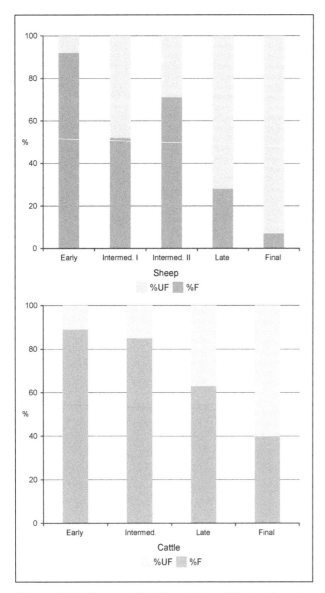

Figure 6.12 Romano-British: epiphyseal fusion data for sheep and cattle postcranial elements

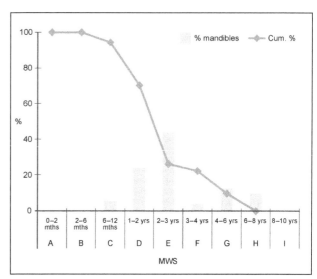

Figure 6.13 Mortality profile for Romano-British sheep based on mandibles retaining 2+ teeth with recordable wear

during the Romano-British period and one that is thought to have originated from the Roman military (Dobney *et al.* 1996, 26–7). Cured shoulder joints of beef have been recorded at a number of contemporary sites in Britain and Europe (Dobney 2001, 40–1; Lauwerier 1988, 71), including the late Romano-British settlement on Amesbury Down (Higbee in prep.).

There is some, albeit limited evidence for the use of carcass by-products. A few sheep and cattle horn cores show signs of having been removed from the frontal bone – a clear indication that the outer sheath was used to manufacture objects. Similarly, a number of worked bone (and antler) objects were recovered from the site, many of which had been fashioned from sheep long bones such as tibiae and metapodials (eg, ONs 1025 and 1026, Fig. 6.10, 2–3).

Other mammals

Horse bones are relatively common in the Romano-British assemblage and account for approximately 8% NISP. Most are from ditches, notably the field ditches, and occur as small groups of disarticulated bones that could potential have come from the same animal(s). For example, the 24 horse bones recovered from the upper fills of solution hollow 6513 are from at least three different animals. Similarly, the 19 bones recovered from slots 6607 and 6537 through enclosure ditch 6203 appear to be from two different animals, as do a skull and pelvis (ABG 26) from field ditch 6219. In some instances, however, the bones were found in articulation, for example the section of vertebral column (ABG 35) from quarry pit group 6215 (Table 6.9).

Butchery marks were noted on 25% of cattle bones, but on only 5% of sheep and 8% of pig bones. Carcasses were processed using both cleavers and knives, and the implement used does not appear to be based on carcass size as is often the case. Cleavers were used to disarticulate and portion the carcass, and split long bones for marrow, while knives were used to skin and fillet. A distinct pattern of butchery marks was noted on 11 cattle scapulae. They include cranio-caudal cut marks on the medial side of the blade, longitudinal cut marks on the caudal side of the blade, cut marks on the cervical margin of the blade, and around the origin of the spine which in most instances has been removed entirely. The evidence indicates that these shoulder joints had been cured for long-term storage, a common practice

All of the horse bones recovered from Romano-British contexts have fused epiphyses and are therefore from adult animals; based on tooth wear it would seem that they range in age from 12–20 years (Levine 1982). The presence of slightly younger animals is suggested by a small number of loose permanent teeth in early wear stages. The measurable bones are all from pony-sized animals with shoulder heights of between 12.1 and 13 hands. Butchery marks were evident on 11 horse postcranial bones, the marks that are consistent with skinning, filleting and disarticulation, and although the evidence is scarce it does at least indicate that horse carcasses were utilised.

Dog bones were recovered from 19 features. The remains are all from adult animals of medium stature and include partial skeletons (ABGs 14 and 1001) from enclosure ditch 6203 and field ditch 6219, respectively, and other small groups of disarticulated but associated bones.

Red deer antler was recovered from four pits and solution hollow 6513. Two of the pieces are worked (ONs 183 and 1009, Fig. 6.10, 1, 7), and at least three of the other pieces are off-cuts from antler-working; this includes the base of a shed antler from pit 5308 (pit group 6233) which has had the brow and bez tines removed using a saw to cut through the basal section of the tine. Roe deer is represented by postcranial bones from two pits and solution hollow 6513. The bones include fragments of pelvis from two different animals, and a fragment of metatarsal.

Birds and fish
The bird bone assemblage includes a few bones from domestic fowl, goose and duck, and two crane bones (tibiotarsus from solution hollow 6513 and ulna from a field ditch), but is largely dominated by corvid remains. These include the remains of two ravens (including ABG 198) from pit 7123, and a crow/rook (ABG 47) from field ditch 6226, as well as several small groups of disarticulated bones from two other pits and solution hollow 6513. It is likely that some of the corvid remains, in particular the remains from 7123, were deliberately deposited as chthonic symbols (relating to the underworld), a common practice during this period (Hambleton and Maltby 2008, 87; Serjeantson and Morris 2011, 103; Serjeantson 1991, 481; Serjeantson 2009, 360).

A single fish vertebra was recovered from the residue of one of the bulk soil samples. It is highly abraded so could not be positively identified to species. The spinal foramen has been widened to provide a large enough hole so that the bone could be worn as a bead (ON 1027, Fig. 6.10, 8). Signs of wear were noted on the edge of the suspension hole from where the thread had repeatedly rubbed against it.

Medieval to Modern

The assemblage includes just 138 identified bones, the majority (72%) of which belong to sheep and are from pit 5006. The pit assemblage includes the disarticulated remains from at least two adults and four neonates. A radiocarbon date (SUERC-50620, 245±30 BP) of 1520–1950 cal AD (at 95% confidence) was obtained on a sheep/goat ulna from this deposit. Pig bones are also relative common and the majority are from pits 7009 and 7019. The disarticulated remains are from a subadult sow aged 21–27 months, and at least two neonates. The partial remains of a horse (ABG 169) were also recovered from pit 6546.

Discussion and Conclusions

The small assemblage of animal bone from Late Neolithic features is dominated by pig and cattle bones. This pattern is in general keeping with basic species proportions for the period as suggested by the results from a review of Neolithic assemblages from sites in southern Britain (Serjeantson 2011). The review suggests that 'the nature of farming and animal management changed greatly in the Late Neolithic when pigs were kept in greater numbers than cattle' (*ibid.*, 35–6). However, there is clearly some local variation to this general trend, with cattle-dominated assemblages recorded from some sites, for example Amesbury Down (Higbee forthcoming).

During the Iron Age and Romano-British period the pastoral economy of the site was one based primarily on sheep farming, and there was little overall change to species proportions between periods. The husbandry strategy also appears to have been fairly stable over this period, with the majority of sheep slaughtered before the age of 3 years, and the majority of cattle maintained into adulthood. The mortality pattern indicates that sheep were intensively managed for prime meat but also wool, while cattle were managed for secondary products and probably traction.

A similar pattern of continuity was recorded at High Post near Salisbury, where sheep accounted for between 55–63% of livestock during the Iron Age and Romano-British period (Higbee 2011, 70–8). At other local sites, however, the economy changed from sheep farming to cattle farming due to the expansion and intensification of arable cultivation, which required larger numbers of cattle for use as traction animals. For example, Amesbury Down (Higbee in prep.), during the late Romano-British period, cattle accounted for 75% of livestock, the majority (37%) of which were maintained beyond the prime meat age, while the nearby 'village-like' settlement at Butterfield Down (Egerton 1996) appears to have been

96

unaffected, continuing with the established local Iron Age tradition of sheep-farming.

The two crane bones recovered from Romano-British contexts are slightly unusual finds given the location and topography of the site. These are large (4.5–7.0 kg) wetland birds that were once common summer visitors to Britain (Boisseau and Yalden 1998; Serjeantson 2009, 23; 2010, 148–9) and it is likely that this particular bird was caught on its migration flight towards a suitable wetland habitat site, such as for example the Somerset Levels. Evidence from later periods indicates that some birds of prey (eg, gyrfalcon or goshawk) can be trained to fly at larger bird species than they would normally take in the wild (Prummel 1997; Serjeantson 2009, 317–8), and it seems likely that this method was also used during the Romano-British period.

Shell
by R.H. Seager Smith

Oyster shells (80 shells, 1339 g) occurred in small groups in 25 features scattered across the site; none was found in the prehistoric features and most were associated with Romano-British pottery. The majority (55% of the total number, 61% by weight) were found in the Romano-British field ditches (44 shells, 817 g), suggesting that the focus of the settlement lay to the north of the excavated area. Both right and left valves were identified, indicating that the oysters were brought to the area whole and prepared for consumption locally, although as similarly small quantities were recorded from Durrington Walls (Wainwright 1971, 122), it is unlikely that they represented more than a very minor food resource.

Chapter 7
Environmental Evidence

Charred Plant Remains

by Sarah F Wyles and Chris J. Stevens

A total of 164 samples were taken from features mainly of Late Neolithic and Romano-British date and processed for the recovery of charred plant remains; 27 of them were selected for full analysis. Three were from Late Neolithic pit group 6283 and posthole alignment 6260 (Table 7.1); the rest were from Romano-British ditches (three samples) and quarry pit groups (five samples) (Table 7.2); other pits (eight samples) (Table 7.3); and pottery kilns (three samples) and ovens (two samples), and single samples from cremation grave 6548, an occupation layer (5489) overlying solution hollow 6257, and solution hollow 6513 (Table 7.4).

All samples were processed using standard flotation methods with the flot collected on a 0.5 mm mesh. For the 27 analysed samples all identifiable charred plant macrofossils were extracted from the flots, together with the 2 mm and 1 mm residues. The flots from seven samples were exceptionally rich in charred plant remains and consequently sub-samples – of which 10% from the finer 0.5 mm fraction and in one case from the 1 mm fraction – were also taken. The remains from these fractions were extracted, identified and multiplied by 10 to provide estimates (indicated by est. in the tables) of the original counts.

Identification was undertaken using stereo incident light microscope at magnifications of up to x40 using a Leica MS5 microscope, following the nomenclature of Stace (1997) for wild species and the traditional nomenclature as provided by Zohary and Hopf (2000, tables 3 and 5), for cereals.

Late Neolithic

The charred plant assemblages from two pits in pit group 6283 were dominated by fragments of hazelnut (*Corylus avellana*) shell, in particular that from pit 7005 (Table 7.1). There were also a few cereal remains some of which were identifiable as wheat (*Triticum* sp.) grain fragments, and a few sloe/hawthorn type (*Prunus spinosa*/*Crataegus monogyna*) thorn/twig fragments. The small assemblage from posthole 6762 contained a few seeds of vetch/wild pea (*Vicia*/*Lathyrus* sp.) and meadow grass/cat's-tail (*Poa*/*Phleum* sp.) and a fragment of hazelnut shell.

The predominance of hazelnut shell fragments in the Late Neolithic pits is typical for this period, and similar assemblages have been recorded from a number of other later Neolithic deposits in the area, such as at Amesbury Down (Wyles and Stevens forthcoming), Old Sarum Water Pipeline (Powell *et al.* 2005) and King Barrow Ridge, Amesbury (Carruthers 1990). This can be seen as indicating the exploitation, and seasonal importance, of wild plant food resources during this period (Moffett *et al.* 1989; Stevens 2007; Robinson 2000).

Table 7.1 Charred plant remains from Late Neolithic pits and postholes

		6283		6260
Group		6283		6260
Cut		7005	7173	6762
Context		7006	7174	6807
Sample		287	303	281
Vol (l)		20	14	4
Flot size (ml)		60	40	30
% roots		55	60	10
Cereals				
Triticum sp. (grain)	wheat	–	1	–
Cereal frag. (est. whole grains)	cereal	1	2	–
Other species				
Corylus avellana L. (fragments)	hazel	86 (3 ml)	10 (< 1 ml)	1
Prunus spinosa/ *Crataegus monogyna* (thorns/twigs)	hawthorn/sloe thorns	1	–	–
Vicia L./*Lathyrus* sp. L.	vetch/wild pea	–	–	1
Poa/*Phleum* sp. L.	meadow grass/cat's-tail	–	–	3
Small seed indet.		–	–	2

Romano-British

Cereal remains were dominant in the majority of the Romano-British assemblages, with chaff elements generally being more numerous than grain. They included remains of hulled wheat, emmer or spelt (*Triticum dicoccum/spelta*) and barley (*Hordeum vulgare*). The majority of identifiable glume bases and spikelet forks were of spelt (*Triticum spelta*) with only a few being identified as probable emmer (*Triticum dicoccum*).

The assemblage from ditch 6208 was dominated by weed seeds, while grain fragments outnumbered chaff elements (Table 7.2). The weed seeds included seeds of fat-hen (*Chenopodium album*), clover/medick (*Trifolium/Medicago* sp.), black-bindweed (*Fallopia convolvulus*), vetch/wild pea (*Vicia/Lathyrus* sp.), and bed straw (*Galium* sp.). There were also a few fragments of Caryophyllaceae capsules.

The samples from ditch 6229 were rich in charred material, in particular that from context 5898 (Table 7.2). They were dominated by cereal remains, with glumes outnumbering grains. Barley grains were more numerous than hulled wheat grains in 5898 and a few of the barley grains showed slight traces of germination. Weed seeds included fat-hen, orache (*Atriplex* sp.), stitchwort (*Stellaria* sp.), black-bindweed, dock (*Rumex* sp.), vetch/wild pea, clover/medick, red bartsia (*Odontites vernus*), bedstraw, narrow-fruited cornsalad (*Valerianella dentata*), rye-grass/fescue (*Lolium/Festuca* sp.), meadow grass/cat's-tail (*Poa/Phleum* sp.), oat (*Avena* sp.) and brome grass (*Bromus* sp.). There were also a few seeds of field madder (*Sherardia arvensis*), broad-fruited cornsalad (*Valerianella rimosa*), corn gromwell (*Lithospermum arvense*) barren brome (*Anisantha sterilis*) and common hemp-nettle (*Galeopsis tetrahit*). Other remains included a few tubers of false oat-grass (*Arrhenatherum elatius* var. *bulbosum*), a stigmatic disc of prickly/long-headed poppy (*Papaver argemone/dubium*) and monocot grass stem and rootlet fragments.

The five samples from quarry pits were all cereal-rich with hulled wheat grains outnumbering those of barley (Table 7.2). Quarry pits 5347 and 5566 were grain-rich, while chaff elements were predominant in quarry pits 5237, 5724 and 6100; large quantities of glume bases and spikelet forks were recorded in particular from quarry pit 5724. Weeds included common fumitory (*Fumaria officinalis*), orache, stitchwort, dock, vetch/wild pea, clover/medick, bedstraw, scentless mayweed (*Tripleurospermum inodorum*), rye-grass/fescue, oat and brome grass. There were also a few seeds of red bartsia, narrow fruited cornsalad, corn gromwell, thorow-wax (*Bupleurum rotundifolium*) and grass vetchling (*Lathyrus nissolia*). Other remains included an immature flax capsule (*Linum usitatissimum*), triangular capsule fragments (possibly of flax), a fragment of hazelnut shell, a false-oat grass tuber, a sloe/hawthorn type (*Prunus spinosa/Crataegus monogyna*) thorn, and monocot grass stem and rootlet fragments.

The very rich assemblage from pit 5756 was dominated by weed seeds, although there were also large quantities of hulled wheat and barley grains together with chaff elements (Table 7.3). The predominant weed seeds were vetch/wild pea. There were also high numbers of seeds of buttercup (*Ranunculus* sp.), goosefoot (*Chenopodium* sp.), blinks (*Montia fontana* subsp. *chondrosperma*), black-bindweed, dock, brassica (*Brassica* sp.), marsh cinquefoil (*Potentilla palustris*), some of which were in a seed head, clover/medick, bedstraw, narrow-fruited cornsalad, cornflower (*Centaurea cyanus*), rye-grass/fescue, oat and brome grass. There were smaller numbers of seeds of common fumitory, stitchwort, corncockle (*Agrostemma githago*), some of which were clearly still in the seed head, knotgrass (*Polygonum aviculare*), sheep's sorrel (*Rumex acetosella* group), shepherd's needle (*Scandix pecten-veneris*), ribwort plantain (*Plantago lanceolata*), red bartsia, hawk's-beard (*Crespis* sp.), and meadow grass/cat's-tail. Other remains included a fragment of hazelnut shell, large numbers of false-oat grass tubers, a few other tubers (one of which had lots of small chambers), monocot grass stem and rootlet fragments, and a small number of possible ergot remains.

All the other pits (including the subrectangular pits) (Table 7.3) were dominated by cereal remains, although pits 5216, 7389 and 7394, and context 7416 in pit 7409 were grain-rich, while pits 5280 and 7095, and context 7415 in pit 7409 were chaff-rich. Barley grains were predominant in pits 5216, 7389, 7394 and 7095 and hulled wheat grains in pit 7409. A whole spikelet of hulled wheat was recovered from pit 7409. Weeds included goosefoot, orache, dock, black-bindweed, vetch/wild pea, clover/medick, corn gromwell, ivy-leaved speedwell (*Veronica hederifolia*), bedstraw, rye-grass/fescue, oat and brome grass. There were also a few seeds of blinks, sheep's sorrel, red bartsia, field madder, cornflower, corncockle, narrow-fruited cornsalad, meadow grass/cat's-tail, oat and brome grass. There was also a stone of hawthorn (*Crataegus monogyna*) and monocot grass stem and rootlet fragments. A few mineralised seeds and nodules were recorded from pit 7389 and 7095.

The assemblages from kilns 7214, 7205 and 7487 were all very rich and dominated by cereal remains, with chaff elements being predominant (Table 7.4). Barley grains were more numerous than those of hulled wheat. Weeds included of small nettle (*Urtica urens*), goosefoot, orache, stitchwort, campion (*Silene* sp.), docks, sheep's sorrel, vetch/wild pea,

Table 7.2 Charred plant remains from Romano-British ditches and quarry pits

		Ditch	Ditch		Quarry pit				
Feature type		Ditch	Ditch			Quarry pit			
Group		6208	6229		6214	6231	6232		
Slot/cut		5196	5896		5347	6100	5237	5566	5724
Context		5160	5901	5898	5343	6104	5248	5633	5804
Sample		3	116	118	33	225	28	57	77
Vol (l)		8	36	32	13	26	8	32	29
Flot size (ml)		250	50	90	50	120	50	150	175
% roots		40	35	35	55	75	60	20	65
% 0.5 mm fraction analysed		–	–	10	–	–	–	–	10
Cereals									
Hordeum vulgare L. *sl* (grain)	barley	3	12	49	2	27	22	18	35
Hordeum vulgare L. *sl* (grain) germinated	barley	1	–	6	–	–	–	–	–
Hordeum vulgare L. *sl* (rachiis frag)	barley	–	6	76	–	3	3	1	–
Triticum dicoccum (Schübl) (grain)	emmer wheat	–	–	1	–	–	–	–	–
T. dicoccum (Schübl) (glume base)	emmer wheat	–	–	cf. 1	–	–	–	–	–
Triticum spelta L. (glume bases)	spelt wheat	4	27	51	1	29	30	30	68
Triticum spelta L. (spikelet fork)	spelt wheat	–	–	3	–	1	1	12	5
Triticum dicoccum/spelta (grain)	emmer/spelt wheat	–	17	30	3	45	59	380	50
T. dicoccum/spelta (spikelet fork)	emmer/spelt wheat	1	7	51	2	18	6	35	72
T. dicoccum/spelta (glume bases)	emmer/spelt wheat	5	233	1545	12	232	147	144	1325
Cereal indet. (grains)	cereal	17	43	183	15	120	70	235	170
Cereal frags (est. whole grains)	cereal	4	70	70	7	60	30	90	45
Cereal frags (culm node)	cereal	–	4	8	2	–	2	9	–
Cereal frags (basal culm node)	cereal	1	3	–	–	–	6	2	–
Other species									
Ranunculus sp.	buttercup	–	–	2	–	–	–	–	2
Papaver argemnone/dubium stigmatic disc	prickly/long-headed poppy	–	1	–	–	–	–	–	3
Fumaria officinalis L.	common fumitory	–	–	1	–	–	–	9	3
Corylus avellana L. (fragments)	hazel	–	–	–	–	–	–	–	1 (<1 ml>
Chenopodiaceae	goosefoot family	5	17	–	1	–	–	–	–
Chenopodium sp.	goosefoot	–	–	80	–	–	–	3	2
Chenopodium album L.	fathen	10	22	7	–	1	2	–	–
Atriplex sp. L.	orache	–	–	212	1	1	4	10	13
Caryophyllaceae (cf. *Agrostemma*) capsules		2	4	–	–	–	–	–	–
Stellaria sp. L.	stitchwort	–	–	20	–	1	1	1	20
Silene sp. L.	campion	–	–	–	–	–	–	2	–
Persicaria lapathifolia/maculosa (L.) Gray/Gray	redshank/pale persicaria	–	–	–	1	–	–	–	–
Polygonum aviculare L.	knotgrass	3	1	2	–	–	–	1	3
Fallopia convolvulus (L.) À. Löve	black bindweed	7	8	3	2	–	2	2	4
Rumex sp. L.	dock	–	2	12	2	–	8	5	40
Brassica sp. L.	brassica	–	–	–	–	–	–	1	–
Prunus spinosa/ Crataegus monogyna (thorns/twigs)	hawthorn/sloe thorns	–	–	–	1	–	–	–	–
Vicia L./*Lathyrus* sp. L.	vetch/pea	6	27	83	4	15	2	15	25
Lathyrus cf. *nissolia* L.	grass vetchling	2	–	–	1	–	–	–	–
Medicago/Trifolium sp. L.	medick/clover	29	38	53	6	14	1	5	18
Medicago sp L.	medick	–	–	12	2	–	–	–	–
Linum usitatissimum L. capsule	flax capsule (immature)	–	–	–	–	–	1	–	–
cf. *Bupleurum rotundifolium*	thorow-wax	–	–	–	1	–	–	–	–
Lithospermum arvense L.	corn gromwell	–	–	5	2	–	–	–	–
Galeopsis cf. *tetrahit*	common hemp-nettle	–	–	2	–	–	–	–	–
Plantago lanceolata L.	ribwort plantain	3	2	3	–	–	1	–	–
Veronica hederifolia L (charred)	ivy-leaved speedwell	–	–	–	–	–	–	–	1
Odontites vernus	red bartsia	–	3	50	2	3	1	1	–
Sherardia arvensis L.	field madder	–	2	5	–	–	–	–	–
Galium sp. L.	bedstraw	5	4	14	2	4	3	14	18
Valerianella dentata (L.) Pollich	narrow-fruited cornsalad	–	1	12	–	–	–	2	–
Tripleurospermum inodorum (L.) Sch. Bip.	scentless mayweed	–	–	1	–	1	2	–	10
Carex sp. L. triganous	sedge trigonous seed	–	4	–	–	–	–	–	–
Carex sp. L. flat	sedge flat seed	1	–	–	–	–	–	–	–
Poaceae (small indet.)	small grass seed	–	–	–	1	–	–	–	–
Lolium sp.	rye grass	2	12	–	1	–	–	–	–
Lolium/Festuca sp.	rye grass/fescue	3	10	67	–	12	14	10	43
Poa/Phleum sp. L.	meadow grass/cat's-tail	–	–	60	3	6	1	1	1
Arrhenatherum elatius var. *bulbosum* (Willd)	false oat-grass tuber	–	–	3	–	–	–	1	–
Avena sp. L. (grain)	oat grain	–	–	14	–	4	5	4	5
Avena sp. L. (awn)	oat awn	–	144	310	–	7	9	1	64
Avena L./*Bromus* L. sp.	oat/brome	3	20	56	3	12	63	22	115
Bromus sp. L.	brome grass	–	–	3	–	3	1	–	2
Anisantha sterilis (L.)	barren brome	–	–	1	–	–	–	–	–
Monocot-stem/rootlet frags		–	7	80	10	2	7	7	3
Bud		–	–	1	–	–	–	–	–
Triangular capsule frags		–	–	–	–	–	–	1	1
Tuber		–	–	–	–	–	–	2	–

Table 7.3 Charred plant remains from Romano-British pits

		Pit				Subrectangular pit			
Feature type									
Cut		5216	5280	5756	7095	7389	7394	7409	7409
Context		5217	5283	5760	7116	7391	7391	7415	7416
Sample		25	31	74	292	327	328	329	330
Vol (l)		35	40	18	16	9	9	10	9
Flot size (ml)		250	60	250	50	25	20	25	120
% roots		65	70	5	45	5	3	3	2
% 1.0mm fraction analysed		–	–	10	–	–	–	–	–
% 0.5mm fraction analysed		10	–	10	–	–	–	–	–
Cereals									
Hordeum vulgare L. *sl* (grain)	barley	190	7	315	72	12	34	7	32
Hordeum vulgare L. *sl* (rachiis frag)	barley	11	3	–	15	–	4	2	–
T. dicoccum (Schübl) (spikelet fork)	emmer wheat	–	–	–	–	–	–	–	cf. 1
Triticum spelta L. (glume bases)	spelt wheat	20	6	120	39	8	4	22	151
Triticum spelta L. (spikelet fork)	spelt wheat	2	–	10	–	–	1	1	12
Triticum dicoccum/spelta (grain)	emmer/spelt wheat	125	6	415	15	8	12	61	657
T. dicoccum/spelta (whole spikelet)	emmer/spelt wheat	–	–	–	–	–	–	–	1
T. dicoccum/spelta (spikelet fork)	emmer/spelt wheat	9	3	110	33	2	–	7	33
T. dicoccum/spelta (glume bases)	emmer/spelt wheat	264	73	300	275	21	18	116	180
Cereal indet. (grains)	cereal	250	22	390	80	19	62	24	110
Cereal frags (est. whole grains)	cereal	125	25	120	35	43	50	35	50
Cereal frags (culm node)	cereal	4	1	18	13	–	2	1	–
Cereal frags (basal culm node)	cereal	–	–	+	2	–	–	–	–
Other species									
Ranunculus sp.	buttercup	–	–	41	6	–	–	–	–
Fumaria officinalis L.	common fumitory	1	–	10	–	–	–	–	–
Urtica urens L.	small neetle	–	–	–	–	–	–	–	–
Corylus avellana L. (fragments)	hazel	4 (<1 ml)	–	1	–	–	–	–	–
Chenopodiaceae	goosefoot family	–	–		–	2 + [1 min]	3	–	–
Chenopodium sp.	goosefoot	43	1	30	7	–	2	1	–
Chenopodium album L.	fathen	4	–	–	–	2	5	–	–
Atriplex sp. L.	orache	47	–	3	10	6	11	2	–
Montia fontana subsp. *Chondrosperma* (Fenzl) Walters	blinks	–	–	30	–	–	1	–	–
Stellaria sp. L.	stitchwort	–	1	10	1	–	5	2	–
Agrostemma githago L.	corncockle	–	–	5	–	–	–	1	2
Agrostemma githago L. (seeds in fruit cluster)	corncockle	–	–	2	–	–	–	–	–
Silene sp. L.	campion	–	–	–	1	–	–	–	–
Persicaria lapathifolia/maculosa (L.) Gray/Gray	redshank/pale persicaria	–	–	–	–	1	6	–	–
Polygonum aviculare L.	knotgrass	5	1	12	2	–	–	–	–
Fallopia convolvulus (L.) À. Löve	black bindweed	8	–	86	6	1	3	–	–
Rumex sp. L.	dock	3	4	171	30	9	8	7	5
Rumex acetosella group Raf.	sheeps sorrel	–	–	20	5	–	–	–	–
Brassica sp. L.	brassica	–	–	31	2	–	–	–	–
Potentilla palustris L.	marsh cinquefoil	–	–	30	–	–	–	–	–
Potentilla palustris L. (seed head/fruit)	marsh cinquefoil	–	–	1 + frags	–	–	–	–	–
Crataegus monogyna Jacq.	hawthorn	–	–	–	–	–	1	–	–
Vicia L./*Lathyrus* sp. L.	vetch/pea	21	4	2486	21	13	10	6	3
Medicago/Trifolium sp. L.	clover/medick	15	7	180	30	4 + [1 min]	37	5	–
Medicago sp L.	medick	–	–	–	–	7	–	–	–
Scandix pecten-veneris L.	shepherd's-needle	–	–	4	–	–	–	–	–
Torilis sp. Adans	hedge-parsley	–	–	–	1	–	–	–	–
Lithospermum arvense L.	corn gromwell	(1 min)	–	1	17	[2 in]	m 8	2	–
Galeopsis cf. *tetrahit*	common hemp-nettle	1	–	–	–	–	–	–	–
Plantago lanceolata L.	ribwort plantain	–	–	20	–	1	–	–	–
Veronica hederifolia L (charred)	ivy-leaved speedwell	–	–	–	14	–	–	–	–
Odontites vernus	red bartsia	–	–	20	–	5	4	1	–
Sherardia arvensis L.	field madder	3	–	–	1	–	–	1	–
Galium sp. L.	bedstraw	49	3	67	12	9	5	5	4
Valerianella dentata (L.) Pollich	narrow-fruited cornsalad	–	–	40	5	–	–	–	–
Cardus/Cirsium	thistle	–	–	1	–	–	–	–	–
Centaurea cyanus L.	cornflower	–	–	124	–	–	–	–	2
cf. *Crepis* sp. L.	hawk's-beard	–	–	10	–	–	–	–	–
Tripleurospermum inodorum (L.) Sch. Bip.	scentless mayweed	–	2	40	3	3	–	–	–
Lolium/Festuca sp.	rye grass/fescue	32	1	40	15	1	6	3	1
Poa/Phleum sp. L.	meadow grass/cat's-tail	20	1	20	5	1	4	–	–
Arrhenatherum elatius Var. *bulbosum* (Willd)	false oat-grass tuber	–	–	108	–	–	–	–	–
Arrhenatherum elatius Var. *bulbosum* (Willd)	false oat-grass stem/root	–	–	+	–	–	–	–	–
Avena sp. L. (grain)	oat grain	14	1	25	11	1	7	1	5
Avena sp. L. (awn)	oat awn	10	2	30	18	–	22	10	–
Avena L./*Bromus* L. sp.	oat/brome	39	3	99	44	3	20	6	7
Bromus sp. L.	brome grass	1	–	21	2	1	2	1	3
Monocot-stem/rootlet frags		1	3	++	14	2	18	1	–
Bud		–	–	–	–	–	–	–	1
Tuber		–	–	2	–	–	–	–	–
?ergot		–	–	6	–	–	–	–	–
Mineralised nodule		=			25		=	–	–

Table 7.4 Charred plant remains from Romano-British kilns, ovens and other contexts

Feature type		Kiln	Kiln	Kiln	Oven	Oven	Cremation grave	Occup. layer	Solution hollow
Cut		7214	7205	7487	6174	7183	6548		6513
Context		7215	7206	7488	6175	7185	6549	5489	6518
Sample		305	331	334	248	300	272	42	266
Vol (l)		20	18	36	38	15	18	7	28
Flot size (ml)		175	50	375	40	50	20	20	60
% roots		15	3	50	60	10	5	50	5
% 0.5 mm fraction analysed		10	10	10	–	–	–	–	–
Cereals									
Hordeum vulgare L. *sl* (grain)	barley	192	30	63	6	6	1	6	595
Hordeum vulgare L. *sl* (grain) germinated	barley	–	–	–	–	7	–	–	3
Hordeum vulgare L. *sl* (rachis frag)	barley	31	22	–	4	–	–	–	2
Hordeum vulgare L. *sl* (palea/lemma frag)	barley	–	–	–	–	–	–	–	+
Triticum spelta L. (glume bases)	spelt wheat	161	127	28	18	–	7	6	10
Triticum spelta L. (spikelet fork)	spelt wheat	3	2	1	–	–	–	–	2
Triticum dicoccum/spelta (grain)	emmer/spelt wheat	43	16	7	5	4	2	5	15
T. dicoccum/spelta (spikelet fork)	emmer/spelt wheat	156	155	12	7	-	2	6	2
T. dicoccum/spelta (glume bases)	emmer/spelt wheat	3061	4527	1078	97	4	13	102	10
Triticum sp. (grain)	wheat	–	–	–	–	–	–	–	–
Cereal indet. (grains)	cereal	220	38	155	15	10	1	20	130
Cereal frags (est. whole grains)	cereal	143	23	65	29	12	4	13	65
Coleoptile frags		–	–	–	–	–	–	2	–
Cereal frags (culm node)	cereal	3	1	–	–	–	–	–	3
Other species									
Ranunculus sp.	buttercup	3	1	–	–	–	–	–	–
Fumaria officinalis L.	common fumitory	2	1	3	–	–	–	–	–
Urtica urens L.	small nettle	10	–	10	–	–	1	–	–
Corylus avellana L. (fragments)	hazel	–	1 (<1 ml)	1 (<1 ml)	1 (< 1 ml)	–	–	–	–
Chenopodiaceae	goosefoot family	–	–	–	1	–	–	–	–
Chenopodium sp.	goosefoot	15	10	12	1	–	–	–	1
Chenopodium urbicum L.	upright goosefoot	–	–	–	–	–	1	–	–
Chenopodium album L.	fathen	–	–	2	–	2	1	–	–
Atriplex sp. L.	orache	2	11	2	3	–	5	–	–
Stellaria sp. L.	stitchwort	10	30	10	–	–	1	–	1
Silene sp.L.	campion	13	21	–	–	–	–	–	–
Persicaria lapathifolia/maculosa (L.) Gray/Gray	redshank/pale persicaria	2	–	–	–	–	–	–	1
Polygonum aviculare L.	knotgrass	4	4	3	–	–	–	–	2
Fallopia convolvulus (L.) À. Löve	black bindweed	2	2	2	–	1	3	2	1
Rumex sp. L.	dock	43	40	116	–	–	6	2	3
Rumex acetosella group Raf.	sheeps sorrel	3	20	–	–	–	–	–	1
Malva sp. L.	mallow	1	–	–	–	–	–	–	–
Brassica sp. L.	brassica	2	1	–	–	–	–	–	1
Vicia L./*Lathyrus* sp. L.	vetch/pea	29	24	38	3	1	4	1	5
Vicia faba	celtic bean	cf. 1	–	–	–	–	–	–	–
Medicago/Trifolium sp. L.	medick/clover	33	18	26	1	9	6	–	1
Medicago sp L.	medick	–	–	–	–	–	5	–	–
Linum usitatissimum L. capsule	flax capsule (immature)	–	–	–	–	–	cf. 1	–	–
Scandix pecten-veneris L.	shepherd's-needle	–	–	–	–	–	–	–	5
Conopodium majus	pignut	19	–	2	–	–	–	–	–
cf. *Bupleurum rotundifolium*	thorow-wax	2	–	–	–	–	–	–	–
Torilis sp. Adans	hedge-parsley	–	10	–	–	–	–	–	–
Hyoscyamus niger L.	henbane	–	–	1	–	–	2	–	–
Lithospermum arvense L.	corn gromwell	6	–	–	–	–	–	–	1
Galeopsis cf. *tetrahit*	common hemp-nettle	1	–	–	–	–	–	–	–
Plantago lanceolata L.	ribwort plantain	1	–	1	1	5	–	–	–
Veronica hederifolia L (charred)	ivy-leaved speedwell	–	4	–	–	–	–	–	–
Odontites vernus	red bartsia	–	10	10	–	–	–	–	–
Sherardia arvensis L.	field madder	–	–	1	–	–	–	–	–
Galium sp. L.	bedstraw	23	33	56	2	5	1	5	5
Sambucus nigra L.	elder	1	–	–	–	–	–	–	–
Valerianella dentata (L.) Pollich	narrow-fruited cornsalad	23	–	–	–	–	–	–	3
Cardus/Cirsium sp.	thistle	–	2	1	–	–	–	–	–
cf. *Crepis* sp. L	hawk's-beard	–	–	1	–	–	–	–	–
Tripleurospermum inodorum (L.) Sch. Bip.	scentless mayweed	–	10	10	–	–	–	–	–
Carex sp. L. flat	sedge flat seed	–	1	–	–	–	–	–	–
Lolium/Festuca sp.	rye grass/fescue	33	63	23	–	–	–	6	–
Poa/Phleum sp. L.	meadow grass/cat's-tail	10	–	20	1	2	–	1	–
Arrhenatherum elatius Var. *bulbosum* (Willd)	false oat-grass tuber	67	34	3	–	–	–	–	–
Arrhenatherum elatius Var. *bulbosum* (Willd)	false oat-grass stem/root	+	+	–	–	–	–	–	–
Avena sp. L. (grain)	oat grain	14	9	18	–	–	–	–	16
Avena sp. L. (spikelet)	oat spikelet	–	–	–	–	–	–	–	1
Avena sp. L. (awn)	oat awn	31	204	21	3	1	–	–	4
Avena L./*Bromus* L. sp.	oat/brome	118	145	64	3	–	3	1	9
Bromus sp. L.	brome grass	3	2	4	–	–	–	–	4
Monocot-stem/rootlet frags		++	4	++	–	2	–	–	2–
Tuber		3	10	–	–	–	–	–	–

clover/medick, hedge-parsley (*Torilis* sp.), red bartsia, bedstraw, narrow-fruited cornsalad, scentless mayweed, rye-grass/fescue, meadow grass/cat's-tail, oat and brome *grass*, with smaller numbers of seeds of mallow (*Malva* sp.), thorow-wax, henbane (*Hyoscyamus niger*), corn gromwell, common hemp-nettle, field madder, thistle (*Carduus/Cirsium* sp.), hawk's-beard and sedge (*Carex* sp.). There were also significant numbers of tubers, including those of pignut (*Conopodium majus*) and false-oat grass, together with monocot grass stem and rootlet fragments.

Oven 6174 produced a chaff-rich assemblage, while the smaller assemblage from oven 7183 was dominated by grains, in particular of barley (Table 7.4), a number of which showed traces of germination. The small weed assemblages included goosefoot, fat-hen, orache, black-bindweed, vetch/wild pea, clover/medick, ribwort plantain, bedstraw, oat, brome grass and meadow grass/cat's-tail.

Weed seeds outnumbered cereal remains in the relatively small assemblage from cremation grave 6548 (Table 7.4). They included dock, vetch/wild pea, clover/medick, henbane, oat/brome grass, black-bindweed, orache and upright goosefoot (*Chenopodium urbicum*); there was also a probable immature flax capsule.

The assemblage from possible occupation layer 5489 mainly consisted of cereal remains, with the chaff elements predominant (Table 7.4); a few coleoptile fragments were noted. The small weed assemblage included black-bindweed, docks, bedstraw and rye-grass/fescue.

The rich assemblage from solution hollow 6513 (context 6518) contained a large quantity of cereal remains, in particular grains of barley (Table 7.4). There were traces of germination on a few of the grains, and a significant number of them were still in hulls rather than being dehusked; barley palea/lemma fragments were also present. The relatively small weed assemblage included vetch/wild pea, sheep's sorrel, shepherd's-needle, bedstraw, narrow-fruited cornsalad, oat and brome grass.

Discussion

The charred cereal assemblages contained hulled wheat and barley. Most of the identifiable hulled wheat remains were spelt, with a few remains of emmer identified in two samples, and typically spelt was the dominant wheat over much of England during the Romano-British period (Greig 1991). Spelt and barley were recorded on other Romano-British sites in the area, such as High Post (Pelling 2011), Coombe Down South, Beach's Barn and Chisenbury Warren (Stevens 2006), and Figheldean (Ede 1993; Hinton 1999), while low levels of emmer

were also recorded at Beach's Barn (Stevens 2006) and Figheldean (Hinton 1999).

Glume waste predominated over estimated grains of glume wheats in all but five samples – from quarry pit 5566, pits 7394, 7409 (context 7416) and 5756, and oven 7183 – although this last deposit was very small. As such the vast majority of assemblages can be ascribed to waste from the dehusking of spikelets of spelt taken from storage. In most of samples grain and/or large weed seeds are dominant over small weed seeds, suggesting that crops were stored as semi-clean spikelets, or, in the case of barley grain, after threshing, winnowing and fine-sieving had been conducted (see Stevens 2003; Hillman 1981; 1984). As such, the waste includes those larger grain or spikelet-sized seeds that often remain with the crop, to be sorted by hand during the dehusking process.

There are, however, a few exceptions to this pattern. Two grain-rich samples (from quarry pit 5566, and context 7416 in pit 7409) may represent the charring of a stored crop of semi-cleaned spikelets, or possibly a charring accident as suggested at Coombe Down South (Stevens 2006). The deposit from pit 7389 may also have contained charred spikelets. The sample from oven 7183 also has more grains than glumes, which might be consistent with waste from a parching accident, although the sample is not rich enough to state this with any certainty.

Three samples, from ditches 6208 and 6229, contained higher proportions of small weed seeds. That weed seeds also dominate over grain, along with occasional seed heads in two of these samples, might indicate that crops were stored in a less processed state. Seed heads and small weed seeds are often removed earlier within the processing sequence, and their presence suggests they had not been removed before the crops were stored.

The assemblages from pottery kilns 7214, 7205 and 7487 were particularly rich in waste from the dehusking of semi-cleaned spikelets. It seems likely that the glume-rich waste was used as tinder for the kilns, although it is possible that the chaff was deliberately used during the firing of the kiln to give a certain effect to the pottery (such as a black finish).

The ovens may have been used for a number of different stages in crop processing (as well as other activities), including drying harvested crops prior to storage, parching spikelets of spelt taken from storage prior to dehusking, and drying malted grain (van der Veen 1989). The assemblage from oven 7183 appears to represent spilt waste from the drying of crops prior to storage, while the germinated barley may indicate its use for malting, although the assemblage is too small to draw firm conclusions. A mixture of germinated and ungerminated grain was also noted in one of the corn-drier deposits at High Post (Pelling 2011). The assemblage from oven 6174, in contrast, is dominated by glume waste from the processing semi-cleaned spikelets. The use of processing waste as fuel for corn-driers during the parching and dehusking of hulled wheats was also seen at High Post (Pelling 2011) and has also been noted elsewhere in the area, such as at Chisenbury Warren and Beach's Barn (Stevens 2006), and further afield (van der Veen 1989). It might be noted that the use of corn-driers for such operations indicate that dehusking was likely to have been carried out on a larger scale than for immediate domestic use, producing clean grain perhaps for the wider settlement.

The interesting assemblage from context 6518 in solution hollow 6513 may be indicative of a deposit of barley being dried before dehusking. Although a few of these grains showed traces of germination, the assemblage is not otherwise reflective of malting.

The weed seeds in these assemblages are generally those recovered from grassland, field margins and arable environments, although there is an indication of the exploitation of a range of soils, with sandier soils indicated by henbane and sheep's sorrel, heavier clay soils by red bartsia and shepherd's-needle, lighter drier calcareous soils by thorow-wax, corn gromwell, field madder, narrow-fruited cornsalad, and broad-fruited cornsalad, and some wetter environments by blinks, marsh cinquefoil and sedge. A similar pattern during this period of growing crops on a range of soil types, but mainly on lighter drier calcareous soils, has been observed on other sites in the area, such as High Post (Pelling 2011).

The presence of both low-growing species such as corn gromwell, field madder, clover, medick and dock, and twining species such as bedstraw, black-bindweed and vetches/wild peas, suggests that the crops were harvested, by sickle, low on the culm with the straw, as at other sites in the area (Stevens 2006; Pelling 2011). A number of species, such as bedstraw, corncockle, field madder and corn gromwell, are believed to be typical of autumn sowing, which is probably the case for spelt and also possibly barley (Jones 1981; Reynolds 1981; Grime et al. 1988).

There is evidence for the occasional collection of material from hedgerows/scrub with the occurrence in a number of assemblages of small numbers of hazelnut shell fragments, sloe/hawthorn thorns, hawthorn stones and elder seeds. Monocot-stem and rootlet fragments were recorded in relatively high numbers in the assemblages from ditch 6229, pit 5756 and kilns 7214 and 7487. False oat-tubers were also noted in significant quantities in the assemblages from pit 5756 and kilns 7214 and 7205, together with pignuts from kilns 7214 and 7487. This may indicate

the occasional burning of turfs or the creation of a fire break around these kilns.

Charcoal
by Dana Challinor

Ten samples were assessed as having potential for charcoal analysis (Wessex Archaeology 2012). The Late Neolithic samples came from posthole alignments 6255 and 6260, and offered the opportunity to examine probable structural remains, with at least one sample, from posthole 6882, representing the remains of an *in situ* charred timber post. The later features were more varied, with samples from a Middle Iron Age cremation grave and two Romano-British pits and two ovens.

The >2 mm charcoal was provided for analysis. A random selection of 30 fragments from several sieve sizes (8 mm, 4 mm and 2 mm) was identified. Given the apparent low taxonomic diversity, a scan of the remaining charcoal was undertaken to look for additional species. The charcoal was fractured and sorted into groups based on the anatomical features observed in transverse section at x10 to x45 magnifications. Representative fragments from each group were then selected for further examination using a Meiji incident-light microscope at up to x400 magnification. Identifications were made with reference to Schweingruber (1990), Hather (2000) and modern reference material. Observations on maturity were made as appropriate. Classification and nomenclature follow Stace (1997).

The charcoal was generally in good condition, with minimal infusion of sediment, and occasional vitrification noted in some fragments. Taxonomic diversity was remarkably low, with only three taxa positively identified: *Quercus* sp. (oak), *Betula* sp. (birch) and Maloideae (hawthorn, apple, pear, service etc.). The apparent absence of spiral thickenings in the Maloideae makes it unlikely that *Malus* sp.(apple) is represented, but the genera are too similar for a positive identification.

The results are presented in Table 7.5, using a key to demonstrate the overwhelming dominance of a single taxon in the assemblages. Much of the oak had characteristically fragmented along the rays, leaving thin slivers from which it was difficult or impossible to determine maturity or to look at growth ring analysis. Nonetheless, several fragments were positively identified as sapwood, with the few heartwood fragments exhibiting only rare tyloses, as though they had only just begun to be laid down. Some of the oak fragments, especially in the Neolithic samples, exhibited narrow rings characteristic of slow growth, but it is difficult to draw interpretations from this as

Table 7.5 Charcoal from the Late Neolithic and Romano-British samples

	Phase	Late Neolithic					MIA	Romano-British			
	Feature type	posthole					crem. grave	quarry pit	subrect. pit	oven	
	Group		6255		6260		–	–	–	–	
	Feature	5074	5918	6002	6882	6882	6548	5497	7409	7183	7245
	Context	5077	5923	6006	6889	6895	6549	5498	7416	7185	7246
					ON 187						
	Sample	81	134	191	282	277	273	43	330	300	307
Quercus sp.	oak	Xs	Xhs	Xhs	Xhs	X	x	Xsr	Xs	–	Xhsr
Betula sp.	birch	–	–	–	–	–		–	–	Xr	–
Maloideae	hawthorn group	–	–	–	–	–	Xr	–	–	–	–

Key: X=dominant; x=present; s=sapwood; h=heartwood; r=roundwood

so much of the oak was too fragmented for accurate observations on growth.

Late Neolithic

All of the charcoal assemblages from the posthole alignments were exclusively composed of oak. The absence of evidence for ring curvature is appropriate for the use of trunkwood for posts, and the identification of sapwood (with a little heartwood evidence) indicates that the wood was not very mature. Although ON 187 was the only confirmed indication of an *in situ* post found during the excavations, it seems likely that all of the oak charcoal in these assemblages derived from structural timber remains. Oak provides excellent timber, and was commonly used in construction (Gale and Cutler 2000, 204).

Iron Age and Romano-British

The dominance of hawthorn group (Maloideae) in Middle Iron Age cremation grave 6548 seems unusual in the light of the other oak-dominated assemblages, but is unlikely to represent any changes in woodland resources, rather a deliberate selection of fuelwood. This unurned burial contained the cremated remains of an adult, along with redeposited pyre debris including burnt animal bone. The quantity of charcoal (approximately 50 fragments) was actually quite low for pyre debris, especially taking into account the relatively large volume of soil (26 l) from which the assemblage derived. It is possible that the Maloideae represent only a small component of the pyre, such as the remains of kindling or brushwood infill, which was picked out with the bone for burial. Pyre structures were commonly constructed with large timbers of oak and ash, which also provided the high calorific values necessary for efficient cremation (Gale 1997, 82), but

hawthorn, service tree and apple wood can make good quality fuel if used in enough quantity (Challinor 2009).

The lack of taxonomic diversity in the assemblages from the Romano-British period is somewhat surprising as some of these, at least, would have derived from domestic activities, which tend to use a greater range of species. The fills of subrectangular pit 7409 and quarry pit 5497 both contained abundant remains of cereals and other plants, suggesting that the charcoal probably derived from crop processing and/or food preparation activities. The apparently exclusive use of oak in these deposits suggests a plentiful supply of oak woodland was available. Likewise, oven 7245 also appears to have been fuelled by oak, although the dominance of birch in oven 7183 indicates that other taxa were used for some firings. The selection of fuelwood may have been influenced by the exact function of the fire, potentially elucidated by the analysis of the charred plant material. Oak makes a high calorific firewood, whereas birch tends to provide a short-lived, intense heat. Additionally, some of the birch came from small diameter roundwood which would be very suitable for use as kindling.

Radiocarbon Dating
by Alistair J. Barclay

Twenty radiocarbon dates were obtained, on short-lived plant remains, animal bone, and cremated and unburnt human bone, from the Scottish Universities Environmental Radiocarbon Centre (SUERC) (Table 7.6). The samples were all selected in conjunction with the project specialists. The dates have been calculated using the calibration curve of Reimer *et al.* (2013) and the computer program OxCal (v4.2.4) (Bronk Ramsey and Lee 2013) and cited at 95% confidence and quoted in the form recommended by Mook (1986), with the end points

Table 7.6 Radiocarbon dates

Lab ref	Sample	Context	Conventional age BP	C(‰)δ^{13}	N δ^{15}	95% calibrated date	Posterior density estimate 95% probability
Posthole alignment 6255							
SUERC-50618	Charcoal: *Quercus* sapwood	Posthole 5918 (5923)	4110±29	-24.6		2870-2570 cal BC	2705-2570 (87.8%) cal BC
SUERC-50614	Charcoal: *Quercus* sapwood	Posthole 5074 (5077)	4091±29	-26.0		2860-2490 cal BC	2670-2565 (89.0%) cal BC
SUERC-50619	Charcoal: *Quercus* sapwood	Posthole 6002 (6006)	4085±29	-25.6		2860-2490 cal BC	2700-2565 (89.1%) cal BC
SUERC-50621	Cattle radius	Posthole 5074 (5076)	4010±32	-23.4	6.2	2620-2460 cal BC	2570-2465 cal BC
SUERC-50624	Cattle humerus	Posthole 6002 (6006)	3915±31	-24.1	5.2	2480-2290 cal BC	2495-2355 (91.3%) cal BC
Posthole alignment 6260							
SUERC-36558	Charcoal: *Quercus* sapwood	Posthole 6882 (6889, ON 187)	4060±35	-26.2		2850-2470 cal BC	2685-2490 (90.0%) cal BC
SUERC-50623	Pig atlas vertebra	Posthole 5087 (5086B)	3999±32	-22.4	6.1	2590-2460 cal BC	2580-2465 cal BC
SUERC-50631	Cattle scapula	Posthole 6817 (6822)	3987±31	-23.8	5.9	2580-2460 cal BC	2570-2460 cal BC
SUERC-50622	Probable aurochs femur	Posthole 5087 (5086A)	3931±31	-22.6	5.7	2560-2300 cal BC	2500-2390 (83.9%) cal BC
Human burials							
SUERC-49176	Human cremated bone	Hollow 7306 (7531)	4000±34	-23.7		2620-2460 cal BC	2585-2460 (94.4%) cal BC
SUERC-49175	Human cremated bone	Cremation 7530 (5190)	2286±34	-24.6		410-230 cal BC	
SUERC-49174	Human cremated bone	Cremation 6548 (6549)	2240±34	-25.4		400-200 cal BC	
SUERC-49173	Human cremated bone	Cremation 5206 (5221)	2156±34	-19.9		360-90 cal BC	
SUERC-49180	Human skull vault	Inhumation 7280 (7284)	2094±34	-19.6	8.9	210-40 cal BC	
Enclosure ditch 6203 and related contexts							
SUERC-50629	Cattle ulna	Pit 6482 (6483)	2010±30	-21.5	3.5	90 cal BC-60 cal AD	
SUERC-36557	Cattle mandible	Ditch cut 5199 (6027)	1995±35	-21.0	3.4	90 cal BC-80 cal AD	
SUERC-50630	Cattle axis vertebra	Ditch cut 6605 (6606)	1902±30	-22.1	3.6	30-210 cal AD	
Solution hollow 6257							
SUERC-50628	Cattle mandible	6176 (6185)	3327±31	-20.8	4.3	1690-1520 cal BC	
SUERC-53037	Horse metapodial	6176 (6145)	2260±25	-22.5	4.3	400-210 cal BC	
Animal burials							
SUERC-50620	Sheep/goat ulna	5006 (5007)	245±30	-22.9	5.3	1520-1950 cal AD	

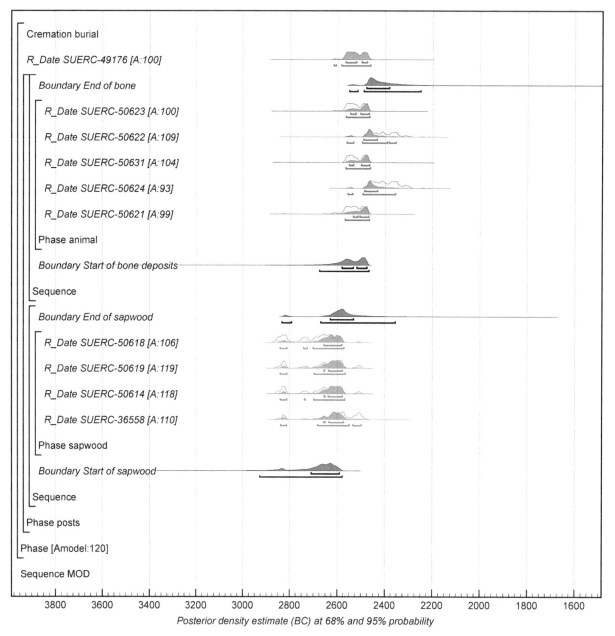

Figure 7.1 Probability distributions of radiocarbon dates for samples associated with the Neolithic posthole alignments and the cremation burial. The square brackets and OxCal key words define the model. For each date two distributions are plotted: one in outline, which is the simple radiocarbon distribution, and a solid one (posterior density estimate), based on the modelled data

rounded outwards to 10 years. The ranges quoted in italics are posterior density estimates derived from mathematical modelling of given archaeological problems. The ranges in plain type have been calculated according to the maximum intercept method (Stuiver and Reimer 1986).

The radiocarbon dating programme had the following aims:

- To date a series of posthole settings and alignments to confirm their suggested Late Neolithic date and to test whether they were broadly contemporaneous;

- To date a series of unaccompanied cremation/inhumation burials;
- To date the large enclosure ditch (6203) and confirm its suggested Late Iron Age date;
- To confirm the date of a series of animal bone deposits.

Late Neolithic Post Settings and Cremation Burial

Radiocarbon dating was used to date a series of postholes and related deposits that formed two

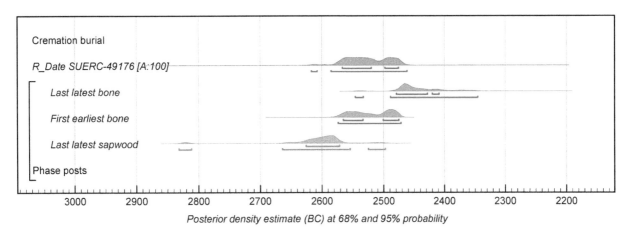

Figure 7.2 Late Neolithic posts and burial: selected parameters based on the model presented in Figure 7.1

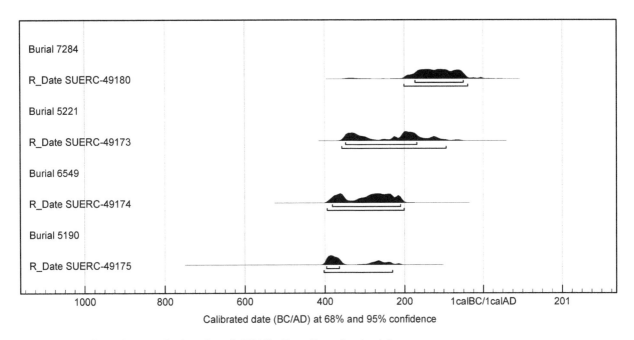

Figure 7.3 Radiocarbon results for selected Middle–Late Iron Age burials

possible post alignments on the site, and a cremation burial.

Posthole alignments 6255 and 6260
A series of 26 mostly undated postholes were found on the site. These formed two intersecting alignments, one running north–south (group 6255: including 5074, 5918 and 6002) and the other WNW–ESE (group 6260: including 5087, 6817 and 6882). Within alignment 6260, one of five more closely spaced postholes (6882) had the remains of a charred post, and others within the two alignments were found to contain charcoal including sapwood (5074, 5918, 6002 and 6889).

During the assessment stage a radiocarbon date, SUERC-36558, had been obtained on the charred oak post (ON 187) in posthole 6882, and this had

returned a date of *2685–2490 cal BC (at 90.0% probability)*. In total, nine radiocarbon dates were obtained from six of the 26 postholes (Table 7.6). Four dates are on sapwood (SUERC-36558, SUERC-50614, SUERC-50618 and SUERC-50619) and five are on fragments of animal bone (SUERC-50621–50624 and SUERC-50631). The sapwood samples are either known, or are assumed, to derive from timber posts, while the animal bone appears to have been mostly deposited, possibly even placed, after the post had been removed or had decayed. The radiocarbon dates are presented in a phased model that makes the assumption that the bone was deposited after the posts were erected; in other words, the phases are contiguous rather than independent. This model has good overall agreement (Amodel 120) (Fig. 7.1).

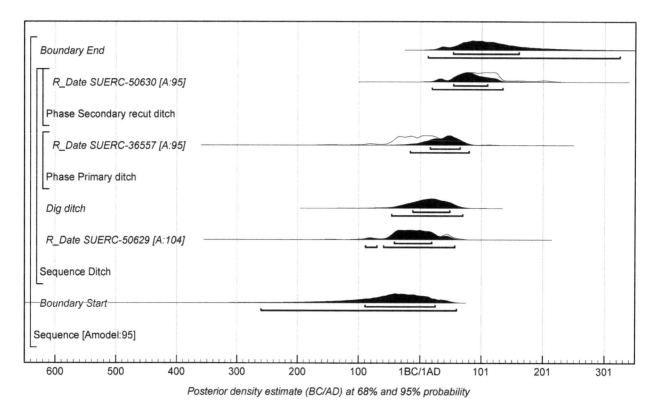

Posterior density estimate (BC/AD) at 68% and 95% probability

Figure 7.4 Radiocarbon dates for enclosure ditch 6203

The four sapwood dates are statistically consistent (X^2-Test: T'=1.2; v=3; T'(5%)=7.8) indicating that they could be of the same age, and their results are modelled in Figures 7.1 and 7.2. Their calibrated date ranges all fall within the 27th to early 25th centuries BC and are consistent with a Late Neolithic date. If it is assumed that the posts were all erected in a single phase of activity then the youngest sapwood date should equate to the date of construction of the post alignments. This is shown in Figure 7.2 and is modelled as *Last_latest_sapwood*, which indicates a construction event at some point during *2745–2580 cal BC (85.9%) at 95% probability*.

The five dates on animal bone are also statistically consistent (X^2-Test: T'=7.4; v=4; T'(5%)=9.5) but are notably later than those on sapwood. Their calibrated date ranges all fall within the 26th to early 24th centuries BC and are consistent with a Late Neolithic or earliest Beaker (British Chalcolithic) date. The earliest animal bone deposit, modelled as *First_animal_bone* was made at some point during *2575–2470 cal BC (at 95% probability)* (see Fig. 7.2). The difference between the latest sapwood date and the earliest animal bone date is between *27 and 122 years (median 80 years:* modelled as *Difference Last sapwood/First animal bone)* which supports the suggestion that the two groups of material represent temporally separate events. Some or all of the animal bone could derive from later activity,

their occurrence being either incidental or as deliberate placements.

Cremation burial in hollow 7306

Radiocarbon dating was also used to date a single cremation deposit found within a hollow below a layer of worked flint. The radiocarbon result (SUERC-49176) indicates that the burial was made during *2585–2460 cal BC (at 94.4% probability)* and is comparable with other Late Neolithic burials within the area (see Chapter 8; Powell and Barclay forthcoming). Figure 7.2 shows that the cremation burial was made after the construction of the post alignments and during the period when the animal bone was accumulating/being deposited in them.

Iron Age Burials and Enclosure Ditch

Radiocarbon dating was used to date four other human burials (three cremation burials and a single inhumation) and deposits associated with the large enclosure ditch.

Human burials

Four other human burials were directly dated, three cremation burials (SUERC-49173–49175) and a single inhumation (SUERC-49180). The cremation burials were all made during the Middle Iron Age (see

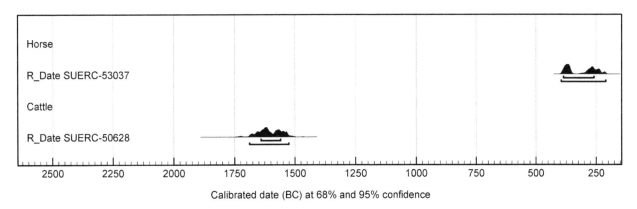

Figure 7.5 Radiocarbon dates for selected animal bone deposits plotted at 95% confidence

Table 7.6 and Fig. 7.3), although they are not statistically consistent and of the same age. The earliest burial (5190: SUERC-49175) could belong to the 4th century BC (410–230 cal BC at 95% confidence, or 400–360 cal BC at 68% confidence). Burial 6549 (SUERC-49174) could be of a similar age or slightly later, whilst burial 5221 (SUERC-49173) is almost certainly later than 5190. All three are earlier than the neonate inhumation burial (7284) which was made at some point during the 2nd or earlier 1st century BC (SUERC-49180), either in the later Middle Iron Age or the Late Iron Age – but probably before the digging of the large enclosure ditch.

Enclosure ditch and associated deposits

Two dates (SUERC-36557 and 50630) were obtained on animal bone recovered from the large enclosure ditch (6203), and a third (SUERC-50629) on animal bone from a pit (6482) apparently cut by the ditch. Two of the dates (SUERC-36557 and SUERC-50629) are statistically consistent and could be of a similar age (90 cal BC–80 cal AD, and 90 cal BC–60 cal AD, respectively), both falling within the Late Iron Age. The third date (SUERC-50630) falls within the early Romano-British period (30–210 cal AD at 95% confidence, or 60–120 cal AD at 68% confidence).

If the assumption is correct that pit 6482 was cut by the ditch then the construction of the ditch can be estimated using the OxCal '*Date*' function (see Fig. 7.4). This would suggest that the ditch could have been constructed during *50 cal BC to 70 cal AD (at 95% probability)* or possibly during *15 BC to 50 cal AD at 68% probability)*, supporting its interpretation as a pre-Conquest earthwork.

Animal Bone Deposits

Three animal bone deposits were radiocarbon dated to confirm their date (Table 7.6). Two, from solution hollow 6257, were dated to see whether they were contemporaneous with the Late Neolithic worked flint from the feature. Part of a cattle mandible in fresh condition from the uppermost deposit (6185) was dated to the Early/Middle Bronze Age (SUERC-50628, 1690–1520 cal BC at 95% confidence). A horse metapodial, from layer 6145 at the edge of the hollow, was also selected for dating because horse is generally accepted as being a later Bronze Age reintroduction. The date on the horse bone (SUERC-53037) confirmed it as belonging to the earlier part of the Middle Iron Age (400–210 cal BC at 95% confidence), and of a similar date to the unurned cremation burials (5187 and 5206) close to the hollow (see above).

Part of a sheep/goat ulna from an animal burial (part of a bone deposit) in feature 5006 was dated to the post-medieval period by SUERC-50620 (1520–1950 cal AD at 95% confidence).

Chapter 8
Discussion

The site at the former MOD Durrington HQ lies just 600 m beyond the north-east corner of the Stonehenge World Heritage Site, in a landscape dense with prehistoric and Romano-British monuments and sites. It is therefore not surprising that the excavation should have uncovered evidence for Neolithic, Iron Age and Romano-British activity. What was less expected was the preservation evidence for a much earlier date. Although the limited exposure of a buried Allerød soil is of importance at this site primarily on account of its environmental potential, it clearly demonstrates the possibility that similar deposits may be preserved more widely along the Avon valley, along with the potential of containing archaeological remains as well.

The Late Neolithic activity – post alignment construction, pit digging and deposition, and the use (and modification) of natural features for mortuary activity and flint knapping, has to be viewed within the context of the wider monumental landscape in the area, although the dominance of particular monuments may conceal the ways that the intervening, apparently empty parts of the landscape could have been extensively occupied and intensely exploited for a wide range of activities – relating to both settlement and ritual. Given the proximity of the great henge enclosure of Durrington Walls it is perhaps not surprising and unexpected that other sites are being discovered in its immediate hinterland especially to the north where relatively little investigation has taken place.

The construction in the Late Iron Age of a substantial defensive 'enclosure' ditch represents a phase of activity, in a period of rapid social change, which was soon to be overrun by wider political events. However, while the defences would have become obsolete after the Roman Conquest, the area of the valley floor which they had enclosed appears to have remained of value for a settlement engaged in mixed farming and small-scale craft and industry. The expansion of Romano-British activity, perhaps closer to the riverbank in the Late Iron Age, right up to the now-levelled boundary suggests that this river valley location was one of particular value in the new economic climate, something which appears to have continued through the Romano-British period and, on the evidence for some of the pottery, possibly into the early post-Roman period.

Late Neolithic

The construction and use of the Late Neolithic monuments that lie along and adjacent to the Avon valley means that this site would have been in an area that witnessed intense and prolonged activity of many and varied forms, relating to settlement and economic activity, as well as monument construction and associated ritual and ceremony. An important feature of this monumental landscape is the numerous spatial connections between different parts of it – by linear monuments of different form and material, by natural features, by lines of site and intervisibility, and by pathways and other routes of communication through it. The two intersecting posthole alignments identified on this site can perhaps best be viewed as further components of a fine-grained web of interconnectivity.

Large-scale post-built structures, both linear and circular, are a relatively common feature of the Late Neolithic monumental landscape, with a long history of use at monuments such as Stonehenge, Woodhenge and Durrington Walls; indeed, the erection of timber posts is a feature identified locally also during the Mesolithic, as in the former Stonehenge car park (Vatcher and Vatcher 1973) and at Amesbury Down (Powell and Barclay forthcoming). Therefore, while the use of a common building material may have invested such timber structures with a degree of symbolic unity, they vary considerably in their form and context, and probably also, therefore, in their meanings and functions. For example, the two intersecting post alignments may have had a very different purpose to the near-contemporary line of postholes excavated on the western edge of Amesbury Down, overlooking the Avon valley to the south (Powell and Barclay forthcoming). Another set of postholes of probable Late Neolithic date cuts the ditch of the Larkhill causewayed enclosure 1 km to the south-west (Matt Leivers pers. comm.).

The east–west post alignment passed just south of natural solution hollow 6257, which was a focus of broadly contemporary flint knapping. Its line, if projected eastwards, would have also passed just south of solution hollow 6513, and although no evidence for contemporary activity was recovered from the latter, this cannot be ruled out, and it is possible that there was some relationship between the post alignment and these two prominent natural features. The intersection of the two alignments lies less than 20 m from hollow 6257; the possible significance of the flint knapping waste in this feature is heightened by the association of similar waste with the cremation burial in the smaller hollow (7306), located between the two larger hollows. The evidence on the site for the digging of pits in which cultural material was deposited, although a more common phenomenon in the landscape, may well also have had some direct relationship to these contemporary features.

None of these features, whether viewed individually or as a group, can be removed from the context of the wider Late Neolithic landscape that they occupy; a landscape of timber posts, stone settings and earthworks that was almost certainly more extensive than is apparent today. This included not only monumental sites such as the Durrington Walls henge less than a kilometre to the south, but also natural features such as the River Avon 300 m to the north-east, whose connections to Durrington Walls and, further downriver at the West Amesbury 'bluestonehenge' (Allen *et al.* 2016), to the Stonehenge Avenue, point to its own potent ritual significance. The piece of 'bluestone' found in a later ditch immediately adjacent to the intersection of the two posthole alignments (6260 and 6255) may be an indication of such a connection (although the possibility that it was a Romano-British trophy or memento curated from Stonehenge cannot be ruled out). It is likely that many elements of the natural landscape, including possibly solution hollows, were invested with symbolic and potentially religious meanings which influenced the types and locations of activities undertaken within and around them.

The orientation of the east–west posthole alignment (6260) matches that of the spur of slightly elevated ground (indicated by the 85 m OD contour), at the edge of the gently rising slope leading up from the Avon valley. Whether the topography was a consideration in establishing its position and alignment is hard to say, although it could have made it a more conspicuous feature in the landscape. It is reasonable to suggest that the north–south alignment continued north beyond its largest posthole (5074, 7.5 m from the northern edge of the excavation), although as this was the only posthole to the north of the east–west alignment, there is at least a case for suggesting that it might have marked the alignment's northern end.

The four radiocarbon dates obtained on oak sapwood from the two alignments (from postholes 5074, 5918, 6002 and 6882) suggest that both were constructed at roughly the same time, and therefore were probably intended to not only to display two orientations, but also their intersection. What their purpose was is unclear, although it is possible that part of their function was to mark routes through the landscape and/or some form of boundary. The east–west alignment, for example, appears to separate the area of pit digging to the south from the area to the north containing evidence for flint knapping at natural hollows – and cremation burial. Whatever their function, such constructions would inevitably have had some symbolic meaning, possibly related to ritual activity.

The radiocarbon dates from the oak sapwood charcoal provide a construction date for the post alignments during *2670–2550 cal BC ((86.6%) at 95% probability)*. This makes them roughly contemporary with the earlier activity during Stonehenge phase 2 (2620–2480 cal BC: Parker Pearson *et al.* 2013, 169) and pre-date the settlement and first phase of the Southern Circle within Durrington Walls (2490–2455 cal BC: Wainwright and Longworth, 1971, 23–38, 204–225; Parker Pearson *et al.* 2013, 169), and probably the raising of the five central trilithons and the surrounding circle of sarsens topped with interlinking lintels (Cleal *et al.* 1995, 524; Parker Pearson *et al.* 2007, 626).

The radiocarbon dates from animal bone (from postholes 5087, 6002, 6817 and 8074), which may provide a date for the decommissioning of the alignments, fall within the range of *2575–2470 cal BC (at 95% probability)*. A date range that is similar to Stonehenge phase 2 (sarsen settings: see above). This appears to have been, in part, a deliberate act involving the removal of some posts, the others possibly having already decayed *in situ*. There does not appear to have been any deliberate deposition of artefacts within the postholes during the alignments' construction, and it was only following their removal or decay that cultural material became incorporated with their postpipe fills and weathering cones, possibly all through natural processes with the material deriving from the surrounding ground surface. However, the occurrence of animal bones in the uppermost fills of some of the postholes, such as cattle scapula fragments in posthole 6817 and pig and cattle bones in postholes 6002 and 6733, could represent commemorative closing deposits as suggested, for example, for similar deposits in postholes at Durrington Walls (Parker Pearson *et al.* 2008, 162–3).

Also possibly related to the decommissioning of the post settings is the occurrence of sarsen in the upper fill of posthole 5074. It is unclear whether this stone had derived from original post packing or had been brought to the site from elsewhere. As noted by Harding and Ixer (see Chapter 6, above) the largest of the three pieces had probably derived from the breaking of a much bigger boulder. In addition, one surface of this stone had been modified and dressed, and it is further noted that one of the two sarsen flakes could have been used as a hammer/pecker possibly to dress sarsen. The absence of any sarsen debitage from the posthole precludes any *in situ* working or breaking. However, the character and date of this material is intriguing given that it is broadly contemporary with the sarsen phase at Stonehenge. It must be noted, however, that sarsen boulders were probably more widespread than they appear today.

The nature of any deposition in the postholes largely contrasts with that in the pits, some of which display evidence for the deliberate deposition of cultural material, including Grooved Ware pottery, worked flints, stone objects, fired clay, animal bone, and the charred remains of wild and cultivated plant foods. The variability in their (surviving) contents, however, suggests the act of a pit's digging may have been as significant as any act of deposition, although what their significance was remains a topic of extended discussion and speculation (eg, Richards and Thomas 1984; Thomas 1999; 2012; Garrow *et al.* 2006).

In the absence of radiocarbon dates from the pits, their chronological relationship to the post settings has not been established, although the occurrence in the upper posthole fills of pottery similar to that in the pits, and the spatial spread of the pits to the south of posthole alignment 6255, suggest that the pits could belong to a subsequent phase. In which case, they may well be relatively contemporary with the settlement activity at Durrington Walls that Parker Pearson *et al.* (2013, 169) place within the late 26th century to mid-25th century BC.

The potential symbolism of below-ground features, perhaps reflected in the digging of and deposition within pits, may have been more emphatically expressed in the activity associated with the two hollows. Although very different features, the recovery from both of them of large quantities of Neolithic flintworking debris may indicate some equivalence in their function and significance.

The smaller hollow is of uncertain origin but appears to have been little more than a shallow depression in the ground, perhaps made visible by different vegetation. However, it was clearly imbued with some significance, first by the mortuary deposit containing cremated human remains placed on its base, then by the episode of flint knapping probably in the immediate vicinity, the waste from which appears to have been deposited fresh into the hollow soon afterwards.

In contrast, the larger solution hollow would have been a very visible landscape feature, and one that is likely to have remained geologically 'active' during prehistory, its fill continuing to subside (even if imperceptibly) into the underlying solution shaft;

however, this makes it hard to establish how deep it was during the Late Neolithic. The potential symbolic significance of such a feature may well help explain why it became a focus of activity, of which the flint knapping may represent only one, and perhaps not the most important, element. As mentioned above, its significance may be reflected in the proximity of the intersection of the two posthole alignments.

The apparent deposition of flint gravel around the sloping edge of the hollow (and possibly further in towards the centre) may have been intended to both modify the feature's appearance and to create a surface on which specific activities could take place. This would have emphasised the significance of the natural geological feature, and turned it into a specifically cultural 'place', possibly one with ritual and religious significance.

Comparable evidence for prehistoric activity around a natural solution hollow was found at the Fir Tree Field Shaft on Cranborne Chase (Green 2007). This had a 10 m-diameter weathering cone at the top, above a narrower vertical shaft, the upper fills containing Beaker pottery, Peterborough Ware and Neolithic Plain Bowl pottery, above Mesolithic flintwork, indicating the longevity of the feature's use.

The most impressive below-ground feature in the Stonehenge landscape is the Wilsford Shaft, 5.5 km to the south-west of the site. The earliest radiocarbon date, both chronologically and stratigraphically, from the 30 m-deep shaft was a fragment of a wooden bucket that has been radiocarbon dated to 3650–3100 BC (OxA-1089; 4640±70 BP, at 95% confidence) (Ashbee *et al.* 1989), raising the possibility that it was constructed in the Early to Middle Neolithic, even though its main period of infilling was the Middle Bronze Age (Darvill 2005, 41).

The ritual significance of shafts in the Neolithic is further indicated by the Monkton Up Wimborne complex, on Cranborne Chase (Green 2000, fig. 52). This comprised a large circular feature, 10 m in diameter and 1.5 m deep, the Chalk natural in the base of which appeared to have been worn smooth by traffic. There was a 7 m-deep shaft on its south-eastern edge, and a grave, containing the multiple burial of four individuals, cut into its northern edge. The hollow was surrounded by a circle of 14 pits, which was passed, within 3 m, by a line of postholes.

The discovery of a Late Neolithic cremation burial (SUERC-49176: *2585–2465 cal BC at 95% probability*) within the complex of features at MOD Durrington once again highlights the importance of routinely radiocarbon dating such deposits, especially where no other cultural material is present. The only other known Late Neolithic cremation burial of this date from near the Durrington Walls complex is the one from Woodhenge (Parker Pearson *et al.* 2013, 168), which has a similar date range of 2580–

2470 BC. At least two other cremation-related deposits are known from Amesbury Down (Powell and Barclay forthcoming) and it is likely that further isolated examples will come to light through new fieldwork or by revisiting archives. There are a growing number of mid- to late Neolithic cremation burials now known from southern England and elsewhere (Willis *et al.* 2016; Powell *et al.* 2015). The discovery of burials away from enclosure cemeteries, such as Stonehenge, is significant as it supports the suggestion that cremation was practiced almost exclusively from the later 4th millennium until the first appearance of Beaker inhumations around the start of the 24th century BC.

Iron Age

By the end of the Iron Age a substantial defensive earthwork had been constructed across the site (see Chapter 4), but the evidence from the immediate area for the patterns of settlement and economic activity which preceded it is limited. Within the site itself this consists largely of a small number of Middle Iron Age cremation burials, and one Middle to Late Iron Age inhumation. The small quantity of Iron Age pottery (just 57 mostly residual sherds) suggests that there was no substantial settlement either on the site or within its immediate vicinity, and although it is possible that some of the undated ditches in the western part of Area 1 are of later prehistoric date, there is also no clear evidence for Iron Age agricultural activity – apart from isolated objects such as a dated horse bone from the solution hollow, and a hooked blade of suggested Iron Age date from an otherwise undated pit.

Similarly, little evidence was recovered from the small, poorly-dated Iron Age kite-shaped Packway enclosure, 600 m south of the site. Although fieldwalking along the flank of the valley has produced small quantities of Iron Age material (Fulford *et al.* 2006), and several Iron Age pits have been recorded both inside and south-west of Durrington Walls (Wainwright 1971), most of the evidence for this period comes from downland sites at higher elevations. Part of an Iron Age settlement has been identified at Larkhill (Matt Leivers pers. comm.), in excavations in advance of the Army Basing Programme, but this activity is similarly localised and small-scale.

There was an Early Iron Age open settlement on the downland south-east of Amesbury, with nearby inhumation burials, and a Middle Iron Age settlement on the adjacent Southmill Hill overlooking the valley (Powell and Barclay forthcoming). While the latter was enclosed by a ditch, it was not substantially defended, in contrast to a number of

Early–Middle Iron Age ditched enclosures which flank the valley, such as at High Post to the south (Powell 2011) and Widdington Farm and Chisenbury Field Barn to the north (Fulford *et al.* 2006).

This pattern of defended downland settlement is largely reflected in the locations of hillforts such as Old Sarum, Ogbury, Lidbury and Casterley Camp, although there is a notable exception in the form of the univallate 'hillfort' of Vespasian's Camp (Hunter-Mann 1999; Jacques *et al.* 2010; Jacques and Phillips 2014, 8), 3 km to the south of the site (Figs 1.1, 1.2). Although this occupies a Chalk ridge up to 45 m above the valley floor, lengths of its rampart on its eastern and southern sides flank the riverbank at the western end of a long eastward meander.

The river clearly remained a feature of considerable and probably strategic importance, with the Avon valley possibly forming part of a major trade route from Hengistbury Head via the Vale of Pewsey to a major Late Iron Age complex near Marlborough (McOmish *et al.* 2002, 86). The Avon is one of a number of major river valleys in Wessex which appears to have acted as foci for hillfort construction (Corney and Payne 2006, 134), and this may have been replicated, by the end of the Iron Age, by the locations of the 'valley fort' at Figheldean, 2 km north of Durrington (Graham and Newman 1993; McKinley 1999) (Fig. 1.2). Many of the settlements on the higher plain appear to have declined and been abandoned towards the end of the Iron Age, a process which may have been mirrored in the developments in the valleys (Fulford *et al.* 2006, 199), with natural features such as rivers and marsh being incorporated into their defences (Harding 1974, 74).

The scale of the Late Iron Age ditch (and suggested bank) at MOD Durrington indicates that the earthwork almost certainly had a defensive purpose, although without further information about its course beyond the site, it is not clear precisely what it was defending. It lies at least 270 m south-west of the outward curve of a large meander in the River Avon, crossing the low spur of ground running from the west. Whether it defined an enclosure, such as that at Figheldean, or represents some other form of more extensive land boundary, has yet to be determined. The Figheldean enclosure, which covered some 8 ha, has been subject to limited excavation along two pipeline trenches, although its full extent has been indicated by a combination of cropmark and geophysical survey (McKinley 1999, fig. 2).

There are a number of similarities between the two sites, not least their valley locations, both lying on the west side of the river at the point of a pronounced outward curve. The Figheldean enclosure had at least two entrances – an in-turned entrance to the west, facing towards the adjacent downland, and one to south pointing down the valley; there may have been another at the north. It may be comparable with a number of 'valley forts' in the middle and upper Thames valley, such as Dyke Hills, Dorchester-on-Thames (Cook 1985) and Cassington Mill, Oxfordshire (Sutton 1966).

The irregular and rather angular line of ditch 6203 is comparable to the western side of the Figheldean enclosure, which McOmish suggested (2002, 83) may have been due to the presence of a pre-existing field system, as was perhaps also the case at Coombe Down, although there was no conclusive evidence for such at this site.

Apart from a small number of pieces of Late Iron Age metalwork and a Durotrigian coin, there was little direct evidence at Figheldean for Late Iron Age occupation, and the cropmarks of possible round-houses could equally be of early Romano-British date. Moreover, the limited extent of its excavation means that the nature of its occupation before the Romano-British period remains uncertain. As at MOD Durrington, the Figheldean ditch, which was up to 7 m wide and 3 m deep and contained only a few sherds of Late Iron Age pottery, appears to have been deliberately infilled with bank material relatively soon after the Roman Conquest, with early Romano-British features cutting the uppermost ditch fill (Graham and Newman 1993, 13–16; McKinley 1999, 30).

One potentially interesting feature of the Figheldean enclosure was the ditch's encompassing, at the south-east, of part of a small round barrow cemetery; at least two of the ring ditches lie within the enclosure, just inside its southern entrance, with one of them appearing to have been enclosed by a small internal plot abutting the enclosure ditch. Whether the incorporation of these two earlier monuments within the enclosure had some deliberate symbolic significance is uncertain, but locations in the landscape may have had long histories, and the enduring replication of patterns of landuse, such as the shared orientations of the Neolithic post alignment and the Late Iron Age ditch (as well as, later, the Romano-British field system) cannot be ruled out.

Romano-British and post-Roman

Given the uncertainty about the nature of the boundary represented by the Late Iron Age 'enclosure' ditch, it is also unclear why the 'enclosure interior' should have become the focus for concentrated activity during the Romano-British period. The ditch appears to have been infilled relatively soon after the Conquest, any defensive

function no longer either required or appropriate in the new political climate. Yet its former line appears to have continued to largely define the southern limit of the later activity.

What seems likely, however, is that there was, in some respects, a substantial degree of continuity from the Late Iron Age into the early Romano-British period. While the dearth of evidence for Late Iron Age activity may indicate that settlement was initially located beyond the site to the north, perhaps closer to the river – the Figheldean enclosure was clearly positioned to dominate the river landscape, and the same may have been the case here – the early Romano-British period saw a rapid expansion of activity up to the boundary of the former site.

It is notable that the main WNW–ESE axis of the Romano-British field system matches approximately the general line within the site of the Iron Age enclosure ditch, both of which follow the line of the low ridge of slightly raised ground that extends into the wide, eastward loop of the River Avon. The Romano-British trackway which crossed the infilled ditch runs from the south, aligned approximately on the narrow gap between Durrington Walls and the river.

The location of settlement structures associated with the Romano-British features was not identified within the site, although it is possible that timber buildings of sleeper-beam construction were present but did not leave identifiable remains. The presence of storage pits, and the large quantities of domestic and agricultural waste suggests that the settlement may have lain immediately north of the site.

Geophysical and air photographic surveys of the Figheldean enclosure show its interior to have been densely occupied with (in addition to the earlier round barrows) numerous circular structures, probably roundhouses of Late Iron Age and/or Romano-British date, lengths of ditch defining small internal plots and possible trackways, and probable pits (McOmish et al. 2002, fig. 3.31). As at MOD Durrington, these features appear to have not extended south beyond the enclosure boundary. Near the centre of the Figheldean enclosure was a small corridor villa, and in the north-east corner a small polygonal enclosure, possibly a shrine (ibid., 83). The recovery from MOD Durrington of fragments of painted wall plaster and several fragments of a Portland Limestone roofing tile provide limited evidence for a substantial building possibly within that 'enclosure' too, while the overall scarcity of identifiable building materials may simply reflect the 'settlement edge' nature of the activity on the site. However, the restricted range of the metalwork finds, which included no high quality items, and the general character of the wider finds assemblage, comprising objects of domestic, agricultural/horticultural and craft/industrial use, suggest that the settlement may not have been of particularly high status.

Nonetheless, the range of features does suggest a substantial agriculturally based community, accessed via a maintained metalled trackway. The arable economy was based around the cultivation of hulled wheat (mostly spelt with some emmer) and barley, with the ovens used for different stages of crop processing. These were relatively insubstantial features compared to the stone-built corn driers found for example at Durrington Walls (Wainwright 1971), Butterfield Down (Rawlings and Fitzpatrick 1996) and High Post (Powell 2011). A range of soils appear to have been cultivated, as indicated by the charred weed seeds, including heavy clay soils, lighter sandier soils and dry calcareous soils, reflecting the varied geology along and flanking the valley floor. The pastoral economy was based largely on sheep-farming, the animals managed mainly for meat but also wool, with cattle also reared mainly for dairy and other secondary products, and probably traction.

In addition to mixed agricultural production and processing, economic activity included on-site pottery manufacture – perhaps by an itinerant potter – and other small-scale craft/industrial activities. These activities appear to have been zoned within an arrangement of field and other plots, the main framework of which appears to have undergone little change during the Romano-British period. Different broad areas of the site areas were devoted to extraction, storage and, activities using fire for drying/curing/smoking etc and pottery production. The two inhumation burials may have been made on or towards the settlements boundaries, at a distance from but potentially in sight of their homes.

The continued occupation of two formerly defended Late Iron Age sites during the early Romano-British period points to the continuing importance of the Avon valley. It appears to have been the focus of settlements which, while relatively small in size compared to the new and more extensive 'villages' on the high downland, appear to have been of generally higher status. There is widespread evidence for settlement on the downs flanking the valley, such as south-west of Durrington Walls (Wainwright 1971), and east and south-east of Amesbury, including multiple cemeteries on Amesbury Down (Rawlings and Fitzpatrick, 1996; McKinley et al. in prep.).

Settlements along the valley include a number of other possible villa sites, such as at Nethavon, Enford Farm and Littlecott (Fulford et al. 2006, 203), and these would have required a road to serve them. Although the course of the Roman road between Sorviodunum (Old Sarum) and Cunetio (Mildenhall, near Marlborough) is largely conjectural, it is thought to cross the downs on the east side of the Avon valley (McOmish et al. 2002, 207). However, this would have been a primarily military road, and the Avon valley may still have been an important trade and communication route serving the surrounding landscape.

The excavation provided little evidence for activity in the post-Roman period, with the later organisation of landscape largely determined by the pattern of settlement and landuse established in the Saxon period, with its two manors – East End and West End – each with a main north–south street and village church. The area appears to have remained as agricultural land through the medieval, post-medieval and modern periods, the few features – ditches and pits (including animal burials) – being concentrated at the east end of the site, probably related to properties along High Street. By the time of the 1839 tithe map these included Red House and the mid-18th-century Parsonage Homestead (later Parsonage Farm), with agricultural plots extending to their west. Parts of the site were purchased by the War Department in 1899 and 1902, with Red House being adopted as the Estate offices in c. 1920. By 1992 the Ministry of Defence owned nearly all the land, the presence of the military stimulating growth of the village in the 20th century.

Bibliography

Adams, J C 1987 *Outline of Fractures.* London, Churchill Livingstone

Adkins, L and Adkins, R A 1985 Neolithic axes from *Roman sites in Britain,* Oxford J Archaeol 4(1), 69–75

Albarella, U and Searjeantson, D 2002 A passion for pork: meat consumption at the British Late Neolithic site of Durrington Walls, in P Miracle and N Milner (eds) *Consuming Passions and Patterns of Consumption,* 33–49. Cambridge, McDonald Institute for Archaeological Research

Allen, M J, Chan, B, Cleal, R, French, C, Marshall, P, Pollard, J, Pullen, R, Richards, C, Ruggles, C, Robinson, D, Rylatt, J, Thomas, J, Welham, K and Parker Pearson, M 2016 Stonehenge's Avenue and 'Bluestonehenge', *Antiquity* 90(352), 991–1008

Allen, S J and Every, R 2006 Worked bone, in Fulford *et al.* 2006, 139

Allen, S J and Seager Smith, R H 2006, in Fulford *et al.* 2006, 121–3

Anderson, A S 1979 *The Roman Pottery Industry in North Wiltshire.* Swindon, Swindon Archaeol Soc Rep 2

Anderson, A S 1980 Romano-British pottery kilns at Purton, *Wilts Archaeol Natur Hist Mag* 72/73 (for 1977/1978), 51–8

Andrews, P 2009 Slag, in J Wright, M Leivers, R Seager Smith and C J Stevens *Cambourne New Settlement: Iron Age and Romano-British settlement on the clay uplands of west Cambridgeshire,* specialist appendices (volume 2: CD). Salisbury, Wessex Archaeology Rep 23

Anon. 2016 Britain in archaeology [Bulford and Tidworth], *British Archaeology* 149, 10

Anon. 2017 The Larkhill causewayed enclosure: rethinking the Early Neolithic Stonehenge landscape, *Current Archaeology* 326, 30–4

Ashbee, P, Bell, M and Proudfoot, E 1989 *Wilsford Shaft excavations, 1960-62.* London, English Heritage Archaeol Rep 11

Aufderheide, A C and Rodriguez-Martin, C 1998 *The Cambridge Encyclopaedia of Human Palaeopathology.* Cambridge, Cambridge Univ Press

Bass, W M 1987 *Human Osteology.* Columbia (MO), Missouri Archaeological Society

Bayley, J and Butcher, S 2004 *Roman Brooches in Britain: a technological and typological study based on the Richborough Collection.* London, Soc Antiq London

Bayley, J, Dungworth, D and Paynter, S 2001 *Archaeometallurgy.* Swindon, English Heritage Centre for Archaeology Guidelines 1

Beek, G C van, 1983 *Dental Morphology: an illustrated guide.* Bristol, Wright PSG

Berry, A C and Berry, R J 1967 Epigenetic variation in the human cranium, *J Anatomy* 101(2), 261–379

Boessneck, J 1969 Osteological differences between sheep (*Ovis aries*) and goat (*Capra hircus*), in D Brothwell and E S Higgs (eds) *Science in Archaeology* (2nd edition), 331–58. London, Thames & Hudson

Boessneck, J, von den Driesch, A, Meyer-Lempennau, U and Weschler-von Ohlen, E 1971 *Das Tierknochenfunde aus dem Oppidum von Manching. Die Ausgrabungen in Manching* 6. Wiesbaden

Boisseau, S and Yalden, D 1998 The former status of the crane *Grus grus* in Britain, *Ibis* 140, 482–500

Booth, A St J and Stone, J F S 1952 A trial flint mine at Durrington, Wiltshire, *Wiltshire Archaeol Natur Hist Mag* 54, 381–8

Bond, J M and O'Connor, T P 1999 *Bones from Medieval Deposits at 16–22 Coppergate and Other Sites in York.* London, CBA, The Archaeology of York 15/5

Bourdillon, J and Coy, J 1980 The animal bones, in P Holdsworth *Excavations at Melbourne Street, Southampton, 1971–76,* 79–121. London, CBA Res Rep 33

Bowen, H C and Smith, I F 1977 Sarsen stones in Wessex: The Society's first investigations in the Evolution of the Landscape Project, *Antiq J* 57(2), 185–96

British Geological Survey, *Geology of Britain Viewer* http://mapapps.bgs.ac.uk/geologyofbritain/home.html [accessed 14 September 2017]

Bronk Ramsey, C and Lee, S, 2013 Recent and planned developments of the Program OxCal, *Radiocarbon* 55 (2–3), 720–30

Brothwell, D R 1972 *Digging Up Bones: the excavation, treatment, and study of human skeletal remains.* London, British Museum (Natur Hist)

Brothwell, D R and Zakrzewski, S 2004 Metric and non-metric studies of archaeological human remains, in M Brickley and J I McKinley (eds) *Guidelines to the Standards for Recording Human Remains*, 24–30. Southampton/Reading, British Association for Biological Anthropology and Osteoarchaeology/Institute of Field Archaeologists

Brown, L 1984 Objects of stone, in B Cunliffe *Danebury: an Iron Age hillfort in Hampshire, Volume 2. The Excavations 1969–1978: the finds*, 407–25. London, CBA Res Rep 52

Buikstra, J E and Ubelaker, D H 1994 *Standards for Data Collection from Human Skeletal Remains*. Fayetteville (AR), Arkansas Archaeol Surv Res Ser 44

Butcher, S 2001 The brooches, in A S Anderson, J S Wacher and A P Fitzpatrick *The Romano-British 'Small Town' at Wanborough, Wiltshire*, 41–69. London, Britannia Monogr 19

Carruthers, W J 1990 Plant and molluscan remains, in Richards 1990, 250–52

Challinor, D 2009 The wood charcoal, in K Powell, G Laws and L Brown, A Late Neolithic/Early Bronze Age enclosure and Iron Age and Romano-British settlement at Latton Lands, Wiltshire, *Wiltshire Archaeol Natur Hist Mag* 102, 22–113

Charlier, P 2012 Toilet hygiene in the classical era, *British Medical J* 345, e8287

Clark, J G D 1928 Discoidal polished flint knives – their typology and distribution, *Proc Prehist Soc E Anglia* 6, 41–54

Clark, J G D 1934 The classification of a microlithic culture: the Tardenoisian of Horsham, *Archaeol J* 90, 52–77

Clark, J G D 1935 Derivative forms of the petit tranchet in Britain, *Archaeol J* 91, 32–58

Cleal, R M J 1995 Pottery fabrics in Wessex in the fourth to second millennia BC, in I Kinnes and G Varndell (eds) *'Unbaked Urnes of Rudely Shape': essays on British and Irish pottery for Ian Longworth*, 185–94. Oxford, Oxbow Books

Cleal, R M J 1999 Introduction: The What, Where, When and Why of Grooved Ware, in R Cleal and A MacSween *Grooved Ware in Britain and Ireland*. Neolithic Studies Group Seminar Papers 3, 1–8. Oxford, Oxbow Books

Cleal, R M J Walker, K E and Montague, R 1995 *Stonehenge in its Landscape: twentieth-century excavations*. London, English Heritage Archaeol Rep 10

Cohen, A and Serjeantson, D 1996 *A Manual for the Identification of Bird Bones from Archaeological Sites*. London, Archetype Publications Ltd

Cook, J 1985 Before the Roman Conquest, in L Cook and T Rowley *Dorchester through the Ages*.

Oxford, Oxford University Dept for External Studies

Corney, M and Payne, A 2006 The regional pattern, in A Payne M Corney and B Cunliffe *The Wessex Hillforts Project: extensive survey of hillforts interiors in central southern England*, 131–50. London, English Heritage

Corney, M, Charlton, M and Morris, N 2014 A Romano-British pottery production centre at Short Street, Westbury, Wiltshire, *Wiltshire Archaeol Natur Hist Mag* 107, 66–76

Crummy, N and Eckardt, H 2003 Regional identities and technologies of the self: nail-cleaners in Roman Britain, *Archaeol. J.* 160, 44–69

Cunliffe, B W 1975 *Excavations at Porchester Castle, Volume I: Roman*. London, Rep Res Comm Soc Antiq London 32

Cunliffe, B W 1991 *Iron Age Communities in Britain: an account of England, Scotland and Wales from the seventh century BC until the Roman conquest* (3rd edition). London, Routledge & Kegan Paul

Cunnington, M E 1929 *Woodhenge*. Devizes, G Simpson & Co.

Curwen, C 1937 Querns, *Antiquity* 11, 133–51

Darvill, T 2005 *Stonehenge World Heritage Site: an archaeological research framework*. London and Bournemouth, English Heritage and Bournemouth University

Darvill, T and Wainwright, G 2009 Stonehenge excavations 2008, *Antiq J* 89, 1–20

Davies, S M 1990 Pottery, (30–45) in P A Rahtz, Bower Chalk 1959: excavations at Great Ditch Bank and Middle Chase Ditch, *Wiltshire Archaeol Natur Hist Mag* 83, 1–49

Dobney, K 2001 A place at the table: the role of vertebrate zooarchaeology within a Roman research agenda, in S James and M Millet, *Britons and Romans: advancing an archaeological agenda*, 36–45. York, CBA Res Rep 125

Dobney, K, Jacques, D and Irving, B 1996 *Of Butchery and Breeds: report on the vertebrate remains from various sites in the City of Lincoln*. Lincoln. Lincoln Archaeol Studies 5

Dobney, K, Jaques, D, Barrett, J and Johnstone, C 2007 *Farmers, Monks and Aristocrats: the environmental archaeology of Anglo-Saxon Flixborough*. Oxford, Oxbow Books, Excavations at Flixborough, Volume 3

Ede, J 1993 Carbonised seed remains, in Graham and Newman 1993, 42–5

Egerton, J 1996 Animal bones, in Rawlings and Fitzpatrick 1996, 35–6

Field, D and McOmish, D 2017 *The Making of Prehistoric Wiltshire*. Stroud, Amberley Publishing

Finnegan, M 1978 Non-metric variations of the infracranial skeleton, *J Anatomy* 125(1), 23–37

Fulford, M G 1975 *New Forest Roman Pottery.* Oxford, BAR 17

Fulford, M G and Timby, J 2001 Ritual piercings? A consideration of deliberately 'holed' pots from Silchester and elsewhere, *Britannia* 32, 293–7

Fulford, M G, Powell, A B, Entwistle, R and Raymond, F 2006 *Iron Age and Romano-British Settlements and Landscapes of Salisbury Plain.* Salisbury, Wessex Archaeology and University of Reading, Wessex Archaeology Rep 20

Gale, R 1997 Charcoal, in A P Fitzpatrick *Archaeological Excavations on the Route of the A27 Westhampnett Bypass, West Sussex, 1992,* 253. Salisbury, Wessex Archaeology Rep 12

Gale, R and Cutler, D 2000 *Plants in Archaeology: identification manual of vegetative plant materials used in Europe and the southern Mediterranean to c. 1500.* Otley, Westbury Publishing and the Royal Botanic Gardens, Kew

Gardiner, J 2008 On the production of discoidal flint knives and changing patterns of specialist flint procurement in the Neolithic on the South Downs, England, in H Fokkens, B J Coles, A L van Gijn, J P Kleijne, H H Ponjee and C G Slappendel (eds) *Between Foraging and Farming: an extended broad spectrum of papers presented to Leendert Louwe Kooijmans,* 235–46. Leiden University Faculty of Archaeology

Garrow, D, Lucy, S and Gibson, D 2006 *Excavations at Kilverstone, Norfolk: an episodic landscape history.* Cambridge, East Anglian Archaeol Rep 113

Gejvall, N G 1981 Determination of burnt bones from prehistoric graves, *OSSA Letters* 2, 1–13

Gerrard, J 2010 Finding the fifth century: a late fourth- and early fifth-century pottery fabric from south-east Dorset, *Britannia* 41, 293–312

Gillings, M, Pollard, J, Wheatley, D and Peterson, R 2008 *Landscape of the Megaliths: excavation and fieldwork on the Avebury monuments, 1997–2003.* Oxford, Oxbow Books

Gingell, C 1992 *The Marlborough Downs: a later Bronze Age landscape and its origins.* Devizes, Wiltshire Archaeol Natur Hist Soc Monogr 1

Graham, A and Newman, C 1993 Recent excavations of Iron Age and Roman-British enclosures in the Avon valley, *Wiltshire Archaeol Natur Hist Mag* 86, 8–57

Grant, A 1982 The use of tooth-wear as a guide to the age of domestic animals, in B Wilson, C Grigson and S Payne (eds) *Ageing and Sexing Animal Bones from Archaeological Sites,* 91–108. Oxford, BAR 109

Green, M 2000 *A Landscape Revealed: 10,000 years on a chalkland farm.* Stroud, Tempus

Green, M 2007 Fir Tree Field shaft, in C French, H Lewis, M J Allen, M Green, R Scaife and J Gardiner *Prehistoric Landscape Development and Human Impact in the Upper Allen Valley, Cranborne Chase,* Dorset, 76–81. Cambridge, McDonald Institute for Archaeological Research

Greig, J R A 1991 The British Isles, in W Van Zeist, K Wasylikowa and K-E Behre (eds) *Progress in Old World Palaeoethnobotany,* 299–334. Rotterdam, Balkema

Grime, J P, Hodgson, J G and Hunt, R 1988 *Comparative Plant Ecology: a functional approach to common British species.* London, Unwin Hyman

Guido, M 1978 *The Glass Beads of the Prehistoric and Roman Periods in Britain and Ireland.* London, Res Rep Comm Soc Antiq London 35

Halstead, P 1985 A study of mandibular teeth from Romano-British contexts at Maxey, in F Pryor and C French *Archaeology and Environment in the Lower Welland Valley, Volume 1,* 219–24. Cambridge, East Anglian Archaeol Rep 27

Halstead, P, Collins, P and Isaakidou, V 2002 Sorting the sheep from the goats: morphological distinctions between the mandibular teeth of adult *Ovis* and *Capra,* *J Archaeol Sci* 29(5), 545–53

Hambleton, E 1999 *Animal Husbandry Regimes in Iron Age Britain: a comparative study of faunal assemblages from British archaeological sites.* Oxford, BAR 282

Hambleton, E and Maltby, M 2008 Faunal remains, in C Ellis and A B Powell *An Iron Age Settlement outside Battlesbury Hillfort, Warminster, and Sites along the Southern Range Road,* 84–93. Salisbury, Wessex Archaeology Rep 22

Harding, D W 1974 *The Iron Age in Lowland Britain* (2015 edition), Routledge & Kegan Paul, London

Harding, P 1992 The flint, in Gingell 1992, 123–33

Harding, P 1995 Flint, in Cleal *et al.* 1995, 368–75

Harding, P n.d. *Worked Flint, Sarsen and Bluestone.* Unpub specialist report of excavations at Stonehenge 2008

Harding, P and Leivers, M forthcoming The worked flint, in Powell and Barclay forthcoming

Hather, J G 2000 *The Identification of Northern European Wood a guide for archaeologists and conservators.* London, Archetype Publications

Higbee, L 2011 Animal bone, in Powell *An Iron Age Enclosure and Romano-British Features at High Post, near Salisbury,* 70–8. Salisbury, Wessex Archaeology

Higbee, L forthcoming Animal bone, in Powell and Barclay forthcoming

Hillman, G C 1981 Reconstructing crop husbandry practices from charred remains of crops, in R J Mercer (ed.) *Farming Practice in British Prehistory*, 123–62. Edinburgh, Edinburgh Univ Press

Hillman, G 1984 Interpretation of archaeological plant remains; the application of ethnographic models from Turkey, in W van Zeist and W A Casparie (eds) *Plants and Ancient man: studies in the palaeoethnobotany*, Proceedings of the 6th symposium of the international work group for Palaeobotanists, 1–42. Rotterdam, Balkema

Hillson, S W 1979 Diet and dental disease, *World Archaeol* 11, 147–62

Hillson, S W 1986 *Teeth*. Cambridge, Cambridge Univ Press

Hinton, P 1999 Charred plant remains, in McKinley 1999, 7–32

Holden, J L, Phakley, P P and Clement, J G 1995a Scanning electron microscope observations of incinerated human femoral bone: a case study, *Forensic Science International* 74, 17–28

Holden, J L, Phakley, P P and Clement, J G 1995b Scanning electron microscope observations of heat-treated human bone, *Forensic Science International* 74, 29–45

Hopkins, R W 1999 *Savernake Ware: a reassessment of the evidence*. Unpubl undergraduate dissertation, University of Bristol

Howard, H 1982 A petrological study of the rock specimens from excavations at Stonehenge, 1979–1980, in Pitts 1982, 104–24

Hunter-Mann, K 1999 Excavations and Vespasian's Camp Iron Age hillfort, *Wiltshire Archaeol Natur Hist Mag* 92, 39–52

Hutcheson, A 1999 Metalwork, in McKinley 1999, 20

Ixer, R and Bevins, R 2011 Craig Rhos-y-felin, Pont Saeson is the dominant source of the Stonehenge rhyolitic 'debitage', *Archaeology in Wales* 50, 21–31

Ixer, R and Bevins, R 2013 Chips off the old block: the Stonehenge debitage dilemma, *Archaeology in Wales* 52, 11–22

Ixer, R and Bevins, R forthcoming Chapter 10. Petrography of bluestones and other lithics, in M Parker Pearson, J Pollard, C Richards, J Thomas, and K Welham *Stonehenge for the Ancestors: the Stonehenge Riverside Project Volume 1*. London, Prehistoric Society

Jackson, R 1988 *Doctors and Disease in the Roman Empire*. London, British Museum Press

Jacques, D, Phillips, T, and Clarke, M 2010 A reassessment of the importance of Vespasian's Camp in the Stonehenge landscape, *PAST* 66, 11–13

Jacques, D and Phillips, T 2014 Mesolithic settlement near Stonehenge: excavations at Blick Mead, Vespasian's Camp, Amesbury, *Wiltshire Archaeol Natur Hist Mag* 107, 7–27

Jarvis, M G, Allen, R H, Fordman, S J, Hazelden J, Moffat, A J and Sturdy, R G 1984 *Soils and Their Use in South East England*. Harpenden, Soil Survey of England and Wales Bulletin 15

Jones, G P 2011 Pottery, in Powell 2011, 47–62

Jones, M K 1981 The development of crop husbandry, in M K Jones and G Dimbleby (eds) *The Environment of Man: the Iron Age to the Anglo-Saxon period*, 95–127. Oxford, BAR 87

Judd, J W 1902 Note on the nature and origin of the rock-fragments found in the excavations made at Stonehenge by Mr Gowland in 1901, *Archaeologia* 58, 106–18

King, A 2005. Animal remains from temples in Roman Britain, *Britannia* 36, 329–69

King N E 1968 The Kennet valley sarsen industry. *Wiltshire Archaeol Natur Hist Mag* 63, 83–93

Lauwerier, R C G M 1988 *Animals in Roman times in the Dutch Eastern River Area*. Nederlanse Oudheden 12/Projest Oostelijk Rivierengebied 1

Lawson, A J 2007 *Chalkland: an archaeology of Stonehenge and its region*. Salisbury, Hobnob Press

Leary, J and Field, D 2013 Ways of understanding prehistoric Silbury Hill, in J Leary, D Field and G Campbell (eds) *Silbury Hill: the largest prehistoric mound in Europe*, 203–22. Swindon, English Heritage

Leivers, M 2017 Robin Hood's other ball? A newly discovered causewayed enclosure at Larkhill, Wiltshire, *PAST* 85, 12–13

Leivers, M forthcoming Worked flint, in A B Powell, Prehistoric deposition, burial and settlement on Salisbury Plain: archaeological investigations along the new military tracks, 2009–12, *Wiltshire Archaeol Natur Hist Mag*

Levine, M 1982 The use of crown height measurements and eruption wear sequences to age horse teeth, in B Wilson, C Grigson and S Payne (eds) *Ageing and Sexing Animal Bones from Archaeological Sites*, 223–50. Oxford, BAR 109

Longworth, 1 1971 The Neolithic pottery in Wainwright and Longworth 1971, 48–155

Longworth, I and Cleal, R 1999 Grooved Ware gazetteer in R Cleal and A MacSween (eds) *Grooved Ware in Britain and Ireland*, 177–206. Oxford, Oxbow Books, Neolithic Studies Group Seminar Papers 3

LRBC = Carson, R A G, Hill, R V and Kent, J P C 1989 *Late Roman Bronze Coinage*, London, Spink

Lyne, M A B, and Jefferies, R S 1979 *The Alice Holt/Farnham Roman Pottery Industry*. London, CBA Res Rep 30

Lyne, M A B 2012 *Archaeological Research in Binstead, Kingsley and Alice Holt Forest, Hampshire*. Oxford, BAR 574

Manchester, K 1983 *The Archaeology of Disease*. Bradford, Bradford Univ Press

Manning, W H 1985 *Catalogue of Romano-British Iron Tools, Fittings and Weapons in the British Museum*. London, British Museum

McKinley, J I 1993a *Human Remains for the Romano-British Area 15 Cemetery, Baldock*. Unpubl report for Letchworth Museum

McKinley, J I 1993b Bone fragment size and weights of bone from modern British cremations and its implications for the interpretation of archaeological cremations, *Int J Osteoarchaeol* 3, 283–7

McKinley, J I 1994a *The Anglo-Saxon Cemetery at Spong Hill, North Elmham. Part 8, The Cremations*. Dereham, East Anglian Archaeol 69

McKinley, J I 1994b Bone fragment size in British cremation burials and its implications for pyre technology and ritual, *J Archaeol Sci* 21, 339–42

McKinley, J I 1995 Human bone, in Cleal *et al*. 1995, 451–61

McKinley, J I 1997 The cremated human bone from burial and cremation-related contexts, in A P Fitzpatrick *Archaeological Excavations on the Route of the A27 Westhampnett Bypass, West Sussex, 1992 Volume 2*, 55–72. Salisbury, Wessex Archaeology Rep 12

McKinley, J I 1999 Further excavations of an Iron Age and Romano-British enclosed settlement at Figheldean, near Netheravon, *Wiltshire Archaeol Natur Hist Mag* 92, 7–32

McKinley, J I 2004a Compiling a skeletal inventory: cremated human bone, in M Brickley and J I McKinley (eds) *Guidelines to the Standards for Recording Human Remains*, 9–12. Southampton/Reading, British Association for Biological Anthropology and Osteoarchaeology/Institute of Field Archaeologists

McKinley, J I 2004b Compiling a skeletal inventory: disarticulated and co-mingled remains, in M Brickley and J I McKinley (eds) *Guidelines to the Standards for Recording Human Remains*, 13–16. Southampton/Reading, British Association for Biological Anthropology and Osteoarchaeology/ Institute of Field Archaeologists

McKinley, J I 2004c The human remains and aspects of pyre technology and cremation rituals, in H E M Cool *The Roman Cemetery at Brougham Cumbria: excavations 1966–67*, 283–309. London, Britannia Monogr 21

McKinley, J I 2004d The cremated bone, 97–103 in V Birbeck and C Moore, Preservation and investigation of Roman and medieval remains at

Hyde Street, Winchester, *Proc Hampshire Fld Club Archaeol Soc* 59, 77–110

McKinley, J I 2006a Human remains from Section 1 of the Channel Tunnel Rail Link, Kent, in *CTRL Scheme-wide Specialist Report Series*. Archaeology Data Service, CTRL digital archive: http://archaeologydataservice.ac.uk/archives/view/ctrl/

McKinley, J I 2006b Cremation ... the cheap option? in C Knusel and R Gowland (eds) *The Social Archaeology of Funerary Remains*, 81–8. Oxford, Oxbow Books

McKinley, J I 2006c Human bone, in A M Chadwick (ed.) Bronze Age burials and settlement and an Anglo-Saxon settlement at Clay Pit Lane, Westhampnett, West Sussex, *Sussex Archaeol Collect* 144, 7–50

McKinley, J I 2008 In the heat of the pyre: efficiency of oxidation in Romano-British cremations – did it really matter? in C A Schmidt and S Sims (eds) *Beyond Recognition: the analysis of burned human remains*, 163–84. Oxford, Levier

McKinley, J I 2009 Human bone, 20–32 in P Andrews, West Thurrock: late prehistoric settlement, Roman burials and the medieval manor house. Channel Tunnel Rail Link Excavations 2002, *Essex Archaeol Hist* 40, 1–77

McKinley, J I 2012 Cremated bone, in J I McKinley and K Egging Dinwiddy *East Kent Access Road (EKAR): human bone*. Unpubl report for Oxford Wessex Archaeology

McKinley, J I 2013a Cremation: excavation, analysis and interpretation of material from cremation-related contexts, in S Tarlow and L Nilsson Stutz *The Oxford Handbook of The Archaeology of Death and Burial*, 147–71. Oxford, Oxford Univ Press

McKinley, J I 2013b *Aldham Mill Hill, Suffolk: cremated bone and mortuary rite*. Unpubl report for Suffolk Archaeological Unit

McKinley, J I 2015 The cremated human bone, in A B Powell *Archaeological Discoveries along the Farningham to Hadlow Gas Pipeline, Kent*. Kent Archaeol Soc eArchaeological report

McKinley, J I, Smith, P and Fitzpatrick, A P 1995 Animal bone from burials and other cremation-related contexts, in A P Fitzpatrick *Archaeological Excavations on the Route of the A27 Westhampnett Bypass, West Sussex, 1992 Volume 2*, 73–7. Salisbury, Wessex Archaeology Rep 12

McOmish, D, Field, D and Brown, G 2002 *The Field Archaeology of the Salisbury Plain Training Area*. Swindon, English Heritage

Mepham, L N 1993 The pottery; The fired clay; The metal objects; The stone, in Graham and Newman 1993, 25–36

Mepham, L N 1997 Iron Age and Romano-British pottery, in I Barnes, C A Butterworth, J W Hawkes and L Smith *Excavations at Thames Valley Park, Reading, 1986–88: prehistoric and Romano-British occupation of the floodplain and a terrace of the River Thames*, 48–66. Salisbury, Wessex Archaeology Rep 14

Mepham, L N 1998 The Pottery, (22–3) in A P Fitzpatrick and A D Crockett, A Romano-British settlement and inhumation cemetery at Eyewell Farm, Chilmark, *Wiltshire Archaeol Natur Hist Mag* 91, 11–33

Mepham, L N 1999 Pottery, in McKinley 1999, 21–3

Mepham, L N 2011 Saxon pottery, in Powell 2011, 62

Millard, J I 1996 The other pottery, in Rawlings and Fitzpatrick, 1996, 27–34

Moffett, L, Robinson, M A and Straker, S 1989 Cereals, fruit and nuts: charred plant remains from Neolithic sites in England and Wales and the Neolithic economy, in A Milles, D Williams and N Gardner (eds) *The Beginnings of Agriculture*, 243–61. Oxford, BAR Int Ser 496

Molleson, T I 1993 The human remains, in D E Farwell and T I Molleson *Poundbury Volume 2: the cemeteries*, 142–214. Dorchester, Dorset Natur Hist Archaeol Soc Monogr 11

Montague, R 1995 Stone, in Cleal *et al.* 1995, 375–90

Mook, W G, 1986 Business Meeting: recommendations/resolutions adopted by the twelfth international radiocarbon conference, *Radiocarbon* 28, 799

Newcomer, M H and Karlin, C 1987 Flint chips from Pincevent, in M H Newcomer and G de G Sieveking (eds) *The Human Uses of Flint and Chert*, Proceedings of the Fourth International Flint Symposium held at Brighton Polytechnic, 33–6. Cambridge, Cambridge Univ Press

Nielsen-Marsh, C, Gernaey, A, Turner-Walker, G, Hedges, R, Pike, A and Collins, M 2000 The chemical degradation of bone, in M Cox and S Mays (eds) *Human Osteology in Archaeology and Forensic Science*, 439–54. London, Greenwich Media Medical

O'Connor, T P 1989 *Bones from Anglo-Scandinavian levels at 16–22 Coppergate*. London, CBA, The Archaeology of York 15/3

Ogden, A R 2005 *Identifying and Scoring Periodontal Disease in Skeletal Material*. Bradford, Biological Anthropology Research Centre, University of Bradford

Ohnuma, K and Bergman, C 1982 Experimental studies in the determination of flaking mode, *UCL Univ London, Inst Archaeol Bull* 19, 161–70

Ortner, D J and Putschar, W G J 1985 *Identification of Pathological Conditions in Human Skeletal Remains.* Washington DC, Smithsonian Institution Press

Papadopoulos, J K 2002 A contextual approach to pessoi (gaming pieces, counters or convenient wipes?), *Hesperia* 71, 423–7

Parker Pearson, M, Cleal, R, Marshall, P, Needham, S, Pollard, J, Richards, C, Ruggles, C Sheridan, A., Thomas, J, Tilley, C, Welham, K, Chamberlain, A, Chenery, C, Evans, J, Knüsel, C, Linford, N, Martin, L, Montgomery, J, Payne, A and Richards, M 2007 The Age of Stonehenge, *Antiquity* 81, 617–39

Parker Pearson, M, Pollard, J, Richards, C, Thomas, J, Tilley, C and Welham, K 2008 The Stonehenge Riverside Project: exploring the Neolithic landscape of Stonehenge, *Documenta Praehistorica* 35, 153–66

Parker Pearson, M, Chamberlain, A, Jay, M, Marshall, P, Pollard, J, Richards, C, Thomas, J, Tilley, C and Welham, K 2009 Who was buried at Stonehenge? *Antiquity* 83, 23–39

Parker Pearson, M, Marshall, M, Pollard, J, Richards, C, Thomas, J and Welham, K 2013 Stonehenge, in H Fokkens and A Harding (eds) *Oxford Handbook of the European Bronze Age*, 159–74. Oxford, Oxford Univ Press

Payne, S 1973 Kill-off patterns in sheep and goats: the mandibles from Asvan Kale, *Anatolian Studies* 23, 281–303

Payne, S 1985 Morphological distinctions between the mandibular teeth of young sheep, *Ovis*, and goats, *Capra*, *J Archaeol Sci* 12, 139–147

Payne, S and Bull, G 1988 Components of variation in measurements of pig bones and teeth, and the use of measurements to distinguish wild from domestic pig remains, *Archaeozoologia* 2, 27–65

Peacock, D P S 1987 Iron Age and Roman quern production at Lodsworth, West Sussex, *Antiq J* 57, 61–85

Pelling, R 2011 Charred plant remains, in Powell 2011, 79–85

Peña, J T 2007 *Roman Pottery in the Archaeological Record*. Cambridge, Cambridge Univ Press

Philpott, R 1991 *Burial Practices in Roman Britain: a survey of grave treatment and furnishing AD, 43–410*. Oxford, BAR 219

Prehistoric Ceramics Research Group (PCRG) 2010 *The Study of Later Prehistoric Pottery: general policies and guidelines for analysis and publication*. Prehistoric Ceramics Research Group Occas Pap 1/2

Pitts, M W 1982 On the road to Stonehenge, *Proc Prehist Soc* 48, 75–132

Pollard, J 2013 The sarsen stone, in J Leary, D Field and G Campbell (eds) *Silbury Hill: the largest*

122

prehistoric mound in Europe, 75–80. Swindon, English Heritage

Poole, C 1984 Objects of baked clay, in B Cunliffe *Danebury: an Iron Age hillfort in Hampshire, Volume 2. The Excavations 1969–1978: the finds*, 398–407. London, CBA Res Rep 52

Powell, A B 2011 *An Iron Age Enclosure and Romano-British Features at High Post, near Salisbury*. Salisbury, Wessex Archaeology

Powell, A B and Barclay, A J forthcoming *Between and Beyond the Monuments: prehistoric activity on the downlands south-east of Amesbury*. Salisbury, Wessex Archaeology

Powell, A B, Allen, M J, Chapman, J, Every, R, Gale, R, Harding, P, Knight, S, McKinley, J I and Stevens, C J 2005 Excavations along the Old Sarum water pipeline, north of Salisbury, *Wiltshire Archaeol Natur Hist Mag* 98, 250–80

Powell, A B, Barclay, A J, Mepham, L, and Stevens, C J, 2015 *Imperial College Sports Ground and RMC Land, Harlington: the development of prehistoric and later communities in the Colne Valley and on the Heathrow Terrace*. Salisbury, Wessex Archaeology Rep 33

PCRG, SGRP and MPRG 2016 *A Standard for Pottery Studies in Archaeology*. Medieval Pottery Research Group

Prummel, W 1997 Evidence for hawking (falconry) from bird and mammal bones, *Int J Osteoarchaeol* 7, 333–8

Rahtz, P A 1963 A Roman villa at Downton, *Wiltshire Archaeol Natur Hist Mag* 58, 303–41

Rawlings, M and Fitzpatrick, A P 1996 Prehistoric sites and a Romano-British settlement at Butterfield Down, Amesbury. *Wiltshire Archaeol Natur Hist Mag* 89, 1–43

Reimer, P J, Bard, E, Bayliss, A, Beck, J W, Blackwell, P G, Bronk Ramsey, C, Buck, C E, Cheng, H, Edwards, R L, Friedrich, Grootes, P M, Guilderson, T P, Haflidason, H, Hajdas, I, Hatté, H, Heaton, T J, Hoffmann, D L, Hogg, A G, Hughen, K A, Kaiser, K F, Kromer, B, Manning, S W, Nui, M, Reimer, R W, Richards, D A, Scott, E M, Southon, J R, Staff, R A, Turney, C S M, and van der Plicht, J, 2013 IntCal13 and Marine13 Radiocarbon Age Calibration Curves, 0–50,000 Years cal BP, *Radiocarbon* 55(4), 1869–1887

Reynolds, P J 1981 New approaches to familiar problems, in M K Jones and G Dimbleby (eds), *The Environment of Man: the Iron Age to the Anglo-Saxon period*, 19–49. Oxford, Brit Archaeol Rep 87

Richards, J C 1990 *The Stonehenge Environs Project*. London, Historic Buildings & Monuments Commission for England Archaeol Rep 16

Richards, C and Thomas, J 1984 Ritual activity and structured deposition in later Neolithic Wessex, in R Bradley and J Gardiner (eds) *Neolithic Studies: a review of some current research*, 189–218. Oxford, BAR 133

Rigby, V 1982 The coarse pottery, in J Watcher and A McWhirr *Early Roman Occupation in Cirencester*, 153–200. Cirencester, Cirencester Excavation Committee

Roberts, C and Cox, M 2003 *Health and Disease in Britain from Prehistory to the Present Day*. Stroud, Sutton

Roberts, C and Manchester, K 1997 *The Archaeology of Disease*. Stroud Sutton

Robinson, M A 2000 Further considerations of Neolithic charred cereals, fruits, and nuts, in A S Fairbairn (ed.) *Plants in Neolithic Britain and Beyond*, 85–90. Oxford, Oxbow Books, Neolithic Studies Seminar Paper 5

Rogers, B and Roddham, D 1991 The excavations at Wellhead, Westbury 1959–66, *Wiltshire Archaeol Natur Hist Mag* 84, 51–60

Rogers, J and Waldron, T 1995 *A Field Guide to Joint Disease in Archaeology*. Chichester, Wiley

Royal Commission on Historical Monuments England (RCHME) 1979 *Stonehenge and its Environs*. Edinburgh, Edinburgh Univ Press

Saunders, P 1997 Excavation of an Iron Age settlement site at Stockton, *Wiltshire Archaeol Natur Hist Mag* 90, 13–25

Scheuer, L and Black, S 2000 *Developmental Juvenile Osteology*. London, Academic Press

Schweingruber, F H 1990 *Microscopic Wood Anatomy* (3rd edition). Swiss Federal Institute for Forest, Snow and Landscape Research

Seager Smith, R H 1996 Pottery; Other artefacts, in J I McKinley and M J Heaton, A Romano-British farmstead and associated burials at Maddington Farm, Shrewton, *Wiltshire Archaeol Natur Hist Mag*, 89, 53–9

Seager Smith, R H 1997 Roman pottery, in R J C Smith, F Healy, M J Allen, E L Morris, I Barnes and P J Woodward *Excavations Along the Route of the Dorchester By-pass, Dorset, 1986–8*, 225–35. Salisbury, Wessex Archaeology Rep 11

Seager Smith, R H 2000 Worked bone and antler, in A J Lawson *Potterne 1982–5: animal husbandry in later prehistoric Wiltshire*, 222–40. Salisbury, Wessex Archaeology Rep 17

Seager Smith, R H 2002 Late Iron Age and Romano-British pottery, in S M Davies, P S Bellamy, M J Heaton and P J Woodward *Excavations at Alington Avenue, Fordington, Dorchester, Dorset, 1984–87*, 93–107. Dorchester, Dorset Natur Hist Archaeol Soc Monogr 15

Seager Smith, R H 2006 Late Iron Age and Roman pottery, in Fulford *et al.* 2006, 113–20

Seager Smith, R H and Davies, S M 1993 Roman pottery, in P J Woodward, S M Davies and A H Graham *Excavations at Greyhound Yard, Dorchester 1981–4*, 202–89. Dorchester, Dorset Natur Hist Archaeol Soc Monogr 12

Sellwood, L 1984 Objects of bone and antler, in B Cunliffe *Danebury: an Iron Age hillfort in Hampshire, Volume 2. The Excavations 1969–1978: the finds*, 371–95. London, CBA Res Rep 52

Serjeantson, D 1991 The bird bones, in B Cunliffe and C Poole (eds) *Danebury: an Iron Age hillfort in Hampshire, Volume 5. The excavations 1979–1988: the finds*, 479–481. London, CBA Res Rep 71

Serjeantson, D 1995 Animal bone, in Cleal *et al.* 1995, 437–51

Serjeantson, D 1996 The animal bone, in S Needham and T Spence (eds) *Refuse and Disposal at Area 16 East Runnymede: Runnymede Bridge research excavations, Volume 2*, 194–224. London, British Museum Press

Serjeantson, D 2006 Food or feast at Neolithic Runnymede?, in D Serjeantson and D Field (eds) *Animals in the Neolithic of Britain and Europe*, 113–34. Oxford, Oxbow Books, Neolithic Studies Group Seminar Papers 7

Serjeantson, D 2009 *Birds*. Cambridge, Cambridge Univ Press

Serjeantson, D 2010 Extinct birds, in T O'Connor and N Sykes (eds) *Extinctions and Invasions: a social history of British fauna*, 146–55. Oxford, Windgather Press

Serjeantson, D 2011 *Review of Animal Remains from the Neolithic and Early Bronze Age of Southern Britain (4000 BC–1500 BC)*. Portsmouth, English Heritage Res Dept Rep Ser 29/2011

Serjeantson, D and Morris, J 2011 Ravens and crows in Iron Age and Roman Britain, *Oxford J Archaeol* 30(1), 85–107

Shaffrey, R 2003 The rotary querns from the Society of Antiquaries' excavations at Silchester, 1890–1909, *Britannia* 34, 143–74

Shaw, M 1979 Romano-British pottery kilns on Camp Hill, Northampton, *Northamptonshire Archaeol* 14, 17–30

Smith, I F 1965 *Windmill Hill and Avebury: excavations by Alexander Keiller 1925–1939*. Oxford, Clarendon Press

Smith, K 1977 The Excavations at Winklebury Camp, Basingstoke, Hampshire, *Proc Prehist Soc* 42, 31–129

Stace, C 1997 *New Flora of the British Isles* (2nd edition). Cambridge, Cambridge Univ Press

Starley, D 2014 Metalworking debris, 235–9 and 360 in N Cooke and A Mudd, *A46 Nottinghamshire: the archaeology of the Newark to Widmerpool Improvement Scheme, 2009*. Cirencester/Salisbury, Cotswold Wessex Archaeology

Stevens, C J 2003 An investigation of consumption and production models for prehistoric and Roman Britain, *Environmental Archaeol* 8, 61–76

Stevens, C J 2006 Charred plant remains, in Fulford *et al.* 2006, 152–8

Stevens, C J 2007 Reconsidering the evidence: towards an understanding of the social contexts of subsistence production in Neolithic Britain, in S Colledge and J Conolly (eds) *The Origin and Spread of Domestic Plants in Southwest Asia and Europe*, 375–89. Walnut Creek (CA), Left Coast Press

Stone, J F S and Young, W E V 1948 Two pits of Grooved Ware date near Stonehenge, *Wiltshire Archaeol Natur Hist Mag* 52, 287–306

Stone, J F S, Piggott, S and Booth, A 1954 Durrington Walls, Wiltshire: recent excavations at a ceremonial site of the early second millennium BC, *Antiq J* 34, 15–77

Stuiver, M, and Reimer, P J, 1986 A computer program for radiocarbon age calculation, *Radiocarbon* 28, 1022–30

Sutton, J E G 1966 Iron Age hill-forts and some other earthworks in Oxfordshire, *Oxoniensia* 31, 28–42

Swan, V 1971 The coarse pottery, in Wainwright 1971, 100–16

Swan, V 1984 *The Pottery Kilns of Roman Britain*. London, Roy Comm Hist Monuments Engl Suppl Ser 5

Sykes, N J 2007 *The Norman Conquest: a zooarchaeological perspective*. Oxford, BAR Int Ser 656

Thomas, J 1999 *Understanding the Neolithic*. London, Routledge & Kegan Paul

Thomas, J 2012 Introduction: beyond the mundane? The humble pit, in H Anderson-Whymark and J Thomas *Regional Perspectives on Neolithic Pit Deposition: beyond the mundane*, 1–12. Oxford, Oxbow Books, Neolithic Studies Group Seminar Papers 12

Timby, J 2001 A reappraisal of Savernake ware, in P Ellis (ed.) *Roman Wiltshire and After: papers in honour of Ken Annable*, 73–84. Devizes, Wiltshire Archaeol Natur Hist Soc

Tomber, R and Dore, J 1998 *The National Roman Fabric Reference Collection: a handbook*. London, MoLAS Monogr 2

Trotter, M and Gleser, G C 1952 Estimation of stature from long bones of American whites and Negroes, *American J Phys Anthropol* 10(4), 463–514

Trotter, M and Gleser, G C 1958 A re-evaluation of estimation of stature bases on measurements of stature taken during life and of long bones after death, *American J Phys Anthropol* 16(1), 79–123

124

Turner, R and Wymer, J J 1987 An assemblage of Palaeolithic hand-axes from the Roman religious complex at Ivy Chimneys, Witham, Essex, *Antiq J* 67, 43–60

Tyrell, A 2000 Skeletal non-metric traits and the assessment of inter- and intra-population diversity: past problems and future potential, in M Cox and S Mays (eds) *Human Osteology in Archaeology and Forensic Science*, 289–306. London, Greenwich Media Medical

van der Veen, M 1989 Charred grain assemblages from Roman-period corn driers in Britain, *Archaeol J* 146, 302–19

Vann, S and Thomas, R 2006 Humans, other animals and disease: a comparative approach towards the development of a standardised recording protocol for animal palaeopathology, *Internet Archaeol* 20(5) https://doi.org/10.11141/ia.20.5

Vatcher, F de M and Vatcher H L 1973 Excavation of three post-holes in Stonehenge carpark, *Wiltshire Archaeol Natur Hist Mag* 68, 57–63

Vaughan, S 2001 Objects of bone and related materials, in A S Anderson, J S Wacher and A P Fitzpatrick *The Romano-British 'Small Town' at Wanborough, Wiltshire*, 322–32. London, Britannia Monogr 19

von den Driesch, A 1976 *A Guide to the Measurement of Animal Bones from Archaeological Sites.* Cambridge (MA), Harvard University Peabody Museum Bulletin 1

Wainwright, G J 1971 The excavation of prehistoric and Romano-British settlements near Durrington Walls, *Wiltshire, Wiltshire Archaeol Natur Hist Mag* 66, 76–128

Wainwright G J and Longworth, I H 1971 *Durrington Walls: excavations 1966–1968*, London, Rep Res Comm Soc Antiq London 29

Wells, C 1982 The human burials, in A McWhirr, L Viner and C Wells *Romano-British Cemeteries at Cirencester*, 135–202. Cirencester, Cirencester Excavation Committee

Wessex Archaeology 2004 *MOD Estate Offices, Durrington, Wiltshire: desk-based assessment of archaeological potential.* Salisbury, unpubl rep 55700.01

Wessex Archaeology 2006 *Defence Estates, Durrington, Wiltshire: report on archaeological field evaluation.* Salisbury, unpubl rep 55701.02

Wessex Archaeology 2011 *MoD Headquarters, High Street, Durrington, Wiltshire: archaeological evaluation report (Phase 2).* Salisbury, unpubl rep 74410.04

Wessex Archaeology 2012 *MOD Headquarters, High Street, Durrington, Wiltshire: archaeological assessment report and updated project design.* Salisbury, unpubl rep 74414.02

Willis, C, Marshall, P, McKinley, J, Pitts, M, Pollard, J, Richards, C, Richards, J, Thomas, J, Waldon, T, Welham, K and Parker Pearson, M 2016 The dead of Stonehenge, *Antiquity* 90(350), 337–356

Wiltshire County Council Archaeology Service 2004 *The Archaeology of Wiltshire's Towns: an extensive urban survey, VERLUCIO.* Trowbridge, Wiltshire County Council, unpubl rep for English Heritage

Wyles, S F and Stevens, C J forthcoming Charred plant remains, in Powell and Barclay forthcoming

Young, C J 1977 *Oxfordshire Roman Pottery.* Oxford, BAR 43

Zohary, D and Hopf, M 2000 *Domestication of Plants in the Old World: the origin and spread of cultivated plants in West Asia, Europe, and the Nile Valley* (3rd edition). Oxford, Clarendon Press